Python Data
With SQL and NOSQL Databases

MW01123577

By

Malhar Lathkar

Distributors:

BPB PUBLICATIONS
20, Ansari Road, Darya Ganj
New Delhi-110002
Ph: 23254990/23254991

BPB BOOK CENTRE
376 Old Lajpat Rai Market,
Delhi-110006
Ph: 23861747

MICRO MEDIA
Shop No. 5, Mahendra Chambers,
150 DN Rd. Next to Capital Cinema,
V.T. (C.S.T.) Station, MUMBAI-400 001
Ph: 22078296/22078297

DECCAN AGENCIES
4-3-329, Bank Street,
Hyderabad-500195
Ph: 24756967/24756400

Published by Manish Jain for BPB Publications, 20, Ansari Road, Darya Ganj, New Delhi-110002 and Printed by Repro India Pvt Ltd, Mumbai

Preface

Almost every other computer application, whether it is a web based application, a standalone data logger, a mobile app or a desktop application with or without GUI, stores and retrieves data from some persistent storage device such as hard disk or a flash drive. Such storage device may either be connected to computer or it may be available on a network. Without this ability to recurrently access, update and retrieve stored data, most computer applications would have been reduced to programmable calculators!

Data storage format depends on the logical structure of data and on the processing logic. Data may be stored in flat computer files, in tables of relational databases or different store formats of NOSQL databases. You will know more about these terms in subsequent chapters of this book.

Back-end process of a computer application stores, modifies and retrieves data in response to front-end user's requirements. Almost every programming language offers tools to interact with files/databases. This book aims to familiarize the reader with Python's functions and modules that handle persistent data processing.

Why Python?

Popularity of Python has increased by many fold recently because of the emergence of powerful libraries for data analysis, visualization and machine learning. These libraries use data stored in different formats such as text files and relational databases. Hence to be a proficient data scientist, it is important to have a sound understanding of Python tools for data persistence.

Features of Python

Python is easy! : So why has Python been so popular? First and foremost, Python is very easy to learn and use. *"Simple is better than Complex"*. This is one of the guiding principles of Python's design philosophy. It has clean and simple syntax resembling to a natural language. It saves a lot of development time.

Open source: Python is free and open source having very active and supportive developer community. As a result plenty of documentation resources, guides tutorials and forums are available in public domain. Any newcomer can access, learn, collaborate and seek advice from community.

Object oriented: Python is completely object oriented, although it supports multiple programming paradigms including functional programming style.

Extensible: Python can be easily integrated with other languages such as C/C++, Java, .NET etc.

Corporate support: Python enjoys a great corporate support. Google for example promotes Python in a big way as Python is extensively used in many of its applications. Many other companies use Python as their development platform.

How this Book is Arranged?

This book assumes reader having no prior knowledge of computer programming. Hence, first two chapters give a quick-start tutorial of Python as if this is reader's first tryst with programming. Third chapter *'Structured Python'* discusses an important programming element called **functions** and **modules**.

As mentioned earlier, Python is a completely object oriented language. Python's implementation of OOP is discussed in fourth chapter.

Fifth chapter is on *File object API of Python*. Most of the users know there are hundreds of files in a computer device, but they don't understand the mechanism of storage and retrieval of data from them. This chapter explains Python's functionality to perform **I/O operation** on computer files.

Next chapter takes a look at modules in Python's standard library that deal with different object serialization techniques such as **pickle** and **marshalling**. It also explains representation of Python objects in the form of CSV, XML document and JSON data.

Relational databases of various flavours are most popular software tools for data storage and retrieval. Products such as Oracle, MySQL, SQLite etc use SQL as underlying language. Chapter 7 intends to introduce **SQL operations**. Since standard Python distribution bundles sqlite3 module, we learn how Python interacts with SQLite. However, any RDBMS product can be interfaced with Python by using corresponding DB-API compliant module.

In order to be compatible with object oriented nature of Python while using relational databases, **Object relational mappers (ORM)** libraries have been developed. Chapter 9 discusses SQLAlchemy, Python's most popular ORM library.

Oracle and MySQL etc. notwithstanding, MS Excel is world's most popular tool to represent data. How do we interact with Excel worksheet through Python? Chapter 10 introduces **openpyxl** and **pandas** packages for the purpose.

While the database ecosystem is dominated by SQL oriented products, NOSQL products are slowly making their mark. Last two chapters of this book intend to introduce two NOSQL products that take two different approaches. MongoDB is document store based database. Cassandra on the other hand is column store database. Python APIs for these two databases have been described along with their native usage.

Installation of Python and other third party libraries is beyond the scope of this book. However, relevant links having downloads and documentation, are cited at appropriate places.

Example codes cited in the book are tested with *Python's 3.7.2* version on Windows platform. Python being a cross-platform language, can be run on any other operating system as well.

I express my sincere gratitude towards **BPB Publications** for bringing out this work and giving me an opportunity to be a part of galaxy of renowned BPB authors.

My parents, who passed away recently in quick succession, would have been extremely proud to hold copy of this book. I humbly dedicate this work in their cherished memory. My family and friends have always backed me wholeheartedly in each of my endeavours. To acknowledge some of them would be injustice to others.

So, let us '*get started!!!*'

Table of Content

About the Author

Malhar Lathkar is an Independent software professional / Programming technologies trainer/E-Learning Subject matter Expert. He is Director, Institute of Programming Language Studies, Rama Computers, Nanded Maharashtra.

He has academic and industry experience of 33 years. His expertise is in Java, Python, C#, IoT, PHP, databases.

Code Bundle

All the code samples used in the book can be found at the following github repository:

https://github.com/bpbpublications/Python-Data-Persistence

"If you can't explain it simply,
you don't understand it well enough."

Albert Einstein

CHAPTER 1
Getting Started

Python is very easy to learn. Well, it is also very easy to start using it. In fact I would encourage trying out one of the many online Python interpreters, get yourself acquainted with the language before going on to install it on your computer.

There are many online resources available to work with Python. Python's official website (*https://www.python.org*) itself provides online shell powered by *http://www.pythonanywhere.com.*

Online Python shells work on the principle of **Read, Evaluate, Print, Loop (REPL).** Such an online Python REPL is available at *https://repl. it/languages/python3.* It can be used in interactive and in scripting mode.

1.1 Installation

Python's official website hosts official distribution of Python at *https:// www.python.org/downloads/.* Precompiled installers as well as source code tarballs for various operating system platforms (Windows, Linux, and Mac OS X) and hardware architectures (32 and 64-bit) are available for download. The bundle contains Python interpreter and library of more than 200 modules and packages.

Precompiled installers are fairly straightforward to use and recommended. Most distributions of Linux have Python included. Installation from source code is little tricky and needs expertise to use compiler tools.

Currently, there are two branches of Python software versions (Python 2.x and Python 3.x) on Python website. At the time of writing, latest versions in both branches are Python 2.7.15 and Python 3.7.2 respectively. **Python Software Foundation (PSF)** is scheduled to discontinue supporting Python 2.x branch after 2019. Hence it is advised to install latest available version of Python 3.x branch.

It is also desirable to add Python's installation directory to your system's PATH environment variable. This will allow you to invoke Python from anywhere in the filesystem.

It is now time to start using Python. Open Windows Command Prompt terminal (or Linux terminal), type *'python'* in front of the prompt as shown below: *(figure 1.1)*

```
C:\Users\acer>python
Python 3.7.2 (tags/v3.7.2:9a3ffc0492, Dec 23 2018,
23:09:28) [MSC v.1916 64 bit (AMD64)] on win32
Type "help", "copyright", "credits" or "license" for
more information.
>>>
```

Figure 1.1 Python Prompt

If a Python prompt symbol >>> (made up of three 'greater than' characters) appears, it means Python has been successfully installed on your computer. **Congratulations**!!!

Most Python distributions are bundled with Python's **Integrated Development and Learning Environment (IDLE)**. It also presents an interactive shell as shown in Figure 1.1. Additionally, it also has a Python aware text editor with syntax highlighting and smart indent features. It also has an integrated debugger.

```
Python 3.7.2 Shell                                                    —  □  ×
File  Edit  Shell  Debug  Options  Window  Help
Python 3.7.2 (tags/v3.7.2:9a3ffc0492, Dec 23 2018, 23:09:28) [MSC v.1916 64 bit
(AMD64)] on win32
Type "help", "copyright", "credits" or "license()" for more information.
>>>
                                                                    Ln: 3  Col: 4
```

1.2 Interactive Mode

The >>> prompt means that Python is ready in **REPL** mode. You can now work with Python interactively. The prompt reads user input, evaluates if it is a valid Python instruction, prints result if it is valid or shows error if invalid, and waits for input again. In this mode, Python interpreter acts as a simple calculator. Just type any expression in front of the prompt and press **Enter**. Expression is evaluated with usual meanings of arithmetic operators used and result is displayed on the next line.

Example 1.1

```
>>> 5-6/2*3
-4.0
>>> (5-6/2)*3
6.0
>>>
```

Python operators follow **BODMAS** order of precedence. There are few more arithmetic operators defined in Python. You will learn about them later in this chapter.

You can assign a certain value to a variable by using '=' symbol. (What is variable? Don't worry. I am explaining it also later in this chapter!) However, this assignment is not reflected in next line before the prompt. The assigned variable can be used in further operations. To display the value of variable, just type its name and press Enter.

Example 1.2

```
>>> length=20
>>> breadth=30
>>> area=length*breadth
>>> area
600
```

Type **'quit()'** before the prompt to return to command prompt.

1.3 Scripting Mode

Interactive mode as described above executes one instruction at a time. However, it may not be useful when you have a series of statements to be repetitively executed. This is where Python's scripting mode is used. Script is a series of statements saved as a file with '**.py**' extension. All statements in the script are evaluated and executed one by one, in the same sequence in which they are written.

The script is assembled by using any text editor utility such as Notepad (or similar software on other operating systems). Start Notepad on Windows computer, enter following lines and save as *'area.py'*

Example 1.3

```
#area.py
length=20
breadth=30
area=length*breadth
print ('area=',area)
```

Open the command prompt. Ensure that current directory is same in which *'area.py'* script (you can call it as a program) is saved. To run the script, enter following command *(figure 1.2)*:

```
C:\Users\acer>python area.py
area= 600
```

Figure 1.2 Running Python Script

1.4 Identifiers

Python identifiers are the various programming elements such as keywords, variables, functions/methods, modules, packages, and classes by suitable name. Keywords are the reserved words with predefined meaning in Python interpreter. Obviously keywords can't be used as name of other elements as functions etc. Python language currently has **33 keywords**. Enter the following statement in Python's interactive console. The list of keywords gets displayed!

Example 1.4

```
>>> import keyword
>>> print (keyword.kwlist)
['False', 'None', 'True', 'and', 'as', 'assert',
'break', 'class', 'continue', 'def', 'del', 'elif',
'else', 'except', 'finally', 'for', 'from', 'global',
'if', 'import', 'in', 'is', 'lambda', 'nonlocal',
'not', 'or', 'pass', 'raise', 'return', 'try',
'while', 'with', 'yield']
```

Apart from keywords, you can choose any name (preferably cryptic but indicative of its purpose) to identify other elements in your program. However, only alphabets (upper or lowercase), digits and underscore symbol ('_') may be used. As a convention, name of class starts with an uppercase alphabet, whereas name of function/method starts with lowercase alphabet. Name of variable normally starts with alphabet, but in special cases an underscore symbol (sometimes double underscore __) is seen to be first character of variable's name.

Some examples of valid and invalid identifiers:

Valid identifiers	Invalid identifiers
name, FileName, yr1sem1, EMP, roll_no, sum_of_dig, _price, __salary, __ function__	123, sub-1, yr1.sem1, roll no, 'price', *marks*

1.5 Statements

Python interpreter treats any text (either in interactive mode or in a script) that ends with Enter key (translated as '\n' and called **newline character**) as a statement. If it is valid as per syntax rules of Python, it will be executed otherwise relevant error message is displayed.

Example 1.5

```
>>> "Hello World"
'Hello World'
>>> Hello world
  File "<stdin>", line 1
    Hello world
            ^
SyntaxError: invalid syntax
```

In the first case, sequence of characters enclosed within quotes is a valid Python string object. However, second statement is invalid because it doesn't qualify as representation of any Python object or identifier or statement, hence the message as **SyntaxError** is displayed.

Normally one physical line corresponds to one statement. Each statement starts at first character position in the line, although it may leave certain leading whitespace in some cases (See **Indents** – next topic). Occasionally you may want to show a long statement spanning multiple lines. The '\' character works as continuation symbol in such case.

Example 1.6

```
>>> zen="Beautiful is better than ugly. \
... Explicit is better than implicit. \
... Simple is better than complex."
>>> zen
'Beautiful is better than ugly. Explicit is better
than implicit. Simple is better than complex.'
```

This is applicable for script also. In order to write expression   you would like to use two separate lines for numerator and denominator instead of a single line as shown below:

Example 1.7

```
>>> a=10
>>> b=5
>>> ratio=(pow(a,2)+(pow(b,2)))/ \
...        (pow(a,2)-(pow(b,2)))
>>>
```

Here **pow()** is a built-in function that computes square of a number. You will learn more built-in functions later in this book.

The use of **back-slash symbol** (\) is not necessary if items in a list, tuple or dictionary object spill over multiple lines. (Plenty of new terms. isn't it? Never mind. Have patience!)

Example 1.8

```
>>> marks=[34,65,92,55,71,
... 21,82,39,60,41]
>>> marks
[34, 65, 92, 55, 71, 21, 82, 39, 60, 41]
```

1.6 Indents

Use of indents is one of the most unique features of Python syntax. As mentioned above, each statement starts at first character position of next available line on online shell. In case of script, blank lines are ignored. In many situations, statements need to be grouped together to form a block of certain significance. Such circumstances are the definitions of function or class, a repetitive block of statements in loop, and so on. Languages such as C/C++ or Java put series of statements in a pair of opening and closing curly brackets. Python uses indentation technique to mark the blocks. This makes the code visually cleaner than clumsy curly brackets.

Whenever you need to start a block, use : symbol as last character in current line, after that press **Enter**, and then press Tab key once to leave a fixed whitespace before writing first statement in new block. Subsequent statements in the block should follow the same indent space. If there is a block within block you may need to press Tab key for each level of block. Look at following examples:

Indented Block in Function

Example 1.9

```
>>> def calculate_tax(sal):
...         tax=sal*10/100
...         if tax>5000:
...                   tax=5000
...         netsal=sal-tax
...         return netsal
...
>>>
```

Indents in Class

Example 1.10

```
>>> class Example:
...         def __init__(self, x):
...                  self.x=x
...                  if x>100:
...                          self.x=100
...
>>>
```

Indents in Loop

Example 1.11

```
>>> for i in range(4):
...        for j in range(4):
...                  print (i,j)
...
```

1.7 Comments

Any text that follows '#' symbol is ignored by Python interpreter. This feature can be effectively used to insert explanatory comments in the program code. They prove to be very useful while debugging and modifying the code. If '#' symbol appears in a line after a valid Python statement, rest of the line is treated as comment.

Example 1.12

```
>>> #this line is a comment
... print ("Hello world!")
Hello world!
>>> print ("hello world again!") #this also a
comment
hello world again!
```

Multiple lines of text which are enclosed within triple quote marks are similar to comments. Such text is called **'docstring'** and appears in definition of function, module and class. You will come across docstrings when we discuss these features in subsequent chapters.

1.8 Data Types

Data and information, these two words are so common nowadays – they are on lips of everybody around us. But many seem to be confused about exact meaning of these words. So much so, people use them almost as if they are synonymous. But they are not.

Computer is a data processing device. Hence, data is a raw and factual representation of objects, which when processed by the computer program, generates meaningful information.

Various pieces of data items are classified in **data types**. Python's data model recognizes the following data types *(figure 1.3)*:

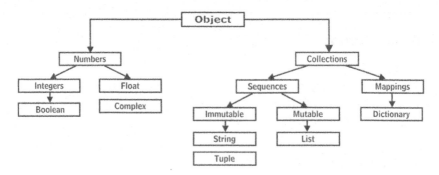

Figure 1.3 Data Types

Number Types

Any data object having numerical value (as in mathematical context) is a Number. Python identifies integer, real, complex, and Boolean as Number types by the built-in type names **int**, **float**, **complex**, and **bool** respectively. Any number (positive or negative) without a fractional component is an integer, and with fractional component is a float. Boolean object represents truth values True and False, corresponding to 1 and 0 respectively.

A number object is created with a literal representation using digit characters. Python has a built-in **type()** function to identify the type of any object.

Example 1.13

```
>>> #this is an integer
... 100
100
>>> type(100)
<class 'int'>
>>> #this is a float
... 5.65
5.65
>>> type(5.65)
<class 'float'>
>>> #this is bool object
... True
True
>>> type(True)
<class 'bool'>
```

Any number with fractional component (sometimes called **mantissa**) is identified as float object. The fractional component is the digits after decimal point symbol. To shorten the representation of a float literal with more digits after decimal point, symbols 'e' or 'E' are used.

Example 1.14

```
>>> #this is float with scientific notation
... 1.5e-3
0.0015
>>> type(1.5e-3)
<class 'float'>
```

Complex number consists of two parts – real and imaginary – separated by '+' or '-' sign. The imaginary part is suffixed by 'j' which is defined as imaginary number which is square root of $\sqrt{-1}$ (. A complex number is represented as **x+yj**.

Example 1.15

```
>>> 2+3j
(2+3j)
>>> type(2+3j)
<class 'complex'>
```

Arithmetic Operators

All number types can undergo arithmetic operations. Addition ('+'), subtraction ('-'), multiplication ('*') and division ('/') operators work as per their traditional meaning. In addition, few more arithmetic operators are defined in Python, which are:

- Modulus or remainder operator ('%'), it returns remainder of division of first operand by second. For example, 10%3 returns 1.
- Exponent operator ('**'), it computes first operand raised to second. For example, 10**2 returns 100.
- Floor division operator ('//') returns an integer not greater than division of first operand by second. For example, 9//2 returns 4.

Example 1.16

```
>>> #addition operator
... 10+3
13
>>> #subtraction operator
... 10-3
7
>>> #multiplication operator
... 10*3
30
>>> #division operator
... 10/3
3.3333333333333335
>>> #modulus operator
... 10%3
1
>>> #exponent operator
... 10**3
1000
>>> #floor division operator
... 10//3
3
```

Sequence Types

An ordered collection of items is called **sequence**. Items in the sequence have a positional index starting with 0. There are three sequence types defined in Python.

1. **String**: Ordered sequence of any characters enclosed in single, double or triple quotation marks forms a string object. Each character in string object is accessible by index.

Example 1.17

```
>>> #string using single quotes
... 'Hello. How are you?'
'Hello. How are you?'
>>> #string using double quotes
... "Hello. How are you?"
'Hello. How are you?'
>>> #string using triple quotes
... '''Hello. How are you?'''
'Hello. How are you?'
```

2. **List**: An ordered collection of data items, not necessarily of same type, separated by comma and enclosed in square brackets [] constitutes a List object. List is a sequence type because its items have positional index starting from 0.

3. **Tuple**: A tuple is also an ordered collection of items, which may be of dissimilar types, each separated by comma and enclosed in parentheses (). Again each item in tuple has a unique index.

Example 1.18

```
>>> ['pen', 15, 25.50, True]
['pen', 15, 25.5, True]
>>> type(['pen', 15, 25.50, True])
<class 'list'>
>>> ('Python', 3.72, 'Windows',10, 2.5E04)
('Python', 3.72, 'Windows', 10, 25000.0)
>>> type(('Python', 3.72, 'Windows',10, 2.5E04))
<class 'tuple'>
```

Apart from type of brackets – [] or () – List and Tuple appears similar. However, there is a crucial difference between them – that of **mutability**. This will come up for explanation just a few topics afterwards.

Mappings Type

A mapping object '*maps*' value of one object with that of other. Python's dictionary object is example of mapping. A language dictionary is a collection of pairs of word and corresponding meaning. Two parts of pair are **key (word)** and **value (meaning)**. Similarly, Python dictionary is also a collection of key:value pairs, separated by comma and is put inside curly brackets {}. Association of key with its value is represented by putting ':' between the two.

Each key in a dictionary object must be unique. Key should be a number, string or tuple. (All are immutable objects). Any type of object can be used as value in the pair. Same object can appear as value of multiple keys.

Example 1.19

```
>>> {1:'one', 2:'two', 3:'three'}
{1: 'one', 2: 'two', 3: 'three'}
>>> type({1:'one', 2:'two', 3:'three'})
<class 'dict'>
>>> {'Mumbai':'Maharashtra',
'Hyderabad':'Telangana', 'Patna':'Bihar'}
{'Mumbai': 'Maharashtra', 'Hyderabad': 'Telangana',
'Patna': 'Bihar'}
>>> type({'Mumbai':'Maharashtra',
'Hyderabad':'Telangana', 'Patna':'Bihar'})
<class 'dict'>
>>> {'Windows':['Windows XP', 'Windows 10'],
'Languages':['Python', 'Java']}
{'Windows': ['Windows XP', 'Windows 10'],
'Languages': ['Python', 'Java']}
>>> type({'Windows':['Windows XP', 'Windows 10'],
'Languages':['Python', 'Java']})
<class 'dict'>
```

1.9 Variables

When you use an object of any of the above types - of any type for that matter – (as a matter of fact everything in Python is an object!) it is stored in computer's memory. Any random location is allotted to it. Its location can be obtained by built-in **id()** function.

Example 1.20

```
>>> id(10)
1812229424
>>> id('Hello')
2097577807520
>>> id([10,20,30])
2097577803464
```

However, in order to refer to same object repetitively with its **id()** is difficult. If a suitable name (by following rules of forming identifier) is given to an object, it becomes convenient while referring to it as and when needed. To bind the object with a name, '=' symbol is used. It is called **assignment operator**.

Here, an int object 5 is assigned a name 'radius'. The **id()** of both is same.

Example 1.21

```
>>> id(5)
1812229264
>>> radius=5
>>> id(radius)
1812229264
```

The name '*radius*' can now be used in different expressions instead of its **id()** value.

Example 1.22

```
>>> diameter=radius*2
>>> diameter
10
>>> area=3.142*radius*radius
>>> area
78.55
>>> circumference=2*3.142*radius
>>> circumference
31.419999999999998
```

Dynamic Typing

Python is a dynamically typed language. This feature distinguishes it from C Family languages like C, C++, Java, and so on. These languages are statically typed. What is the difference?

The difference is the manner in which a variable behaves. In statically typed languages, variable is in fact a named location in the memory. Moreover it is configured to store data of a certain type before assigning it any value. Data of any other type is not acceptable to the respective language compiler. Type of Variable is announced first, and data of only that type is acceptable. This makes these languages statically typed.

Look at following statements in a Java program. A string variable is declared and assigned a string value. However, if we try storing value of any other type then Java compiler reports error.

Example 1.23

```
String somevar;
somevar="some string value";
somevar=999;
```

Java Compiler error

```
Error: incompatible types: int cannot be converted
to java.lang.String
```

On the other hand a variable in Python is not bound permanently to a specific data type. In fact, it is only a label to an object in memory. Hence, Java-like prior declaration of variable's data type is not possible, nor is it required. In Python, the data assigned to variable decides its data type and not the other way round.

Let us define a variable and check its **id()** as well as **type()**.

Example 1.24

```
>>> somevar='some string value'
>>> id(somevar)
2166930029568
>>> type(somevar)
<class 'str'>
```

'*somevar*' is a string variable here. But it's just a label. So you can put same label on some other object.

Let us assign an integer to '*somevar*' and check **id()** as well as **type()** again.

Example 1.25

```
>>> somevar=999
>>> id(somevar)
2166929456976
>>> type(somevar)
<class 'int'>
```

Two things to note here:

1. You didn't need prior declaration of variable and its type.

2. Variable's type changed according to data assigned to it. That's why Python is called **dynamically typed language**.

Sequence Operators

As described earlier, string, list, and tuple objects are sequence types. Obviously, arithmetic operators won't work with them. However, the symbols '+' and '*' can. In this context, they are defied as concatenation and repetition operator respectively.

The concatenation operator ('+') appends contents of second operand to first. Of course both operands must be of same type.

Example 1.26

```
>>> #concatenation of strings
...
>>> str1='Hello World.'
>>> str2='Hello Python.'
>>> str1+str2
'Hello World.Hello Python.'
>>> #concatenation of lists
...
>>> list1=[1,2,3,4]
>>> list2=['one','two','three','four']
>>> list1+list2
[1, 2, 3, 4, 'one', 'two', 'three', 'four']
>>> #concatenation of tuples
...
>>> tup1=(1,2,3,4)
>>> tup2=('one','two','three','four')
>>> tup1+tup2
(1, 2, 3, 4, 'one', 'two', 'three', 'four')
```

Repetition operator ('*****') concatenates multiple copies of a sequence. Sequence to be replicated is first operand, second operand is an integer that specifies the number of copies.

Example 1.27

```
>>> #repetition operator with string
...
>>> str1='Hello.'
>>> str1*3
'Hello.Hello.Hello.'
>>> #repetition operator with list
...
>>> list1=[1,2,3,4]
>>> list1*3
[1, 2, 3, 4, 1, 2, 3, 4, 1, 2, 3, 4]
>>> #repetition operator with tuple
... tup1=(1,2,3,4)
>>> tup1*3
(1, 2, 3, 4, 1, 2, 3, 4, 1, 2, 3, 4)
```

Index operator ('**[]**') extracts an item at given position in a sequence. As you know, sequence is an ordered collection of items and each item has a positional index starting from 0. The expression seq[i] fetches i[th] item from given sequence.

Example 1.28

```
>>> #indexing of string
...
>>> str1='Monty Python and the Holy Grail'
>>> str1[21]
'H'
>>> #indexing of list
...
>>> list1=[1,2,3,4,5,6,7,8,9,10]
>>> list1[6]
7
>>> list1=['Python', 'Java', 'C++', 'Ruby',
'Kotlin']
>>> list1[3]
'Ruby'
>>> #indexing of tuple
...
>>> tup1=(-50, 3.142, 2+3j, True, 50)
>>> tup1[2]
(2+3j)
```

Slice operator ('[:]') fetches a part of sequence object. The expression has two integers on either side of ':' symbol inside square brackets. First integer is index of first item in the sequence and second integer is index of next item upto which slice is desired. For example seq[I,j] returns items from i[th] position to (j-1)[th] position. First integer is 0 by default. Second integer defaults to last index of sequence. Remember index starts from 0.

Example 1.29

```
>>> #slicing of string
... str1='Monty Python and the Holy Grail'
>>> str1[13:16]
'and'
>>> list1=['Python', 'Java', 'C++', 'Ruby', 'Kotlin']
>>> list1[1:3]
['Java', 'C++']
>>> tup1=(-50, 3.142, 2+3j, True, 50)
>>> tup1[2:4]
((2+3j), True)
```

There are two '*Membership*' operators in Python. The **in** operator checks if an operand exists as one of the items in given sequence and returns True if so, otherwise it returns False. The **not in** operator does the opposite. It returns False if operand doesn't belong to given sequence, otherwise it returns True.

Example 1.30

```
>>> #membership operator with string
...
>>> str1='Monty Python and the Holy Grail'
>>> 'Holy' in str1
True
>>> 'Grill' not in str1
True
>>> #membership operator with list
...
>>> list1=['Python', 'Java', 'C++', 'Ruby', 'Kotlin']
>>> 'C#' in list1
False
>>> 'Ruby' not in list1
```

```
False
>>> #membership operator with tuple
...
>>> tup1=(-50, 3.142, 2+3j, True, 50)
>>> 3.142 in tup1
True
>>> 3.142 not in tup1
False
```

Mutability

As already mentioned, everything in Python is object. A Python object is either mutable or immutable. What is the difference?

To put it simply, the object whose contents can be changed in place is **mutable**. As a result, changes are not possible in contents of **immutable** object. Of the built-in objects numbers, string, and tuple objects are immutable. On the other hand, list and dictionary objects are mutable.

Let us try to understand concept of mutability with the help of **id()** function that we have earlier used. First define a variable and assign an integer to it.

Example 1.31

```
>>> x=100
>>> id(x)
1780447344
```

Remember that a variable is just a label of object in memory. The object is stored in a location whose **id()** is given as shown in example 1.31 above. (The location is allotted randomly. So, when you try it on your machine, it may be different.) To understand what goes on inside the memory, have a look at diagram *(figure 1.4)* below. The *figure 1.4 (a)* shows a label assigned to an integer object 100.

Next, assign x to another variable y.

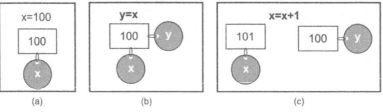

Figure 1.4 Storage of object inside the memory

Example 1.32

```
>>> y=x
>>> id(y)
1780447344
>>> y
100
```

Figure 1.4 (b) shows that **id()** of y is same as **id()** of x. It means both x and y are labels of same object in memory, in this case the number 100.

Now, increment x by 1 (x=x+1). A new integer object 101 is located at different location and it is bound to name x. Now x label is detached from 100 but y still remains on 100. (refer *figure 1.4 (c))*

Example 1.33

```
>>> x=x+1
>>> x
101
>>> id(x)
1780447376
>>> id(y)
1780447344
```

id(x) has changed but **id(y)** remains as earlier.

It is clear that the location containing object 100 doesn't get replaced by 101, instead it is stored in new location. Hence, we say that a Number object is immutable.

String and tuple objects are also immutable. If we try to change the sequence of characters in a string or any of items in a tuple, **TypeError** message appears effectively meaning that items in a string/tuple sequence can't be altered because they are immutable.

Example 1.34

```
>>> str1='Hello World'
>>> str1[6]
'W'
>>> str1[6]='z'
Traceback (most recent call last):
  File "<stdin>", line 1, in <module>
TypeError: 'str' object does not support item
assignment
```

```
>>> tup1=(-50, 3.142, 2+3j, True, 50)
>>> tup1[1]
3.142
>>> tup1[1]=2.303
Traceback (most recent call last):
  File "<stdin>", line 1, in <module>
TypeError: 'tuple' object does not support item
assignment
```

This restriction doesn't apply to list or dictionary objects. You can add, remove, or modify a list or dictionary. Hence, they are mutable.

Following code demonstrates how an item in list/dictionary is modified.

Example 1.35

```
>>> list1=['Python', 'Java', 'C++', 'Ruby',
'Kotlin']
>>> list1[2]='C#'
>>> list1
['Python', 'Java', 'C#', 'Ruby', 'Kotlin']
>>> dict1={'Mumbai':'Maharashtra',
'Hyderabad':'Telangana', 'Patna':'Bihar'}
>>> dict1['Hyderabad']='Andhra Pradesh'
>>> dict1
{'Mumbai': 'Maharashtra', 'Hyderabad': 'Andhra
Pradesh', 'Patna': 'Bihar'}
```

Addition/removal of items in list and dictionary is being explained later in this chapter. That brings us to one of the questions left unanswered earlier. What is the difference between list and tuple? Now the answer is clear. Tuple is immutable. List is mutable.

1.10 Built-in Functions

Python interpreter contains a number of built-in functions. These functions can always be used. You have come across a couple of them in previous sections (**type()** and **id()**). In this section few more built-in functions are being introduced. Some of them will come up for discussion in subsequent chapters. Full list of built-in functions is attached in appendix A.

Number Conversion Functions

A numeric object of one type can be converted to other by using following built-in functions. These functions have name that is same as the built-in data type.

1. **int()**: Function returns an integer from a float, or a string of digit characters.

Example 1.36

```
>>> #float to integer
...
>>> int(10.55)
10
>>> int(0.546)
0
>>> #int from string
... int('12')
12
```

String of digits returns to integer according to decimal number system i.e. base is assumed to be 10. For conversion of string to octal, or hexadecimal integer, the function needs the base – 8 or 16 as second parameter. Knowing '*12*' in octal is equivalent to 10 (Ten) and '*12*' in Hexadecimal is equivalent to 18 (Eighteen). Incidentally, the alphabets ABCDEF are also Hexadecimal digits and hence get converted to their integer equivalents.

Example 1.37

```
>>> int('12',8)
10
>>> int('12',16)
18
>>> int('C',16)
12
```

2. **float()**: Function returns a float object from any number or a string containing valid floating point number representation, either with decimal point or with scientific notation symbol e or E.

Example 1.38:

```
>>> #float from string with decimal notation
...
>>> float('3.142')
3.142
>>> #float from scientific notation
...
>>> float('1.501E2')
150.1
```

3. **complex()**: Function creates a complex number object out of two parameters given to it. First parameter is treated as real part of complex number and real part is second one multiplied by imaginary number j makes up the imaginary part. So, complex(x,y) returns x+yj.

Second argument is optional and is considered 0 by default. Both arguments can be integer, float, or even a complex number.

Example 1.39

```
>>> #complex from integer parameters
...
>>> complex(5,6)
(5+6j)
>>> #complex from float parameters
...
>>> complex(2.2,-3.5)
(2.2-3.5j)
>>> #complex from complex number parameters
...
>>> complex(2+3j,1+2j)
4j
```

When second parameter is a complex number, the result is calculated by multiplying it with 1+0j and adding first parameter to it. Hence,

Example 1.40

```
2+3j+(1+2j)*1.0j = 4j
```

If first parameter is a string representation of complex object, there shouldn't be second parameter. There shouldn't be any space within the string.

Example 1.41

```
>>> #complex from string
...
>>> complex('1+2j')
(1+2j)
>>> #space not allowed
...
>>> complex('1 + 2j')
Traceback (most recent call last):
File "<stdin>", line 1, in <module>
ValueError: complex() arg is a malformed string
```

Conversely real and imaginary components can be separated by a complex number object using '*real*' and '*imag*' attributes.

Example 1.42

```
>>> c1=complex('1+2j')
>>> #real part
...
>>> c1.real
1.0
>>> #imaginary part
... c1.imag
2.0
```

4. **bool():** Function evaluates given parameter and returns True or False. It needs one parameter. If it is a non-zero number, or an expression that evaluates to non-zero number, the function returns True, otherwise it returns False.

Example 1.43

```
>>> #boolean value of integer
...
>>> bool(20)
True
>>> bool(-11)
True
>>> bool(0)
False
>>> bool(10-5*2)
False
>>> bool(10%2)
False
```

A non-empty sequence as well as a dictionary object as parameter makes this function True.

Example 1.44

```
>>> #boolean value of sequence
...
>>> bool([1,2,3])
True
>>> bool([])
False
>>> bool('') #empty string
False
>>> bool('Hello')
True
>>> bool((1,2,3)) #tuple
True
>>> bool(())
False
>>> bool({1:'one',2:'two'}) #dictionary
True
>>> bool({})
False
```

The **bool()** function also returns True if it receives any logical expression that evaluates to True. Under all other circumstances, **bool()** returns False.

Example 1.45

```
>>> #boolean value of logical expression
...
>>> bool(10>5)
True
>>> bool(3 in [1,2,3,4])
True
```

Built-in Mathematical Functions

This section introduces some important mathematical functions from built-in function library.

1. **abs()** : Function returns absolute value of the parameter, which can be integer, float, or complex number.

Example 1.46

```
>>> #absolute of integer
...
>>> abs(-256)
256
>>> #absolute of integer
...
>>> abs(1.2E-3)
0.0012
>>> #absolute of complex
...
>>> abs(2-3j)
3.605551275463989
```

Absolute value of complex number a+bj is calculated as $\sqrt{a^2 + b^2}$

2. divmod(): Function performs division of two parameters and returns division and remainder in the form of a tuple.

Example 1.47

```
>>> a=divmod(10,3)
>>> a
(3, 1)
```

3. pow(): Function performs exponent computation. It takes two numeric parameters. **pow(x,y)** returns x to the power y (or x raised to y). This is equivalent to exponent operator x**y

Example 1.48

```
>>> pow(10,2)
100
>>> pow(27,1/3)
3.0
```

4. round(): Function returns a number by rounding the parameter to precision of desired digits before/after decimal point. First parameter is the number to be rounded. Second parameter is the digits upto which it is to be rounded. If digit at position next to desired precision is greater than 5, then last digit is increased by 1 and remaining digits are dropped.

Example 1.49

```
>>> round(123.453467,4)
123.4535
>>> round(123.453467,2)
123.45
>>> round(123.453467,1)
123.5
```

If the second parameter is 0, then the entire fraction part is considered. If it is greater than 0.5, return value of **round()** function is integer part +1, otherwise only integer part is returned.

Example 1.50

```
>>> round(123.453467,0)
123.0
>>> round(10/6,0)
2.0
```

If second parameter is negative, then integer part is rounded towards left of decimal point.

Example 1.51

```
>>> round(123.453467,-1)
120.0
>>> round(123.453467,-2)
100.0
```

Sequence Functions

Following functions act on sequence objects (also called **iterables**) such as string, list and tuple.

1. **max()** : In case of list or tuple consisting of numeric items (excluding complex numbers), largest number is returned. If list/tuple is made of strings, the one appears last in alphabetical order is returned. For a string object, **max()** function returns a character with highest ASCII value.

2. **min()** : Function returns smallest number from list/tuple of numeric items. The string that appears first in alphabetical order is returned by this function if list/tuple is made up of string items. For a single string, **min()** function returns a character with lowest ASCII value.

Example 1.52:

```
>>> #max/min of numeric items
...
>>> tup1=(-50, 3.142,True, 50, pow(8,2),1.001e-2)
>>> max(tup1)
64
>>> min(tup1)
-50
>>> #max/min of string items
...
>>> list1=['Python', 'Java', 'C++', 'Ruby', 'Kotlin']
>>> max(list1)
'Ruby'
>>> min(list1)
'C++'
>>> #max/min in a string
...
>>> str1='Monty Python and the Holy Grail'
>>> max(str1)
'y'
>>> min(str1)
' '
```

3. **len()** : In addition to sequence types, this function is also used with dictionary object. It returns number of items in sequence/dictionary.

Example 1.53

```
>>> str1='Monty Python and the Holy Grail'
>>> len(str1)
31
>>> list1=['Python', 'Java', 'C++', 'Ruby', 'Kotlin']
>>> len(list1)
5
>>> tup1=(-50, 3.142,True, 50, pow(8,2),1.001e-2)
>>> len(tup1)
6
>>> dict1={'Mumbai':'Maharashtra',
'Hyderabad':'Telangana', 'Patna':'Bihar'}
>>> len(dict1)
3
```

4. **list()** : Function returns a new list object. If there is no parameter given, an empty list object is created. If a string parameter is used, its

each character becomes an item in the list object. If tuple parameter is used, it returns a mutable version of same items.

Example 1.54

```
>>> list()
[]
>>> list('Hello Python')
['H', 'e', 'l', 'l', 'o', ' ', 'P', 'y', 't', 'h',
'o', 'n']
>>> tup1=(-50, 3.142,True, 50, pow(8,2),1.001e-2)
>>> list(tup1)
[-50, 3.142, True, 50, 64, 0.01001]
```

5. **tuple()** :Function returns a new tuple object. If no parameter is given, then an empty tuple object is created. If a string parameter is used, its each character becomes an item in the tuple object. If parameter is a list, it returns a immutable version of same items.

Example 1.55

```
>>> tuple()
()
>>> tuple('Hello Python')
('H', 'e', 'l', 'l', 'o', ' ', 'P', 'y', 't', 'h',
'o', 'n')
>>> list1=(-50, 3.142,True, 50, pow(8,2),1.001e-2)
>>> tuple(list1)
(-50, 3.142, True, 50, 64, 0.01001)
```

6. **str()** :Function returns a string representation of any Python object. If no parameter is given an empty string is returned.

Example 1.56

```
>>> str()
' '
>>> str(1101)
'1101'
>>> str(3.142)
'3.142'
>>> str([1,2,3])
'[1, 2, 3]'
>>> str((1,2,3))
'(1, 2, 3)'
>>> str({1:'one',2:'two',3:'three'})
"{1: 'one', 2: 'two', 3: 'three'}"
```

IO functions

Python's built-in function library has **input()** and **print()** functions. The former reads user input and latter displays output. These functions are meant more for scripting mode rather than interactive mode, although you can them in Python shell as well.

1. **input()** : When this function is encountered, Python interpreter waits for input from input device, the default being keyboard. The function returns a string object made up of all keys entered by user until Enter key. You can use a string parameter inside function parentheses to prompt the user about what to input. The return value of function is usually stored in a string variable for further processing.

Example 1.57
```
>>> name=input('enter your name :')
enter your name :
```
Keystrokes from user form a string object and is assigned to variable on left.

Example 1.58
```
>>> name=input('enter your name_')
enter your name :Ramkrishna
>>> name
'Ramkrishna'
```

2. **print()** : Function displays value of one or more objects on Python console (if used in interactive mode) or **DOS** window (if used in scripting mode). In interactive mode, any expression anyway echoes in next line when entered in front of Python prompt >>>.

Example 1.59
```
>>> 2+2
4
>>> print (2+2)
4
```

This function plays very important role in displaying output in scripting mode as we shall see soon.

There can be multiple comma separated parameters in function's parentheses. Their values are separated by ' ' although separation character can be changed if you want. For example if you want ',' between two values, use **sep** parameter.

Example 1.60

```
>>> name='Ram'
>>> age=20
>>> marks=50
>>> print (name, age, marks)
Ram 20 50
>>> print (name, age, marks, sep=',')
Ram,20,50
```

Python scripts become extremely powerful with use of **input()** and **print()** functions. Result of a certain process with different user inputs can be displayed as following :

First, using suitable text editor, type and save following code as *'hello.py'*.

Example 1.61

```
#hello.py
name=input('enter your name:')
print ('Hello', name, 'how are you?')
```

Now, run this script from command line *(figure 1.5)*:

```
C:\Users\acer>python hello.py
enter your name:Maya
Hello Maya how are you?
```

Figure 1.5 Command Prompt

Run it again with different input and get corresponding output.*(figure 1.6)*

```
C:\Users\acer>python hello.py
enter your name:Mahesh
Hello Mahesh how are you?
```

Figure 1.6 Command Prompt

Remember that **input()** function always returns a string object. What if you want numeric input from user? This is where you have to use different number conversion functions (like **int()**, **float()** and so on.) we studied earlier. Following script reads length and breadth from user and computes area of rectangle.

Example 1.62

```
#area.py
length=int(input('enter length:'))
breadth=int(input('enter breadth:'))
area=length*breadth
print ('area=',area)
```

Output: *(figure 1.7)*

```
C:\Users\acer>python area.py
enter length:20
enter breadth:30
area= 600

C:\Users\acer>python area.py
enter length:25
enter breadth:35
area= 875
```

Figure 1.7 Command Prompt

The **print()** function issues an EOF character ('\n') at the end. Output of next **print()** statement appears below current line. To make it appear in same line, specify '*end*' parameter to some other character such as ' '. Look at the following modified version of '*area.py*' script:

Example 1.63

```
#area.py
length=int(input('enter length:'))
breadth=int(input('enter breadth:'))
area=length*breadth
print ('length:',length, 'breadth:', breadth, end='
')
print ('area=',area)
```

Output *(figure 1.8)*

```
C:\Users\acer>python area.py
enter length:20
enter breadth:30
length: 20 breadth: 30 area= 600
```

Figure 1.8 Command Prompt

1.11 Methods of Built-in Data Type Classes

Python built-in object of a certain type is characterized by attributes and methods, and as defined in built-in class of corresponding name. Methods defined in **str** class for example are available for use to each string object. So is the case of list, tuple, and dictionary objects.

In this section, some commonly used methods of built-in type classes are described. (Two new terms pop up here – class and methods. You'll come to know about them in chapter on Object oriented programming. For the time being treat a method as a function only.)

String Methods

Various methods in **str** class fall in following categories:

Related to Case of Alphabets

1. **capitalize()**: Method changes first letter of given string to uppercase and returns another string object.

Example 1.64

```
>>> str1='python string'
>>> str2=str1.capitalize()
>>> str2
'Python string'
```

2. **lower()**: Method returns a string object by replacing all alphabets in given string with respective lowercase equivalents.

Example 1.65

```
>>> str1='Python String'
>>> str2=str1.lower()
>>> str2
'python string'
```

3. **upper()**: Method ensures that the resulting string consists of all uppercase alphabets.

Example 1.66

```
>>> str1='Python String'
>>> str2=str1.upper()
>>> str2
'PYTHON STRING'
```

4. `title()`: Method titlecases the string having first alphabet of each word in uppercase.

Example 1.67

```
>>> str1='python string'
>>> str2=str1.title()
>>> str2
'Python String'
```

5. `swapcase()`: Method replaces uppercase alphabets by lowercase and vice versa.

Example 1.68

```
>>> str1='Simple is Better than Complex.'
>>> str2=str1.swapcase()
>>> str2
'sIMPLE IS bETTER THAN cOMPLEX.'
>>> str1=str2.swapcase()
>>> str1
'Simple is Better than Complex.'
```

Find/Replace Methods

1. **find()**: Method returns index of first occurrence of a substring in given string. If not found, the method returns -1

Example 1.69

```
>>> str1='Simple is Better than Complex.'
>>> str1.find('pl')
3
>>> str1.find('bet')
-1
```

2. **index()**: Method is similar to find() except this one raises **ValueError** if the substring is not found.

Example 1.70

```
>>> str1='Simple is Better than Complex.'
>>> str1.index('pl')
3
>>> str1.index('bet')
Traceback (most recent call last):
  File "<stdin>", line 1, in <module>
ValueError: substring not found
```

3. **replace()**: Method requires two string parameters. All occurrences of first parameter get replaced by second parameter.

Example 1.71

```
>>> str1='all animals are equal. Some are more
equal'
>>> str1.replace('are', 'were')
'all animals were equal. Some were more equal'
```

4. **count()**: Method returns an integer corresponding to number of times a substring occurs in given string.

Example 1.72

```
>>> str1='Simple is Better than Complex.'
>>> str1.count('pl')
2
```

Methods Returning Boolean Result

1. **isalpha()**: Method returns True if all characters in given string are alphabetic i.e a-z or A-Z.

Example 1.73

```
>>> str1='BpbOnline'
>>> str1.isalpha()
True
>>> str2='BPB Publications'
>>> str2.isalpha()
False
```

2. **isdigit()**: Method returns True if the string is made of all digits. If not, it returns False.

Example 1.74

```
>>> str1='8860322236'
>>> str1.isdigit()
True
>>> str1='(+91)8860322236'
>>> str1.isdigit()
False
```

3. **islower()**: If all alphabets in given string are in lowercase, this method returns True otherwise returns False.

Example 1.75

```
>>> str1='pythonrocks'
>>> str1.islower()
True
```

4. **isupper()**: Method returns True if all alphabets in given string are in uppercase not considering other characters.

Example 1.76

```
>>> str1='IIT JEE'
>>> str1.isupper()
True
```

5. **startswith()**: Method returns True if given string has substring parameter or any of string items is in a tuple parameter. If it doesn't, then False is returned.

Example 1.77

```
>>> name='Mr. John'
>>> name.startswith('Mr')
True
>>> name='Dr. Watson'
>>> name.startswith(('Mr', 'Dr'))
True
```

6. **endswith()**: Method checks whether the substring parameter is at the end of given string and returns True if so, otherwise returns False. The substring to be checked can also be in the tuple parameter.

Example 1.78

```
>>> name='Mr. John'
>>> name.endswith('on')
False
>>> name='Dr. Watson'
>>> name.endswith(('on', 'hn'))
True
```

Join/split

1. **join()**: Method concatenates all string objects in a list or tuple. Items in list/tuple are separated by given string object.

Example 1.79

```
>>> list1=['Python','C++','Ruby','Kotlin']
>>> sep=' and '
>>> sep.join(list1)
'Python and C++ and Ruby and Kotlin'
>>> list1=['192','168','0','1']
>>> sep='.'
>>> sep.join(list1)
'192.168.0.1'
```

2. **split()**: Method separates splits given string into parts wherever the substring parameter is found. The parts are returned in the form of a list object.

Example 1.80

```
>>> str1='all animals are equal. Some are more
equal'
>>> str1.split(' ')
['all', 'animals', 'are', 'equal.', 'Some', 'are',
'more', 'equal']
>>> str1='192.168.0.1'
>>> str1.split('.')
['192', '168', '0', '1']
```

3. **strip()**: If no parameter is present in the parentheses of this method, then leading and trailing spaces are removed. The parameter can be a string of one or more characters. It acts as a set of characters to be removed.

Example 1.81

```
>>> str1='    Hello Python    '
>>> str1.strip()
'Hello Python'
>>> str1='all animals are equal'
>>> str1.strip('alu')
' animals are eq'
```

4. **format()**: Method returns a formatted string by interpolating placeholders in the given string by values of objects. Values of parameters in the method's parentheses fillup the place holders marked by {}.

Example 1.82

```
>>> name='Virat Kohli'
>>> runs=10385
>>> print ('{} is Captain of India. He has scored {}
runs in ODI.'.format(name,runs))
Virat Kohli is Captain of India. He has scored 10385
runs in ODI.
```

The curly bracket placeholders in the string are filled in the same order in which parameters appear in parentheses. You can also refer to the parameter by name and use them in any order.

Example 1.83

```
>>> name='Virat Kohli'
>>> runs=10385
>>> print ('{nm} is Captain of India. He has scored
{r} runs in ODI.'.format(r=runs,nm=name))
Virat Kohli is Captain of India. He has scored 10385
runs in ODI.
```

Python also supports C style string formatting using '**%**' sign as substitution character. The format specification symbols (like **%d, %f, %c**, and so on; famously used in **printf()** statement of C program) are available for use in Python too.

Example 1.84

```
>>> name='Virat Kohli'
>>> runs=10385
>>> print ("%s is Captain of India. He has scored %d
runs in ODI." % (name,runs))
Virat Kohli is Captain of India. He has scored 10385
runs in ODI.
```

List Methods

As described earlier, list is a mutable data type. It means, it is possible to change the contents of a list object after it has been defined. In this section you will learn to handle methods in list class that can add/modify/remove items in list object.

1. **append()** : Method adds new item at the end of given list.

Example 1.85

```
>>> list1=['Python','C++','Ruby','Kotlin']
>>> list1.append('JS')
>>> list1
['Python', 'C++', 'Ruby', 'Kotlin', 'JS']
>>>
```

2. **insert()**: Method needs two parameters. Second parameter is the new object to be added. First parameter is the index at which it will be inserted. Again, sequence index starts from 0.

Example 1.86

```
>>> list1=['Python','C++','Ruby','Kotlin']
>>> list1.insert(2,'Java')
>>> list1
['Python', 'C++', 'Java', 'Ruby', 'Kotlin']
>>>
```

3. **count()**: Method returns an integer corresponding to number of times a certain item appears in given list.

Example 1.87

```
>>> list1=[3,5,9,3,6]
>>> list1.count(3)
2
>>> str1='all animals are equal. Some are more
equal'
>>> list1=str1.split(' ')
>>> list1
['all', 'animals', 'are', 'equal.', 'Some', 'are',
'more', 'equal']
>>> list1.count('are')
2
>>>
```

4. **index()**: Method returns index of first occurrence of a certain value if found in given list. If it is not found, then the method raises **ValueError**.

Example 1.88

```
>>> list1=['all', 'animals', 'are', 'equal.',
'Some', 'are', 'more', 'equal']
>>> list1.index('are')
2
>>> list1.index('were')
Traceback (most recent call last):
  File "<stdin>", line 1, in <module>
ValueError: 'were' is not in list
>>>
```

5. **reverse()**: Order of items in given list is reversed by using this method.

Example 1.89

```
>>> list1=['Python', 'C++', 'Ruby', 'Kotlin', 'JS']
>>> list1.reverse()
>>> list1
['JS', 'Kotlin', 'Ruby', 'C++', 'Python']
>>>
```

6. **sort()**: Items in the given list object are rearranged in ascending order unless the method's '*reverse*' parameter set to True.

Example 1.90

```
>>> list1=['Python', 'C++', 'Ruby', 'Kotlin', 'JS']
>>> list1.sort()
>>> list1
['C++', 'JS', 'Kotlin', 'Python', 'Ruby']
>>> list2=['all', 'animals', 'are', 'equal.',
'Some', 'are', 'more', 'equal']
>>> list2.sort(reverse=True)
>>> list2
['more', 'equal.', 'equal', 'are', 'are', 'animals',
'all', 'Some']
>>>
```

7. **remove()**: Method causes removal of an item's first occurrence from given list. If the item to be removed is not found in list, then ValueError is raised.

Example 1.91

```
>>> list1=['all', 'animals', 'are', 'equal.',
'Some', 'are', 'more', 'equal']
>>> list1.remove('are')
>>> list1
['all', 'animals', 'equal.', 'Some', 'are', 'more',
'equal']
>>> list1=['all', 'animals', 'are', 'equal.',
'Some', 'are', 'more', 'equal']
>>> list1.remove('were')
Traceback (most recent call last):
  File "<stdin>", line 1, in <module>
ValueError: list.remove(x): x not in list
>>>
```

8. **pop ()** : Method is similar to **remove()** method. However, this method returns the removed item. The **pop()** method by default removes last item in the list. If it contains index parameter, item at specified index is removed and returned.

Example 1.92

```
>>> list1=['Python', 'C++', 'Ruby', 'Kotlin', 'JS']
>>> lang=list1.pop()
>>> lang
'JS'
>>> list2=[31,55,90,35,60]
>>> num=list2.pop(2)
>>> num
90
>>>
```

9. **clear ()** : Method removes all items in given list.

Example 1.93

```
>>> list1=['Python', 'C++', 'Ruby', 'Kotlin', 'JS']
>>> list1.clear()
>>> list1
[]
>>>
```

If you remember, tuple is an immutable object. As a result, above methods performing addition, removal, sorting, and so on; can't be used with tuple. Only **count ()** and **index ()** methods are available for a tuple object. Their behaviour is similar to list methods of same name.

Dictionary Methods

Like List, a dictionary object is also mutable. However, dictionary is not a sequence. Its items do not have index. So, index based insertion or removal is not supported. Following methods are defined in built-in dictonary class:

1. **get()** : Method retrieves value component corresponding to key parameter.

Example 1.94

```
>>> dict1={'Mumbai':'Maharashtra',
'Hyderabad':'Telangana', 'Patna':'Bihar'}
>>> dict1.get('Patna')
'Bihar'
>>>
```

2. **pop()** : Method removes k-v pair item from given dictionary object corresponding to key parameter, an returns its value component.

Example 1.95

```
>>> dict1={'Mumbai':'Maharashtra',
'Hyderabad':'Telangana', 'Patna':'Bihar'}
>>> state=dict1.pop('Mumbai')
>>> state
'Maharashtra'
>>>
```

3. **popitem()** : Method returns a k-v pair in the form of a tuple.

Example 1.96

```
>>> dict1={'Mumbai':'Maharashtra',
'Hyderabad':'Telangana', 'Patna':'Bihar'}
>>> t=dict1.popitem()
>>> t
('Patna', 'Bihar')
>>>
```

4. **update()**: Method is used to add new k-v pair item as well as modify value of existing key. The **update()** method takes another dictionary object as parameter. There may be one or more items in it. If its key is not used in given dictionary, a new k-v pair is added. If key is already present, its value is replaced by new value. This process takes place for all items in the dict parameter.

In following code snippet, dict1 is updated by adding a new state-capital pair.

Example 1.97

```
>>> dict1={'Maharashtra':'Bombay','Andhra Pradesh':
'Hyderabad', 'UP':'Lucknow'}
>>> dict1.update({'MP':'Bhopal'})
>>> dict1
{'Maharashtra': 'Bombay', 'Andhra Pradesh':
'Hyderabad', 'UP': 'Lucknow', 'MP': 'Bhopal'}
>>>
```

The initial dictionary object gets update by another dict parameter. Capitals of two states are modified and one pair is added.

Example 1.98

```
>>> dict1={'Maharashtra': 'Bombay', 'Andhra
Pradesh': 'Hyderabad', 'UP': 'Lucknow', 'MP':
'Bhopal'}
>>> dict2={'Andhra
Pradesh':'Amaravati','Telangana':'Hyderabad',
'Maharashtra':'Mumbai'}
>>> dict1.update(dict2)
>>> dict1
{'Maharashtra': 'Mumbai', 'Andhra Pradesh':
'Amaravati', 'UP': 'Lucknow', 'MP': 'Bhopal',
'Telangana': 'Hyderabad'}
>>>
```

You can also add a new k-v pair simply by assigning value to unused key by following syntax:

```
dict1[newkey]=value
```

Here is an example:

Example 1.99

```
>>> dict1={'Maharashtra': 'Bombay', 'Andhra
Pradesh': ' Hyderabad', 'UP': 'Lucknow', 'MP':
'Bhopal'}
>>> dict1['Maharashtra']='Mumbai'
>>> dict1
{'Maharashtra': 'Mumbai', 'Andhra Pradesh': '
Hyderabad', 'UP': 'Lucknow', 'MP': 'Bhopal'}
>>>
```

Dictionary View Methods

1. **items()**: Method returns a view object consisting of two-item tuples, one for each k-v pair. This view object can be converted to a list of k-v tuples.

Example 1.100

```
>>> dict1={'Maharashtra': 'Mumbai', 'Andhra
Pradesh': 'Amaravati', 'UP': 'Lucknow', 'MP':
'Bhopal', 'Telangana': 'Hyderabad'}
>>> items=dict1.items()
>>> items
dict_items([('Maharashtra', 'Mumbai'), ('Andhra
Pradesh', 'Amaravati'), ('UP', 'Lucknow'), ('MP',
'Bhopal'), ('Telangana', 'Hyderabad')])
>>> list(items)
[('Maharashtra', 'Mumbai'), ('Andhra Pradesh',
'Amaravati'), ('UP', 'Lucknow'), ('MP', 'Bhopal'),
('Telangana', 'Hyderabad')]
>>>
```

2. **keys()**: Method returns a view object consisting all keys in given dictionary. This view object can be converted to a list of keys.

Example 1.101

```
>>> dict1={'Maharashtra': 'Mumbai', 'Andhra
Pradesh': 'Amaravati', 'UP': 'Lucknow', 'MP':
'Bhopal', 'Telangana': 'Hyderabad'}
>>> keys=dict1.keys()
>>> keys
dict_keys(['Maharashtra', 'Andhra Pradesh', 'UP',
'MP', 'Telangana'])
>>> list(keys)
['Maharashtra', 'Andhra Pradesh', 'UP', 'MP',
'Telangana']
>>>
```

3. **values()**: Method returns a view object consisting of all values in given dictionary. This view object can be converted to a list of values.

Example 1.102

```
>>> dict1={'Maharashtra': 'Mumbai', 'Andhra
Pradesh': 'Amaravati', 'UP': 'Lucknow', 'MP':
'Bhopal', 'Telangana': 'Hyderabad'}
>>> values=dict1.values()
>>> values
dict_values(['Mumbai', 'Amaravati', 'Lucknow',
'Bhopal', 'Hyderabad'])
>>> list(values)
['Mumbai', 'Amaravati', 'Lucknow', 'Bhopal',
'Hyderabad']
>>>
```

All view objects returned by items(), keys(), and values() methods get automatically refreshed whenever the underlying dictionary object gets updated.

Example 1.103

```
>>> dict1={'Maharashtra':'Bombay','Andhra Pradesh':
'Hyderabad', 'UP':'Lucknow'}
>>> items=dict1.items()
>>> keys=dict1.keys
>>> values=dict1.values
>>> items
dict_items([('Maharashtra', 'Bombay'), ('Andhra
Pradesh', 'Hyderabad'), ('UP', 'Lucknow')])
>>> dict2={'Andhra
Pradesh':'Amaravati','Telangana':'Hyderabad',
'Maharashtra':'Mumbai'}
>>> dict1.update(dict2)
>>> items
dict_items([('Maharashtra', 'Mumbai'), ('Andhra
Pradesh', 'Amaravati'), ('UP', 'Lucknow'),
('Telangana', 'Hyderabad')])
>>>
```

We have thus reached the end of fairly lengthy introductory chapter of this book. As mentioned in the preface, this (and next) chapter is intended to be a quick-start tutorial to Python. So try and explore Python as much as you can with Python's interactive shell.

Next chapter explains how Python's scripting mode works. Python's conditional and looping techniques are also discussed there.

CHAPTER 2

Program Flow Control

In the previous chapter, although we briefly discussed the scripting mode of Python interpreter, we mostly worked with Python in interactive mode. It is definitely useful in getting acquainted with the features and syntax of Python especially while learning. It doesn't prove to be useful though, if you want to execute certain set of instructions repeatedly. In case, if you want to automate a certain process, scripting mode is needed. As we saw in previous chapter, script is executed from command prompt as follows *(figure 2.1)*:

```
C:\Users\acer>python hello.py
enter your name..Akshay
Hello Akshay how are you?
```

Figure 2.1 Command prompt

A program is a set of instructions, which is saved as a script and can be executed together as and when needed. A Python program is simply a text file with **.py** extension and contains one or more than one Python statements. Statements are executed in the order in which they are written in script.

Statements in a program follow **input-process-output** pattern sequentially. However, it is useful only in very simplistic problems, where one or more inputs are collected, processed and, result of process is displayed. More realistic and real world problems require appropriate decisions to be taken depending on varying situations. In other words, we definitely want program to have '*decision*' taking ability.

Many a times an entire process, or a part of it, may be required to be executed repeatedly until a situation arrives or is encountered. In such case, default sequential flow of program is diverted back to one of earlier statements, thereby constituting a '*loop*'.

The decision statements and looping statements are essential part of any programming language. In this chapter, you will learn to use Python keywords implementing decision control (**if, else,** and **elif**) and repetition control (**while** and **for**).

Both these programming constructs, decision and repetition controls are implemented conditionally i.e. based on whether a certain logical expression that evaluates to Boolean value (True or False). Python uses set of comparison operators to form a logical expression.

The symbols >, <, >=, and <= carry their conventional meaning. The '==' symbol is defined as *'is equal to'* operator that returns True if both operands are equal and False otherwise. The '!=' symbol acts as the opposite. It may be called *'not equal to'* operator and returns False if operands are equal.

Example 2.1

```
>>> a=10
>>> b=5
>>> a>b
True
>>> a<b
False
>>> a>=b*2
True
>>> a*2<=b*4
True
>>> a==b*2
True
>>> a/2!=b
False
>>>
```

2.1 Decision Control

Python's if keyword constructs a conditional statement. It evaluates a boolean expression and executes indented block of statements following it. The block is initiated by putting ':' symbol after the expression. (Indentation was already explained in previous chapter.) Following skeleton shows typical usage of **if** statement and conditional block in a Python script:

Example 2.2

```
#using if statement
if expression==True:
        #block of one or more statements
        statement1
        statement2
        . . .

        . . .
        end of if block
#rest of the statements
```

Let us try to understand this with the help of a simple example. Following script computes tax on employee's salary @10% if it is greater than or equal to 50,000. No tax is deducted if salary is less than 50,000.

Example 2.3

```
#tax1.py
salary=int(input("enter salary.."))
tax=0
if salary>=50000:
        #tax @10%
        tax=salary*10/100
net_sal=salary-tax
print ("Salary={} tax={} net payable={}".
format(salary, tax, net_sal))
```

Save above script as '**tax1.py**' and run it from command prompt as shown below *(figure 2.2)*:

```
C:\python37>python tax1.py
enter salary..75000
Salary=75000 tax=7500.0 net payable=67500.0

C:\python37>python tax1.py
enter salary..30000
Salary=30000 tax=0 net payable=30000

C:\python37>
```

Figure 2.2 if Statement

Python also provides **else** keyword. If there is another block of statements to be executed when the expression in **if** statement happens to be no True (False), it appears as:

Example 2.4

```
#using if statement
if expression==True:
        #if block
        statement1
        statement2
        . . .
        . . .
        #end of if block
else:
        #else block
        statement1
        statement2
        . . .
        . . .
        #end of else block
#rest of the statements
```

To show use of **else** block, let us modify previous example of computation of tax, assuming that tax is calculated 5% for salary<50000.

Example 2.5

```
#tax2.py
salary=int(input("enter salary.."))
tax=0
if salary>=50000:
        #tax @10%
        tax=salary*10/100
else:
        #tax@5%
        tax=salary*5/100
net_sal=salary-tax
print ("Salary={} tax={} net payable={}".
format(salary, tax, net_sal))
```

Two sample executions of above script (**tax2.py**) are as shown below (*figure 2.3*):

```
C:\python37>python tax2.py
enter salary..60000
Salary=60000 tax=6000.0 net payable=54000.0
C:\python37>python tax2.py
enter salary..20000
Salary=20000 tax=1000.0 net payable=19000.0


C:\python37>
```

Figure 2.3 if - else Statement

Python also has **elif** keyword. Before using it in a Python script, let us modify above tax calculation program to include few more tax slabs. Tax rate for salary above 50,000 is same @10%. However, 5% tax is imposed for salary between 25,001 – 50,000. Employee with salary between 10,001 – 25000 pays 2% tax, and anything below it requires no tax to be deducted. The script looks like as:

Example 2.6

```
#tax3.py
salary=int(input("enter salary.."))
tax=0
if salary>=50000:
        #tax @10%
        tax=salary*10/100
else:
        if salary>25000:
                #tax @5%
                tax=salary*5/100
        else:
                if salary>10000:
                        #tax @2%
                        tax=salary*2/100
                else:
                        #no tax
                        print ("No tax applicable")
net_sal=salary-tax
print ("Salary={} tax={} net payable={}".
format(salary, tax, net_sal))
```

Here's the output showing different tax slabs *(figure 2.4)*:

```
C:\python37>python tax3.py
enter salary..60000
Salary=60000 tax=6000.0 net payable=54000.0

C:\python37>python tax3.py
enter salary..40000
Salary=40000 tax=2000.0 net payable=38000.0

C:\python37>python tax3.py
enter salary..18000
Salary=18000 tax=360.0 net payable=17640.0

C:\python37>python tax3.py
enter salary..5000
No tax applicable
Salary=5000 tax=0 net payable=5000

E:\python37>
```

Figure 2.4 if – else blocks

While the output is satisfactory as per the expectations, the code (**tax3. py**) looks a little clumsy because of increasing indent level of successive if blocks which fall in else part of previous if statement. This is where use of **elif** keyword provides a more elegant way to avoid these indentations and combine empty else with subsequent if block. General syntax of if – elif – else usage is as shown below:

Example 2.7

```
#using elif statement
if expr1==True:
        #first block

        ...
        #end of first block
elif expr2==True:
  #second block. executes if expr1 is False  and
expr2 is true.

        ...
```

```
        #end of second block
elif exp3==True:
        #third block. executes if expr2 is false and
expr3 is true
        . . .
        #end of third block
else:
        #else block. executes if all preceding
expressions are false
        . . .
        end of else block
#rest of the statements
```

In this structure, there is one if block, followed by one or more elif blocks and one else block at the end. Each subsequent elif is evaluated if previous expression fails. Last else block is run only when all previous expressions turn out to be not true. Importantly all blocks have same level of indentation. Here, is another version of **tax3.py** which uses **elif** blocks.

Example 2.8

```
#tax4.py
salary=int(input("enter salary.."))
tax=0
if salary>=50000:
        #tax @10%
        tax=salary*10/100
elif salary>25000:
        #tax @5%
        tax=salary*5/100
elif salary>10000:
        #tax @2%
        tax=salary*2/100
else:
        #no tax
        print ("No tax applicable")
net_sal=salary-tax
print ("Salary={} tax={} net payable={}".
format(salary, tax, net_sal))
```

Output of course will be similar as before.

2.2 Repetition

Python's keywords to construct conditional statements are more or less similar to those found in other languages such as C/C++, Java, and so on. Same is with the repletion control statements. Python has keywords - **while** and **for** - using which a loop can be formed in a program. While their usage is similar to that of other languages, there are certain Python specific changes.

As mentioned in the beginning of this chapter, by default the statements in a program are executed sequentially. However, instead of going to next instruction, if program flow redirected to any of earlier steps, it results in repetitive execution of part of statements in the script.

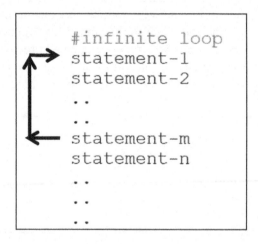

Figure 2.5 Infinite loop

If, as shown in figure 2.5, we somehow manage to make the program go back to statement-1 after statement-m (instead of next in line), the result will be a continuous execution of statements 1 to m which won't stop on its own and it forms a loop called as **infinite loop**. Obviously this situation is never desired. Instead, we should have a mechanism by which repetition is conditional. The while keyword does exactly the same – it constructs a **conditional loop.**

2.3 while Statement

The **while** keyword constructs a conditional loop. Python interpreter evaluates boolean expression and keeps on executing the subsequent uniformly indented block of statements as long as it holds true. The moment it is no longer true, the repetition stops and program flow proceeds to next statement in the script. A syntactical representation of usage of **while** loop is as follows:

Example 2.9

```
#using while statement
while expression==True:
        #while block
        . . .
        end of while block
#rest of the statements
```

One way to control repetition is to keep its count and allow next round of execution of block till count exceeds a desired limit. In the following code snippet, the block executes repeatedly till count is <= 5.

Example 2.10

```
#while-1.py
count=0
while count<5:
        #count repetitions
        count=count+1
        print ("This is count number",count)
print ("end of 5 repetitions")
```

Output *(figure 2.6)*:

```
E:\python37>python while-1.py
This is count number 1
This is count number 2
This is count number 3
This is count number 4
This is count number 5
end of 5 repetitions

E:\python37>
```

Figure 2.6 while Loop

The expression in **while** statement is executed before each round of repetition (also called **iteration**). Here is another example to consolidate your understanding of while loop.

Following code generates the list of numbers in Fibonacci series. First two numbers in the list are 0 and 1. Each subsequent number is the sum of previous two numbers. The **while** loop in the code adds next 10 numbers. The iterations are counted with the help of variable 'i'. sum of numbers at i^{th} and $(i+1)^{th}$ position is appended to the list till 'i' reaches 10.

Example 2.11

```
#fibolist.py
FiboList=[]
i=0
max=1
FiboList.append(i)
FiboList.append(max)
while i<10:
        #next number is sum of previous two
        max=FiboList[i]+FiboList[i+1]
        FiboList.append(max)
        i=i+1
print ('Fibonacci series:',FiboList)
```

Output *(figure 2.7)*:

```
E:\python37>python fibolist.py
Fibonacci series: [0, 1, 1, 2, 3, 5, 8, 13, 21, 34,
55, 89]

E:\python37>
```

Figure 2.7 Fibonacci Series

2.4 for Keyword

Like many other languages, Python also provides for keyword to construct a loop. However, Python's for loop is a little different from others. Instead of count based looping mechanism, Python's **for** loop iterates over each item in a collection object such as list, tuple, and so on.

Python's sequence type objects are the collections of items. These objects have an in-built iterator. Iterator is a stream that serves one object at a time until it is exhausted. Such objects are also called **iterables**. Python's **for** loop processes one constituent of an iterable at a time till it is exhausted. The general form of usage of for statement is as follows:

Example 2.12

```
#using for loop
for obj in iterable:
        #for block
        #processing instructions of each object
        . .
        end of block
```

Unlike the **while** loop, any other Boolean expression is not required to control repetition of this block. Let us take a simple example. If you want to calculate square of each number in a list, use for loop as shown below:

Example 2.13

```
#for-1.py
numbers=[4,7,2,5,8]
for num in numbers:
        sqr=num*num
        print ('sqaure of {} is {}'.format(num,sqr))
```

Output *(figure 2.8)*:

```
E:\python37>python for-1.py
sqaure of 4 is 16
sqaure of 7 is 49
sqaure of 2 is 4
sqaure of 5 is 25
sqaure of 8 is 64

E:\python37>
```

Figure 2.8 for Loop

Just as a list, a tuple or string object is also an iterable. Following code snippet uses a **for** loop to traverse the characters in a sentence and count number of words in it assuming that a single space (' ')separates them.

Example 2.14

```
#for-2.py
sentence='Simple is better than complex and Complex
is better than complicated.'
wordcount=1
for char in sentence:
        if char==' ':
                wordcount=wordcount+1
print ('the sentence has {} words'.
format(wordcount))
```

Output *(figure 2.9)*:

```
E:\python37>python for-2.py
the sentence has 11 words

E:\python37>
```

Figure 2.9 Output

2.5 Using range

Python's built-in **range()** function returns an immutable sequence of numbers that can be iterated over by **for** loop. The sequence generated by **range()** function depends on three parameters.

The start and step parameters are optional. If it is not used, then start is always 0 and step is 1. The range contains numbers between start and stop-1, separated by step. Consider an example 2.15:

Example 2.15

```
range(10) generates 0,1,2,3,4,5,6,7,8,9

range(1,5) results in 1,2,3,4

range(20,30,2) returns 20,22,24,26,28
```

We can use this range object as iterable as in the example 2.16. It displays squares of all odd numbers between 11-20. Remember that last number in the range is one less than stop parameter (and step is 1 by default)

Example 2.16

```
#for-3.py
for num in range(11,21,2):
        sqr=num*num
        print ('sqaure of {} is {}'.format(num,sqr))
```

Output *(figure 2.10)*:

```
E:\python37>python for-3.py
sqaure of 11 is 121
sqaure of 13 is 169
sqaure of 15 is 225
sqaure of 17 is 289
sqaure of 19 is 361
```

Figure 2.10 range Function

In previous chapter you have used **len()** function that returns number of items in a sequence object. In next example, we use **len()** to construct a range of indices of items in a list. We traverse the list with the help of index.

Example 2.17

```
#for-4.py
numbers=[4,7,2,5,8]
for indx in range(len(numbers)):
        sqr=numbers[indx]*numbers[indx]
        print ('sqaure of {} is {}'.
format(numbers[indx],sqr))
```

Output *(figure 2.11):*

```
E:\python37>python for-4.py
sqaure of 4 is 16
sqaure of 7 is 49
sqaure of 2 is 4
sqaure of 5 is 25
sqaure of 8 is 64

E:\python37>
```

Figure 2.11 Output

Have a look at another example of employing for loop over a range. Following script calculates factorial value of a number. Note that factorial of n (mathematical notation is **n!**) is cumulative product of all integers between the range of 1 to n.

Example 2.18:

```
#factorial.py
n=int(input("enter number.."))
#calculating factorial of n
f=1
for i in range(1,n+1):
        f=f*i
print ('factorial of {} = {}'.format(n,f))
```

Output *(figure 2.12):*

```
E:\python37>python factorial.py
enter number..5
factorial of 5 = 120
```

Figure 2.11 Factorial example

2.6 for loop with dictionary

Dictionary object is not iterable as it is an unordered collection of k-v pairs. However, its views returned by methods – **items()**, **keys()**, and **values()** – do return iterables. So, it is possible to use for statement with them. Following code snippet displays each state-capital pair in given dictionary object.

Example 2.19

```
#for-5.py
dict1={'Maharashtra': 'Bombay', 'Andhra Pradesh':
'Hyderabad', 'UP': 'Lucknow', 'MP': 'Bhopal'}
for pair in dict1.items():
        print (pair)
```

Output *(figure 2.12)*:

```
E:\python37>python for-5.py
('Maharashtra', 'Bombay')
('Andhra Pradesh', 'Hyderabad')
('UP', 'Lucknow')
('MP', 'Bhopal')

E:\python37>
```

Figure 2.12 Output

As you can see, each pair happens to be a tuple. You can easily unpack it in two different variables as follows:

Example 2.20

```
#for-6.py
dict1={'Maharashtra': 'Bombay', 'Andhra Pradesh':
'Hyderabad', 'UP': 'Lucknow', 'MP': 'Bhopal'}
for k,v in dict1.items():
        print ('capital of {} is {}.'.format(k,v))
```

Output *(figure 2.13)*:

```
E:\python37>python for-6.py
capital of Maharashtra is Bombay.
capital of Andhra Pradesh is Hyderabad.
capital of UP is Lucknow.
capital of MP is Bhopal.

E:\python37>
```

Figure 2.13 Output

The **keys()** and **values()** methods also return iterables. The
keys() view returns collection of keys. Each key is then used to fetch
corresponding value by **get()** method of dictionary object.

Example 2.21

```
#for-7.py
dict1={'Maharashtra': 'Bombay', 'Andhra Pradesh':
'Hyderabad', 'UP': 'Lucknow', 'MP': 'Bhopal'}
for k in dict1.keys():
        state=k
        capital=dict1.get(k)
        print ('capital of {} is
{}.'.format(state,capital))
```

2.7 Repetition Control

A looping construct is normally designed to make a certain number of
repetitions. For example, the Boolean expression in while statement
decides how many times the block will be repeatedly executed. In case of
for loop, it is decided by the length of iterable.

But what if a situation requires early termination of loop? Consider an
example: your program gives the user 10 chances to guess a secret number.
Obviously, user input and comparison logic forms body of the loop.
However, if user guesses it right earlier than stipulated chances, naturally
the loop should terminate without undergoing all repetitions. Following
figure 2.14 explains this scenario:

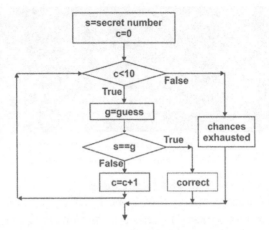

Figure 2.14 Early termination of loop

Python's **break** keyword serves exactly this purpose. This keyword appears in a conditional statement inside loop's body. If and when the statement evaluates to true, the break statement causes current loop to be abandoned before the stipulated number of repetitions.

Following Python code implements figure 2.14 flowchart algorithm. To start with a random integer is set as secret number. (The **randint()** function is defined in built-in random module. More about it in next chapter.) The while loop gives 10 chances for user to guess it correctly, but terminates early if user gets it right.

Example 2.22

```
#secret-number.py
import random
secret=random.randint(1,10)
chances=0
while chances<10:
        guess=int(input('enter your guess..'))
        if guess==secret:
                print ('you got that right!')
                break
        print ('try again..')

        chances=chances+1
        if chances==10:
                print ('chances exhausted. secret
number is:',secret)
```

Output of above code is shown below. However your result is likely to be different because secret number is generated randomly.

Output *(figure 2.15)*

```
E:\python37>python secret-number.py
enter your guess..1
try again..
enter your guess..2
try again..
enter your guess..3
try again..
enter your guess..4
you got that right!
```

Figure 2.15 break Statement

Python also has **continue** keyword which is more or less opposite to break. Instead of breaking out of current loop, when encountered, continue sends program control back to beginning of loop. Remaining statements in current iteration will not be executed.

Typical scenario of continue in a loop is like this:

A loop accepts five numbers from user and displays the sum. However, if a negative number is input, user is forced to input again. The negative number is kept away from sum operation. Look at the following flowchart *(figure 2.16)*:

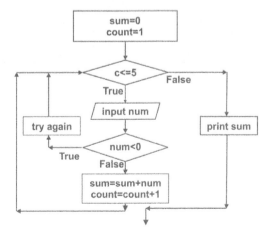

Figure 2.16 Continue in a loop

Following Python code implements above algorithm *(figure 2.16)*.

Example 2.23

```
#continue-example.py
count=1
sum=0
while count<=5:
        num=int(input('enter a number..'))
        if num<0:
                print ('negative number is not
accepted. Try again..')
                continue
        sum=sum+num
        count=count+1
print ('sum=',sum)
```

Output *(figure 2.17)*:

```
E:\python37>python continue-example.py
enter a number..2
enter a number..4
enter a number..-1
negative number is not accepted. Try again..
enter a number..6
enter a number..-9
negative number is not accepted. Try again..
enter a number..3
enter a number..1
sum= 16

E:\python37>
```

Figure 2.17   continue Statement

else Statement with Loop

This might be a bit of surprise to you if you know any C family language (e.g. C, C++, Java, C#, and so on.) The **else** keyword is normally used to describe action to be taken when the expression in if statement is false. While this usage is also defined in Python, **else** is also used along with looping constructs, both **while** and **for**.

When constructing a loop, you can use optional **else** block just after loop's body. Rest of the statements follow after the **else** block. The else block comes into play after loop is over, but before leaving the loop.

Example 2.24

```
#else with loop
while expression==True:
        #while block
        . .
        #end of while block
else:
        #else block
        . .
        #end of else block
#ret of the statements
. .
```

Following code is typical use case of **else** with a loop. The objective is to determine whether input number is prime or not. The number is successively divided by all numbers between 2 and n. If any number is able to divide it without leaving remainder, it is a prime. After completion of loop, **else** block displays message of prime number.

Example 2.25

```
#else-in-loop.py
num=int(input("enter a number.."))
x=2
while x<num:
        if num%x==0:
                print ("{} is not
prime.".format(num))
                break
        x=x+1
else:
    print ("{} is prime.".format(num))
print ('end of program')
```

Note that the else block won't come into picture if loop breaks prematurely as it would happen in case the number is not prime. Here is the output of above script:

Output *(figure 2.18)*:

```
E:\python37>python else-in-loop.py
enter a number..31
31 is prime.
end of program

E:\python37>python else-in-loop.py
enter a number..24
24 is not prime.
end of program

E:\python37>
```

Figure 2.18 Output

It is possible to provide else block to for loop also. You can try writing above prime number example using **for** loop.

Hint: You may have to use **range()** function in it.

2.8 Nested Loops

Nesting is a very popular term in programming parlance. It indicates existence of a certain entity inside another which is of same type. If you have a situation where an if statement appears inside another if statement, it is termed as **nested if**. Similarly a loop within another loop constitutes nested loops. It is also possible to have nested functions, classes, and so on. We are going to discuss nested loops here.

As mentioned above, nested loop means existence of loop within loop. Following diagram illustrates the situation (figure 2.19):

```
    # nested loops
┌── while expr1==True :
│           #outer loop
│           ..
│       ┌── while expr2==True :
│       │                   #inner loop
│       │                   ..
│       └─►                 #end of inner loop
│           ..
└─►         #end of outer loop
```

Figure 2.19 Nested loop

What happens when such nesting of loop is done? Each repetition of outer loop encounters inner loop which has to complete its own repetitions before next round of outer loop starts. As a result if outer loop is designed to perform m iterations and inner loop is designed to perform n iterations, the innermost statement will be executed mXn times.

There are number of instances around us where looping activities are performed in nested manner. The clock for example has three loops. Outer loop counting hours has a nested loop for minutes, which in turn has a seconds loop.

Any type of loop (**while** or **for**) can appear in any other type. However, in practice we find nesting of for loops. Following example displays all prime numbers between 1 and 100. Outer loop iterates over a range object. Inner loop checks whether each number in outer range is prime or not.

Example 2.26

```
#nestedfor.py
for num in range(1,101):
        for x in range(2,num):
                if num%x==0:
                        break
                x=x+1
        else:
                print (num,sep=' ', end=' ')
```

Output *(figure 2.20)*:

```
E:\python37>python nestedfor.py
1 2 3 5 7 11 13 17 19 23 29 31 37 41 43 47 53 59 61
67 71 73 79 83 89 97
E:\python37>
```

Figure 2.20 Nested Loop

2.9 List Comprehension

Python supports many functional programming features. List comprehension is one of them. This technique follows mathematical set builder notation. It is a very concise and efficient way of creating new list by performing a certain process on each item of existing list. List comprehension is considerably efficient than processing a list by for loop.

Suppose we want to compute square of each number in a list and store squares in another list object. We can do it by a **for** loop as shown below:

Example 2.27

```
#new list with loop
list1=[4,7,2,5,8]
list2=[]
for num in list1:
        sqr=num*num
        list2.append(sqr)
print ('new list:', list2)
```

The new list will store squares of existing list.

List comprehension method achieves same result more efficiently. List comprehension statement uses the following syntax:

```
newlist = [x for x in sequence]
```

We use above format to construct list of squares by using list conmprehension.

Example 2.28

```
>>> list1=[4,7,2,5,8]
>>> list2=[num*num for num in list1]
>>> list2
[16, 49, 4, 25, 64]
>>>
```

We can even generate a dictionary or tuple object as a result of list comprehension.

Example 2.29

```
>>> list1=[4,7,2,5,8]
>>> dict1=[{num:num*num} for num in list1]
>>> dict1
[{4: 16}, {7: 49}, {2: 4}, {5: 25}, {8: 64}]
>>>
```

List comprehension works with any iterable. Nested loops can also be used in a list comprehension expression. To obtain list of all combinations of characters from two strings:

Example 2.30

```
>>> list1=[x+y for x in 'ABC' for y in '123']
>>> list1
['A1', 'A2', 'A3', 'B1', 'B2', 'B3', 'C1', 'C2',
'C3']
>>>
```

The resulting list stores all combinations of one character from each string.

We can even have **if** condition in list comprehension. Following statement will result in list of all non-vowel alphabets in a string.

Example 2.31

```
>>> consonents=[char for char in "Simple is better
than complex" if char not in ['a','e','i','o','u']]
>>> consonents
['S', 'm', 'p', 'l', ' ', 's', ' ', 'b', 't', 't',
'r', ' ', 't', 'h', 'n', ' ', 'c', 'm', 'p', 'l',
'x']
>>>
```

Conditionals and looping constructs are two most important tools in programmer's armoury. Along with them, we also learnt about controlling repetition with break and continue statements.

Next chapter introduces the concept of structured programming through the use of functions and modules.

CHAPTER 3
Structured Python

Previous two chapters explained some basic features of Python, which will empower you to develop programming solution for just about any algorithm. Now it's time to learn how to make the solution more tidy, efficient, and easy to maintain.

In previous chapter, **factorial.py** code calculates factorial value of a number. Based on same algorithm, let us calculate combination of two numbers. In mathematics, a combination is a selection of items from a collection, such that (unlike permutations) the order of selection does not matter. Its mathematical notation is $_nC_r$. Following script uses **for** loop in its solution.

Example 3.1

```
#combinations.py
n=int(input("enter n.."))
r=int(input("enter r.."))
t=n-r
#calculating factorial of n - fn
fn=1
for i in range(1,n+1):
        fn=fn*i
#calculating factorial of r - fr
fr=1
for i in range(1,r+1):
        fr=fr*i
#calculating factorial of t - tr
ft=1
for i in range(1,t+1):
        ft=ft*i
combinations=fn/(fr*ft)
print ("C({},{})={}".format(n,r, combinations))
```

Output *(figure 3.1)***:**

```
E:\python37>python combinations.py
enter n..5
enter r..2
C(5,2)=10.0
E:\python37>python combinations.py
enter n..10
enter r..5
C(10,5)=252.0
```

Figure 3.1 Output

Looks alright isn't it? However, looking at above code, the thing that strikes immediately is that it uses for loop thrice to calculate factorial value of three numbers. Following code is the alternative solution to the same problem but appears to be cleaner and more concise.

Example 3.2

```
#combinations-2.py
#calculate factorial
def factorial(x):
        f=1
        for i in range(1,x+1):
                f=f*i
        return f
n=int(input("enter n.."))
r=int(input("enter r.."))
combinations=factorial(n)/
(factorial(r)*factorial(n-r))
print ("C({},{})={}".format(n,r, combinations))
```

3.1 Function

Function is called as a structured approach of program development. Idea is to break the algorithm into one or more smaller, independent, and reusable blocks of instructions. Each such block, designed to perform a single task is known as **function**. It is called wherever it is required in main routine of the program. When called, each function performs the process as defined in it and returns the control back to main routine. *(figure 3.2)*

```
                      # function
         ┌──────→ def AFunction ( ):
         │               # function docstring
         │               . . .
      ①                  . . .
         │               . . .
         │  ┌─②────────── return
         │  │
         │  #main routine
         │  . . .
         └──│── AFunction ( )
         └──→ . . .

            . . .
            AFunction ( )
            . . .
```

Figure 3.2 Function

Thus function is an important building block of any software. Python interpreter itself has quite a few in-built functions. You have already come across some of them. In addition, standard Python installation a library of many built-in modules (nearly 500 modules are bundled in standard Python distribution), each one having some functions defined in it. While built-in functions are always available, functions in other built-in modules have to be explicitly loaded. Remember we used a **randint()** function to generate a random integer as a secret number in previous chapter (secret-number.py). Let us look at another function that calculates square root of a number. The **sqrt()** function is defined in math module. (The math module itself contains nearly 50 functions.) You need to **import** this module for that purpose.

Example 3.3

```
>>> import math
>>> math.sqrt(100)
10.0
>>>
```

As you can see, Python interpreter has access to large number of predefined functions, either built-in or in built-in modules. You can employ these functions in your program as per requirement. You can of course develop your own function if you don't find a suitable function in any of the built-in modules. These built-in modules are appropriately named to indicate type of functions in them. Examples are **math** module (having mathematical functions) and **random** module (having random number generation functions).

Built-in modules are generally written in C and bundled with Python interpreter in precompiled form. A built-in module may be a Python script (with **.py** extension) containing useful utilities. A module may contain one or more functions, classes, variables, constants, or any other Python resources.

To display list of all available modules, use following command in Python console:

```
>>> help('modules')
```

Python has **import** keyword to load all contents of a module in current namespace of Python interpreter. Functions can then be called using **dot operator** as follows:

Example 3.4

```
import module
module.function([arguments if any])
```

Python also provides **from** keyword that allows only specified functions from a module rather than all functions. The **sqrt()** function from **math** module can also be imported as follows:

Example 3.5

```
>>> from math import sqrt
>>> sqrt(100)
10.0
>>>
```

We shall first get ourselves acquainted with some of the frequently required functions in built-in modules before we learn how to define and use own functions.

3.2 math **Module**

As you would expect, **math** built-in module is one of the most frequently used. Various functions which are often required are defined in this module.

Functions for computing all trigonometric ratios are present in math module. All these functions calculate respective ratio of an angle given in radians. Knowing that 30 degrees is roughly equal to 0.5236, various ratios are calculated as follows:

Example 3.6

```
>>> import math
>>> math.sin(0.5236)
0.5000010603626028
>>> math.cos(0.5236)
0.866024791582939
>>> math.tan(0.5236)
0.5773519017263813
>>>
```

The math module also has two functions to convert measure of angle in degrees to radians and vice versa.

Example 3.7

```
>>> math.radians(30)
0.5235987755982988
>>> math.degrees(0.52398)
30.021842549264875
>>>
```

Two important mathematical constants are defined in this module. They are **Pic (π)** and **Euler's number (e)**

Example 3.8

```
>>> math.e
2.718281828459045
>>> math.pi
3.141592653589793
>>>
```

We have used **sqrt()** function from **math** module. Likewise the module has **pow()**, **log()**, and **exp()** functions.

Example 3.9

```
>>> math.sqrt(25)
5.0
>>> math.pow(5,2)
25.0
>>> math.log(10) #natural logarithm using math.e as
base
2.302585092994046
>>> math.log10(100) #standard logarithm using 10 as
base
2.0
>>>
```

The **mod operator (%)** and **floor operator (//)** was introduced earlier. This module contains similar functions (**remainder()** and **floor()**). Another **ceil()** function in this module returns nearest integer of division operation.

Example 3.10

```
>>> math.remainder(10,6) #Difference between
numerator and closest integer multiple of
denominator
-2.0
>>> math.floor(10/6) #Returns the largest integer <=
given float
1
>>> math.ceil(10/6) #Returns the smallest integer >=
float
2
>>>
```

3.3 os Module

This is another module containing useful utilities for manipulating files and directories programmatically. The usual operating system commands for directory management have equivalents in this module. There is **mkdir()** function that creates a new directory inside current directory by default. To create it at any other location in file system, its absolute path has to be given.

Example 3.11

```
import os
os.mkdir('newdir') # inside current directory
os.mkdir('c:\\newdir') #in C drive
```

The **chdir()** function (to set current working directory) and **rmdir()** function (to remove a directory) also take relative path by default. A **getcwd()** function is also available to know which is the current working directory. All these operations are demonstrated in following interpreter session:

Example 3.12

```
>> import os
>>> os.mkdir("newdir") #new directory in current
path
>>> os.chdir("newdir") #set current directory
>>> os.getcwd() #displays current working directory
'E:\\python37\\newdir'
>>> os.rmdir("newdir") #shouldn't be current
directory and should be empty
Traceback (most recent call last):
  File "<stdin>", line 1, in <module>
FileNotFoundError: [WinError 2] The system cannot
find the file specified: 'newdir'
>>> os.chdir("..") #sets current directory to parent
directory
>>> os.getcwd()
'E:\\python37'
>>> os.rmdir("newdir") #now it can be deleted
>>> os.listdir() #returns list of files and
directories in current path
['abcdemo.py', 'aifftest.py', 'checkindent.py',
'clbr.py', 'combinations-2.py', 'combinations.py',
'comprehension1.py', 'conditionals.jpg', 'continue-
example.py', 'data_class.py', 'DLLs', 'Doc', 'else-
in-loop.py', 'equitriangle.py', 'fibolist.py',
'findertest.py', 'for-1.py', 'for-2.py', 'for-3.
py', 'for-4.py', 'for-5.py', 'for-6.py', 'for-7.
py', 'gcexample.py', 'hello.py', 'include', 'Lib',
'libs', 'LICENSE.txt', 'modfinder.py', 'modspec.
py', 'module1.py', 'module2.py', 'mydb.sqlite3',
'myfunctions.cover', 'myfunctions.py', 'mymain.
cover', 'mymain.py', 'nestedfor.py', 'newdirbak',
```

```
'NEWS.txt', 'out.aiff', 'out.au', 'out.mp3',
'out.wma', 'polar.png', 'python.exe', 'python3.
dll', 'python37.dll', 'pythonw.exe', 'report.txt',
'runpyexample.py', 'sample.wav', 'Scripts', 'secret-
number.py', 'securepwd.py', 'sound.aiff', 'sound.
wav', 'sqrmodule.py', 'structexample.py', 'tabdemo.
py', 'tax1.py', 'tax2.py', 'tax3.py', 'tax4.
py', 'tcl', 'testindent.py', 'Tools', 'triangle.
py', 'trianglebrowser.py', 'vcruntime140.dll',
'warningexample.py', 'wavetest.py', 'while-1.py', '_
threadexample.py', '__pycache__']
>>>
```

The os module also has functions to create a new file and perform read/ write operations on it. We shall learn about these functions in chapter on File Handling.

3.4 sys Module

This module defines some important system-specific parameters and functions. In this section you will learn one such parameter which is useful in scripting mode of Python.

sys.argv stores a list of all command line arguments provided to Python script. We know that **input()** function in a Python script is used to collect user inputs. However, inputs can also be given to script from command line. They are made available to the program in the form of this list object. For example:

```
E:\python37>python example.py aa bb
```

This is the command line to execute *'example.py'* providing *'aa'* and *'bb'* as arguments. Three strings are stored in sys.argv list and can be accessed in the script. Name of script – **sysexample.py** in this case is stored at **sys.argv[0].** Other arguments are stored at successive indexes. Let sysexample.py script be as follows:

Example 3.13

```
#example.py
import sys
args=sys.argv
print ("Hello {}".format(sys.argv[1]))
```

It is now executed from command line. *(figure 3.3)*

```
E:\python37>python sysexample.py Python
Hello Python
E:\python37>python sysexample.py Java
Hello Java
```

Figure 3.3 Command line

We are going to learn few more built-in modules and their functions in following chapters:

- **Serialization :** csv module, picke module, dbm module, json module.

- **DB-API :** sqlite3 module, pymysql module, pyodbc module.

3.5 User Defined Functions

As mentioned earlier, it is possible to define a custom function if you don't find a suitable one in the collection of predefined functions. It is popularly called as user defined function. So, let us proceed to define a new function and learn how to use it.

Python provides **def** keyword for this purpose. This keyword is followed by a suitable identifier and in front of which give parentheses. The parentheses may or may not have anything inside. This is followed by function block of one or more statements of uniform indent level. A formal outline of function definition appears like this:

Example 3.14

```
#defining a function
def AFunction([p1,p2,..]):
        'function docstring as first line in function
block'
        ..
        ..
        return [value]
```

As always you'll use ':' symbol to start a block. You may write a string literal as explanatory string for the function. It is called docstring and is optional. Something similar to comment but is treated as value of function's __doc__ attribute.

Subsequent lines can have any number of valid Python statements as demanded by function's processing logic. Last statement of the block should be **return** indicating that program's control is going back to the position from where this function was called. You may put an expression in its front if it is required that this function should not just return but return with a value (most of the times, result of the function).

How should this user defined function be called? Just use its name as a Python statement anywhere in the code after it has been defined. Of course you need to provide adequate parameters if the function's definition contains any.

So, let us define a function with the name '**zen**' and no parameters. When called, it will print a couple of lines from '*Zen of Python*' – a set of guiding principles that govern design philosophy of Python.

Example 3.15

```
#function-1.py
def zen():
        'Zen of Python'
        print ('Beautiful is better than ugly.
Explicit is better than implicit.')
        print ('Simple is better than complex.
Complex is better than complicated.')
        return
#call above function
zen()
print ('Docstring:', zen.__doc__)
```

Output *(figure 3.4)*:

```
E:\python37>python function-1.py
Beautiful is better than ugly. Explicit is better
than implicit.
Simple is better than complex. Complex is better
than complicated.
Docstring: Zen of Python
```

Figure 3.4 Output

Note that docstring – the first line in function block is not executed by interpreter but is recognized as value of __doc__ attribute.

3.6 Function with Parameters

A parameter (also called argument) is certain data passed on to the function while calling it. In previous section (**sys** module) showed how command line arguments passed to a Python script can be processed by using **sys.argv** parameter. Similarly one or more parameters can be passed to function from inside script. Values of received parameters are then processed inside the function.

Two things must be kept in mind here. First, the function should be defined taking into consideration the number of parameters it is going to receive. Secondly, the function call should ensure it passes adequate number of parameters as anticipated in function's definition. Variables used in function's definition to receive passed values are often called formal arguments. Actual arguments are the values passed while calling.

In following script, **LoveU()** function is defined with one argument with a formal name as '*lang*'. Its value is used in the function to print relevant message. User input is passed to this function as actual argument.

Example 3.16

```
#function-2.py
def LoveU(lang):
        'function with one parameter'
        print ('I love {}'.format(lang))
        return
#call above function
lang=input('enter name of a language..')
LoveU(lang)
```

Output *(figure 3.5)*

```
E:\python37>python function-2.py
enter name of a language..Python
I love Python
E:\python37>python function-2.py
enter name of a language..Hindi
I love Hindi
```

Figure 3.5 passing parameter

3.7 return Keyword

The **return** keyword at the end of function block is merely to indicate that program flow would be returned to calling position after the block is over. Use of return is optional in the sense program flow anyway goes back to calling position even if it is not used. However, if you intend to send some data back to calling environment, then return keyword must be used along with the expression to be returned.

Following script is a simple example of a function returning its result. It defines **add()** function to receive two numbers, perform addition, and return the result.

Example 3.17

```
#func-with-return.py
def add(num1,num2):
        'function assumes a two numbers to be
passed'
        result=num1+num2
        return result
#call above function
x=int(input('enter a number..'))
y=int(input('enter another number..'))
z=add(x,y)
print ('addition of {} and {} is {}'.format(x,y,z))
```

Output *(figure 3.6)*

```
E:\python37>python func-with-return.py
enter a number..100
enter another number..200
addition of 100 and 200 is 300
```

Figure 3.6 return Statement

3.8 Required Arguments

The statement that calls a function should pass exactly same number of values as number of actual arguments in its definition, otherwise Python raises **TypeError** as in following example, where the function is defined with two parameters but there is an attempt to call it with three values.

Example 3.18

```
#function-3.py
def LoveU(lang1, lang2):
        'function with two parameters'
        print ('I love {} and {}'.format(lang1, lang2))
        return
#call above function
LoveU('Hindi', 'Python', 'Java')
```

Output *(figure 3.7)*

```
E:\python37>python function-3.py
Traceback (most recent call last):
  File "function-3.py", line 7, in <module>
    LoveU('Hindi', 'Python', 'Java')
TypeError: LoveU() takes 2 positional arguments but
3 were given
E:\python37>
```

Figure 3.7 Output

Values passed to a function are picked up by formal arguments in positional order. Since Python doesn't enforce static typing, any formal argument may hold any type of data. However, there still may be error raised inside a function if treatment of the variable is not as per its value.

Look at following script. The function in it receives two values. First one is expected to be a string and second a number. The function calculates length of string – the first parameter and determines if the number – second argument – is odd/even. Therefore, the function receives two values but with mismatching types, **TypeError** is raised when trying to compute **len()** on a number data type.

Example 3.19

```
#function-4.py
def function(string,num):
        'function assumes a string and number to be
passed'
        print ('parameter received', string, num)
        print ('length of string:', len(string))
        if num%2==0:
```

```
            print (num,' is ','even')
        else:
                print (num, ' is ','odd')
        return
#call above function
function ('Hello', 10)
function (10, 'Hello')
```

Output *(figure 3.8)*:

```
E:\python37>python function-4.py
parameter received Hello 10
length of string: 5
10  is  even
parameter received 10 Hello
Traceback (most recent call last):
  File "function-4.py", line 13, in <module>
    function (10, 'Hello')
  File "function-4.py", line 5, in function
    print ('length of string:', len(string))
TypeError: object of type 'int' has no len()
```

Figure 3.8 Output

3.9 Parameter with Default Value

You can have a function that defines one or more parameters with default value. If the function call doesn't explicitly give any value to the said parameter, the default will be used inside the function. If however, the call does pass a value, it will override the default set in function's definition.

Example 3.20

```
#func-with-default.py
def dress(trouser, shirt='White'):
        print ('Trouser is {}. Shirt is {}'.
format(trouser,shirt))
dress('Black')
dress('Blue','Green')
```

You can see that second argument is having a default value. First call doesn't give any value to it, so default is used. Second call overrides the default value. The output demonstrates this behaviour *(figure 3.9)*:

```
E:\python37>python func-with-default.py
Trouser is Black. Shirt is White
Trouser is Blue. Shirt is Green
```

Figure 3.9 Default arguments

There is one precaution to be taken. Arguments with default value must appear after the required arguments in the parameter list of function definition.

3.10 Keyword Arguments

We now know that the values passed to a function are read as per the order in which parameters are defined. However, if you do want to pass values out of order, use the parameter's name as keyword. Following code snippet will illustrate the point:

Example 3.21

```
#func-with-keywords.py
def division(num, denom):
        div=num/denom
        print ('numerator:{} denominator: {}
division: {}'.format(num,denom,div))
division(10,2)
division(2,10)
division(denom=2, num=10)
```

In first two cases, first argument becomes numerator and second becomes denominator as values are picked up by formal parameter names as per the order. In last case, name of the parameter is used as keyword so that even if values are passed out of order, they go in desired parameters of the function.

Output *(figure 3.10)*

```
E:\python37>python func-with-keywords.py
numerator:10 denominator: 2 division: 5.0
numerator:2 denominator: 10 division: 0.2
numerator:10 denominator: 2 division: 5.0
```

Figure 3.10 Keyword arguments

Note that in above example, use of keyword arguments is optional. To force compulsory use of keyword arguments, use '*' as one parameter in parameter list. All parameters after * become keyword only parameters. Any parameters before * continue to be positional parameters.

Above example is modified so that both parameters are made keyword-only by putting * as first parameter in the list. Now if you try to call **division()** function without specifying keywords, TypeError is raised.

Example 3.22

```
#func-with-kwonly.py
def division(*,num, denom):
        div=num/denom
        print ('numerator:{} denominator: {}
division: {}'.format(num,denom,div))
division(denom=2, num=10)
division(10,2)
```

Output *(figure 3.11)*

```
E:\python37>python func-with-kwonly.py
numerator:10 denominator: 2 division: 5.0
Traceback (most recent call last):
  File "func-with-kwonly.py", line 7, in <module>
    division(10,2)
TypeError: division() takes 0 positional arguments
but 2 were given
```

Figure 3.11 Keyword-only arguments

Python uses the mechanism of keyword arguments and arguments with default value very extensively in defining built-in functions and methods. One such example is **int()** function.

In fact we had discussed **int()** function in chapter 1. It can be used as per two prototype definitions:

```
int([x])
int(x, base=10)
```

In first definition, the parameter x should be a number. The function returns its integer part. In second case, x must be a string containing digits only. Second parameter – base has a default value of 10. But it can be 2, 8, 16, and so on. i.e. base of binary, octal, or hexadecimal number system. The string is then converted to number accordingly. The base parameter can be used like a normal positional argument or keyword argument.

Example 3.23

```
>>> #converts float to int
...
>>> int(123.45)
123
>>> #converts string to number with default base 10
- decimal number system
...
>>> int('121')
121
>>> #converts string with hexadecimal digits -
base=16 as positional argument
...
>>> int('121',16)
289
>>> #converts string with hexadecimal digits -
base=16 as keyword argument
...
>>> int('121',base=16)
289
```

3.11 Function with Variable Arguments

We have already seen how arguments can be passed to Python script from command line. All arguments are stored in a list object (**sys.argv**). On similar lines, if a function is called by passing variable number of arguments from within script, they are stored in a parameter prefixed with '*'. It is a list object of all values passed. Treat it as a normal list object and process it accordingly within the function. Following script is a very appropriate example of function with variable parameters.

Example 3.24

```
#func-with-var-args.py
def addall(*nums):
        ttl=0
        for num in nums:
                ttl=ttl+num
        return ttl
total=addall(10,20,50,70)
print ('Total of 4 numbers:',total)
total=addall(11,34,43)
print ('Total of 3 numbers:',total)
```

Output *(figure 3.12)*:

```
E:\python37>python func-with-var-args.py
Total of 4 numbers: 150
Total of 3 numbers: 88
```

Figure 3.12   Variable arguments

3.12 User Defined Modules

A module is a collection of Python objects such as functions, classes, and so on. Python interpreter is bundled with a standard library consisting of large number of built-in modules, some of which we got acquainted with. Just as built-in modules, you can create collection of your own functions and import them in an interactive Python session or in another script.

Any Python script (having **.py** extension) can be used as a module. The idea behind user defined module is the same as that of built-in module. If entire programming solution involves quite a large number of functions and classes, in that case putting all definitions in a single script is likely to be troublesome. Better way is to organize them in separate modules. Functions and classes of similar relevance are kept in one module. Such an approach makes the code easier to maintain.

First of all let us put some functions in a script called *'mymodule.py'*.

Example 3.25

```python
'docstring of mymodule'
def isprime(num):
        x=2
        for x in range(2,num):
                if num%x==0:
                        return False
        else:
                return True
def iseven(num):
        if num%2==0:
                return True
        else:
                return False
def isleap(num):
        if num%4==0:
                return True
        else:
                return False
```

We can now import any function from this module in interactive interpreter session, just as we imported math module.

Example 3.26

```
>>> import mymodule
>>> mymodule.isprime(43)
True
>>> mymodule.isprime(72)
False
>>> mymodule.iseven(28)
True
>>> mymodule.iseven(93)
False
>>> mymodule.isleap(2019)
False
>>> mymodule.isleap(1996)
True
>>>
```

It is also possible to import this module in another Python script. Here is an example script *'moduledemo.py'*

Example 3.27

```
#moduledemo.py
import mymodule
print ('calling isprime function from mymodule')
n=int(input('enter a number..'))
retval=mymodule.isprime(n)
if retval==True:
        print ('{} is a prime number'.format(n))
else:
        print ('{} is not a prime number'.format(n))
```

Output *(figure 3.13)*:

```
E:\python37>python moduledemo.py
calling isprime function from mymodule
enter a number..39
39 is not a prime number
E:\python37>python moduledemo.py
calling isprime function from mymodule
enter a number..97
97 is a prime number
```

Figure 3.13 import Statement

__name__ attribute

As is often said, everything in Python is an object. Likewise, module – whether built-in or user defined - is also an object of module class.

Example 3.28

```
>>> #module object - built-in module
...
>>> import math
>>> type(math)
<class 'module'>
>>> #module object - user defined module
...
>>> import mymodule
>>> type(mymodule)
<class 'module'>
```

Module object is characterized by various attributes. One of the important attributes of module object is __name__ and it has a peculiar behaviour.

Inside Python's interactive shell, the __name__ attribute returns '__main__'. It is the name of top level namespace in which Python interpreter is running. However, value of an imported module's __name__ attribute is name of the module itself (excluding **.py** part from script's name)

Example 3.29

```
>>> #__name__ attribute of interactive shell
...
>>> __name__
'__main__'
>>> # __name__ attrbute of imported module
...
>>> import math
>>> math.__name__
'math'
>>> import mymodule
>>> mymodule.__name__
'mymodule'
```

This is also the same in case of a Python script. When a certain script is run from command line, Python is running in scripting mode. Hence value of __name__ in the script is '**__main__**'. So also, __name__ attribute of a module imported in the script is its name itself. Run following code from command line.

Example 3.30

```
#moduledemo-1.py
import mymodule
print ('__name__ of top level module:', __name__)
print ('__name__ of imported mymodule:', mymodule.__name__)
```

Output *(figure 3.14)*

```
E:\python37>python moduledemo-1.py
__name__ of top level module: __main__
__name__ of imported mymodule: mymodule
```

Figure 3.14 __name__ attribute

A script having function definitions may also have certain executable code also in it. What happens if it is imported in another script? Let us see. Open **mymodule.py** and add statements that call **iseven()** function after definitions.

Example 3.31

```
'docstring of mymodule'
def isprime(num):
        x=2
        for x in range(2,num):
                if num%x==0:
                        return False
        else:
                return True
def iseven(num):
        if num%2==0:
                return True
        else:
                return False
def isleap(num):
        if num%4==0:
                return True
```

```
        else:
                return False
##add following statements
n=int(input('enter a number..'))
retval=iseven(n)
if retval==True:
        print ('{} is even'.format(n))
else:
        print ('{} is odd'.format(n))
```

Now if the **moduledemo.py** is run (it imports mymodule in it). Look at the result. *(figure 3.15)*

```
E:\python37>python moduledemo.py
enter a number..23
23 is odd
calling isprime function from mymodule
enter a number23
23 is a prime number
```

Figure 3.15 Output

You find that the executable part in imported module also runs. Obviously we don't want this to happen. We do want the executable code to run when module script is invoked but not when it is imported. The peculiar behaviour of __name__ attribute comes in handy here. As we saw, its value happens to be '__main__' when a module script is run, but __name__ attribute takes up its name when imported. So we have to test this attribute and run the executable code only if it is '__main__'. Modify the **mymodule code** as follows:

Example 3.32

```
'docstring of mymodule'
def isprime(num):
        x=2
        for x in range(2,num):
                if num%x==0:
                        return False
        else:
                return True
def iseven(num):
```

```
        if num%2==0:
                return True
        else:
                return False
def isleap(num):
        if num%4==0:
                return True
        else:
                return False
#modify as follows:
if __name__=='__main__':
        n=int(input('enter a number..'))
        retval=iseven(n)
        if retval==True:
                print ('{} is even'.format(n))
        else:
                print ('{} is odd'.format(n))
```

You can run **mymodule.py** independently but wouldn't affect execution of **moduledemo.py**. *(figure 3.16)*

```
E:\python37>python moduledemo.py
calling isprime function from mymodule
enter a number..11
11 is a prime number
```

Figure 3.16 Output

3.13 Package

Concept of package takes Python's modular approach to next level. A package is a collection of modules. All modules having functionality of certain common features are stored in one folder. Python's standard library contains some packages that are collection of modules. For example **Tkinter** package, which is Python's implementation of **TCL/Tk UI toolkit**, consists of several modules such as tkinter. ttk, tkinter.messagebox, tkinter.commondialog, and so on. The importlib is another Python package in standard library that has multiple modules (importlib.abc, importlib.util, importlib.machinery, and so on.) You can build your own package having multiple but related modules under one folder. Let us see how it can be done.

In addition to Python modules, the folder should have a special file named as **__init__.py** for it to be recognized as a package by Python interpreter. This file is also useful to build a packaging list of functions from various modules under the folder.

So, let us build a package named as '*MyPackage*'. First of all, create a new folder at some suitable location in filesystem (for example c:\testpackage) and a subfolder under it. Name the subfolder as '*MyPackage*'. Go on to save following module scripts in it.

Example 3.33

```
#addfunctions.py
def add(num1,num2):
        result=num1+num2
        return result
def addall(*nums):
        ttl=0
        for num in nums:
                ttl=ttl+num
        return ttl
```

```
#mathfunctions.py
def sum(x,y):
    return x+y
def average(x,y):
    return (x+y)/2
def power(x,y):
    return x**y
```

```
#myfunctions.py
def isprime(num):
        x=2
        for x in range(2,num):
                if num%x==0:
                        return False
        else:
                return True
def iseven(num):
        if num%2==0:
                return True
        else:
```

```
                  return False
def isleap(num):
       if num%4==0:
                  return True
       else:
                  return False
```

In addition to above, create an empty __init__.py in Mypackage folder. The folder structure should appear as shown below *(figure 3.17)*:

```
C:\TestPackage
|    example.py
|
|____MyPackage
        addfunctions.py
        mathfunctions.py
        myfunctions.py
        __init__.py
```

Figure 3.17 Folder Structure

The **example.py** file in '*TestPackage*' folder is at the same level with MyPackage folder. We shall add code in it a little later.

Next, open command prompt window while in TestPackage directory and start Python. The child directory in it, MyPackage is recognized as a legitimate Python package because it does contain __init__.py, so you can import any module available in it. The usage is shown below:

```
C:\TestPackage>python
>>>
```

Example 3.34

```
>>> from MyPackage import addfunctions
>>> addfunctions.addall(1,2,3,4)
10
>>> from MyPackage import myfunctions
>>> myfunctions.isprime(67)
True
>>> from MyPackage import mathfunctions
>>> mathfunctions.power(10,2)
100
```

What is more, it is possible to required function by name from any module.

Example 3.35

```
>>> from MyPackage.mathfunctions import power,
average
>>> power(5,4)
625
>>> average(20,30)
25.0
```

This is where __init__.py file plays an important role. It can provide package level access to certain functions chosen from various modules. Let us modify the __init__.py script as shown below:

Example 3.36

```
#__init__.py
from .mathfunctions import average
from .addfunctions import addall
from .myfunctions import isprime, iseven
```

Now what does this __init__.py script do? It allows a function to be accessed by name of package and not by name of module in which originally defined. To verify this behaviour, save following script as '*example.py*' in parent folder ('*testpackage*')

Example 3.37

```
#example.py
import MyPackage
#calling isprime function
num=int(input('enter a number..'))
retval=MyPackage.isprime(num)
if retval==True:
        print ("{} is a prime number".format(num))
else:
        print ("{} is not a prime number".format(num))
#addall function
result=MyPackage.addall(10,20)
print ("Result of addition:",result)
```

Output *(figure 3.18)*

```
C:\TestPackage>python example.py
enter a number..23
23 is a prime number
Result of addition: 30
```

Figure 3.18 package example

In above discussion, we learned how to create a package and use it from inside its parent folder. It is also possible to install the package for system wide use. However, this book's scope doesn't cover its explanation. At this juncture, it is sufficient to state that it can be achieved by using setuptools module from Python's standard library. You can also upload your package to Python package Index repository (**https://pypi.org//**). The procedure is explained in detail on the website itself.

However it is important to know how to install a new package in your computer's Python library. Latest versions of Python com with **pip** utility.

3.14 Virtual Environment

Before we actually try and install a package from **PyPi** repository, let us understand what a virtual environment is and what are its advantages. When you install Python at a certain location in file system (ex. C:\python37), the interpreter can be invoked from anywhere provided Python executable is include in system's PATH. The folder containing library modules and packages is also set relative to Python's installation directory (C:/Python37/Lib). Naturally, when new packages/modules are installed, they will be done in this folder.

You would often be required to use a package developed by a third party (not by python.org) for a certain purpose. Package developers normally make incrementing versions of same package available. So, you may install an upgraded version of some package, and end up breaking functionality of one of your scripts because it is not compatible with the latest version! This is where setting up virtual environment proves handy.

Virtual environment helps you to keep your library isolated from global installation. It allows you to test functionality of newer version of package without creating conflict with earlier version. You can have as many side by side environments as you want. Each one of them has its own library and other directories.

Python's standard library contains **venv** module that helps you to create a named virtual environment using following command:

```
E:\python37>python -m venv e:\SQLAlchemyEnv
```

(**Note:** We shall be using this virtual environment later in the book when we discuss **SQLAlchemy** package.)

This command will create a new folder with the given name inside which it has a local copy of Python interpreter, library, and other supporting utilities. The Python executable lies in Scripts subfolder.

Before starting Python interpreter (don't start now, otherwise it will start global copy of Python!), we need to activate this newly created environment. For this purpose, the Scripts folder contains a batch file '**activate.bat**'. *(figure 3.19)*

```
E:\SQLAlchemyEnv>scripts\activate
(SQLAlchemyEnv) E:\SQLAlchemyEnv>python
Python 3.7.2 (tags/v3.7.2:9a3ffc0492, Dec 23 2018,
23:09:28) [MSC v.1916 64 bit (AMD64)] on win32
Type "help", "copyright", "credits" or "license" for
more information.
>>>
```

Figure 3.19 Virtual environment

Name of the virtual environment appears to the left of command prompt. We can now invoke Python interpreter using executable's copy available locally.

The Scripts folder is preloaded with **pip** utility (stands for **Python package installer**). This is our key to install any package from **PyPi** repository in Libs folder of current environment. Let us install **SQLAlchemy** package in **SQLAlchemyEnv** with following command *(figure 3.20)*:

```
(SQLAlchemyEnv) E:\SQLAlchemyEnv>scripts\pip3 in-
stall sqlalchemy
Collecting sqlalchemy
  Downloading https://files.pythonhosted.org/pack-
ages/c6/52/73d1c92944cd294a5b165097038418abb6a235f-
5956d43d06f97254f73bf/SQLAlchemy-1.2.17.tar.gz
(5.7MB)
    100% |████████████████████████████████| 5.7MB
119kB/s
Installing collected packages: sqlalchemy
  Running setup.py install for sqlalchemy ... done
Successfully installed sqlalchemy-1.2.17
```

Figure 3.20 Using pip utility

How do you confirm whether installation was successful? Just try importing newly installed package. If Python doesn't throw up any error, the installation is done correctly. You can also check version of installed package by typing the following command *(figure 3.21)*:

```
>>> import sqlalchemy
>>> sqlalchemy.__version__
'1.2.17'
```

Figure 3.21 Output

So there you are. We have come a long way starting from basics of Python. Next chapter introduces you to a modern approach towards programming – Object oriented methodology.

CHAPTER 4
Python - OOP

Object oriented programming paradigm has emerged as a cornerstone of modern software development. Python too is a predominantly object oriented language, although it supports classical procedural approach also. Python's implementation of OOP is a little different from that of C++ and Java, and is in keeping with **'Simple is better than Complex'** – one of the design principles of Python. Let us not go into much of theory of object oriented programming methodology and its advantages. Instead, let us dive straight into Python's brand of OOP!

Everything in Python is an **object**. This statement has appeared more than once in previous chapters. What is an object though? Simply put, object is a piece of data that has a tangible representation in computer's memory. Each object is characterized by attributes and behaviour as stipulated in a template definition called **class**. In Python, each instance of any data type is an object representing a certain class. Python's built-in **type()** function tells you to which class an object belongs to. *(figure 4.1)*

```
>>> num=1234
>>> type(num)
<class 'int'>
>>> complexnum=2+3j
>>> type(complexnum)
<class 'complex'>
>>> prices={'pen':50, 'book':200}
>>> type(prices)
<class 'dict'>
>>>
```

Figure 4.1 type() function

Each Python object also possesses an attribute **__class__** that returns class. *(figure 4.2)*

```
>>> num.__class__
<class 'int'>
>>> complexnum.__class__
<class 'complex'>
>>> prices.__class__
<class 'dict'>
>>>
```

Figure 4.2 Python object

Hence, it is clear that num is object of **int** class, complexnum is object of **complex** class, and so on. As mentioned above, an object possesses attributes (also called **data descriptors**) and methods as defined in its respective class. For example, the **complex** class defines **real** and **imag** attributes that return real and imaginary part of complex number object. It also has **conjugate()** method returning a complex number with imaginary part of opposite sign. *(figure 4.3)*

```
>>> complexnum=2+3j
>>> #attributes
...
>>> complexnum.real
2.0
>>> complexnum.imag
3.0
>>> #method
...
>>> complexnum.conjugate()
(2-3j)
```

Figure 4.3 'complex' class object

In above example, **real** and **imag** are the instance attributes as their values will be different for each object of **complex** class. Also, **conjugate()** method is an instance method. A class can also have class level attributes and methods which are shared by all objects. We shall soon come across their examples in this chapter.

Built-in data types in Python represent classes defined in builtins module. This module gets loaded automatically every time when the interpreter starts. The class hierarchy starts with **object** class. The builtins module also defines Exception and built-in functions (many of which we have come across in previous chapters).

The following diagram rightly suggests that built-in classes (**int, float, complex, bool, list, tuple, and dict**) are inherited from object class. Inheritance incidentally is one of the characteristic features of Object Oriented Programming Methodology. The **__bases__** attribute of each of these classes will confirm this.

Python's built-in function library also has **issubclass()** function to test if a certain class is inherited from other. We can use this function and confirm that all built-in classes are sub classes of object class.

Interestingly, class is also an object in Python. Another built-in function **isinstance()** returns True if first argument is an object of second argument which has to be a class. By the way, **type()** of any built-in class returns **type** which happens to be a metaclass of which all classes are objects, is itself a subclass of object as its base class. *(figure 4.4)*

```
CLASSES
    object
    |- BaseException
    |   |-- Exception(s)
    |   |   |-- Warning(s)
    |   |-- GeneratorExit
    |   |-- KeyboardInterrupt
    |   |-- SystemExit
    |- bytearray
    |- bytes
    |- classmethod
    |- complex
    |- dict
    |- enumerate
    |- filter
    |- float
    |- frozenset
    |- int
    |- |- bool
    |- list
    |- map
    |- memoryview
    |- property
    |- range
    |- reversed
    |- set
    |- slice
    |- staticmethod
    |- str
    |- super
    |- tuple
    |- type
    |- zip
    FUNCTIONS
    DATA
    FILE
```

Figure 4.4 Built-in Classes

Following interpreter activity shows that bool class is derived from int class, which is a sub class of object class and also an object of object class!

Example 4.1

```
>>> isinstance(int, object)
True
>>> issubclass(bool, int)
True
>>> int.__bases__
(<class 'object'>,)
>>> isinstance(int, object)
True
```

Each class also has access to another attribute **__mro__** (method resolution order) which can show class hierarchy of inheritance. The bool class is inherited from int and int from object.

Example 4.2

```
>>> bool.__mro__
(<class 'bool'>, <class 'int'>, <class 'object'>)
```

As mentioned above, **type()** on any built-in class returns **type** class which in turn is both a subclass and instance of object class.

Example 4.3

```
>>> type(bool)
<class 'type'>
>>> type.__bases__
(<class 'object'>,)
>>> isinstance(type, object)
True
>>> issubclass(type, object)
True
```

Other important constituents of Python program such as functions or modules are also objects, as following interpreter activity demonstrates:

Example 4.4

```
>>> #function from a module
...
>>> import math
>>> type(math.sqrt)
<class 'builtin_function_or_method'>
>>> #built-in function
...
>>> type(id)
<class 'builtin_function_or_method'>
>>> #user defined function
...
>>> def hello():
...     print ('Hello World')
...
>>> type(hello)
<class 'function'>
>>> #module is also an object
...
>>> type(math)
<class 'module'>
```

We have used **range()** function in connection with for loop. It actually returns a range object which belongs to range class.

Example 4.5

```
>>> #range is also an object
...
>>> obj=range(10)
>>> type(obj)
<class 'range'>
>>> >>> range.__bases__
(<class 'object'>,)
```

4.1 class Keyword

Apart from various built-in classes, user can define a new class with customised attributes and methods. Just as a built-in class, each user defined class is also a subclass of object class. The keyword '**class**' starts definition of a new class.

Example 4.6

```
>>> #user defined class
...
>>> class MyClass:
...      pass
...
>>> type(MyClass)
<class 'type'>
>>> MyClass.__bases__
(<class 'object'>,)
>>> issubclass(MyClass, object)
True
```

User defined name is mentioned just besides the **class** keyword and is followed by ':' symbol to initiate an indented block containing its attributes and methods. In this case the class body contains just one statement **pass** which is a no-operation keyword.

Above code clearly indicates that user defined class is subclassed from object class. It means that any Python class, built-in or user defined is either directly or indirectly inherited from parent object class. To underline this relationship explicitly, the MyClass can very well be defined as follows:

Example 4.7

```
>>> class MyClass(object):
...      pass
...
>>> MyClass.__bases__
(<class 'object'>,)
```

Now we can have objects of this class. The library function **dict()** returns an empty dictionary object. Similarly **MyClass()** would return an empty object because our new class doesn't have any attributes defined in it.

Example 4.8

```
>>> obj1=MyClass()
>>> obj2=MyClass()
```

It is very easy to add attributes to this newly declared object. To add 'myname' attribute to obj1, give following statement:

```
>>> obj1.myname='Ashok'
```

There is also a built-in **setattr()** function for this purpose.

```
>>> setattr(obj1, 'myage',21)
```

The second argument to this function may be an existing attribute or a new one. Third argument is the value to be assigned. You can even assign a function to attribute as shown below:

Example 4.9

```
>>> def aboutme(obj):
...       print ('My name is {} and I am {} years
old'.format(obj.myname,obj.myage))
...
>>> setattr(MyClass, 'about', aboutme)
>>> obj1.about()
My name is Ashok and I am 21 years old
```

So you have been able to add new attributes to an individual instance or class. Even from outside the class! If you have honed your object oriented programming skills by learning Java or C++, this might send shivers down your spine! On the face of it, this seems to be violation of very idea of class which is a template definition of object's attributes. Don't worry; we will soon make a Python class work as per OOP guidelines.

4.2 Constructor

We provide a constructor method to our class to initialize its object. The **__init__()** method defined inside the class works as a constructor. It takes reference to the object as first positional argument in the form of a special variable called '**self**'. Java/C++ programmers will immediately relate this to '**this**' variable. A method with '**self**' argument is known as an **instance method**. Save the following script as **myclass.py**. It provides two instance variables (**myname** and **myage**) and **about()** method.

Example 4.10

```
#myclass.py
class MyClass:
        def __init__(self):
                self.myname='Ashok'
                self.myage=21
        def about(self):
                print ('My name is {} and I am {}
years old'.format(self.myname,self.myage))
```

Let us use this script as a module, import **MyClass** from it and have its object.

Example 4.11

```
>>> from myclass import MyClass
>>> obj1=MyClass()
>>> obj1.myname
'Ashok'
>>> obj1.myage
21
>>> obj1.about()
My name is Ashok and I am 21 years old
```

So, now each object will have same attributes and methods as defined in the class. However, attributes of each object will be initialized with same values as assigned in **__init__ ()** method. To counter this, we can have a parameterized constructor, optionally with default values. Modify **myclass.py** as follows:

Example 4.12

```
#myclass.py
class MyClass:
        def __init__(self, name=None, age=None):
                self.myname=name
                self.myage=age
        def about(self):
                print ('My name is {} and I am {}
years old'.format(self.myname,self.myage))
```

Now we can have objects having attributes with different values.

Example 4.13

```
>>> from myclass import MyClass
>>> obj1=MyClass('Ashok', 21)
>>> obj2=MyClass('Asmita',20)
>>> obj1.about()
My name is Ashok and I am 21 years old
>>> obj2.about()
My name is Asmita and I am 20 years old
```

However, does this process prevent dynamic addition of attribute to an object/class? Well, not really.

Example 4.14

```
>>> setattr(obj1,'marks',50)
>>> obj1.marks
50
```

So, how do we ensure that the object will have only those attributes as per the class definition? The answer is __**slots**__.

4.3 __slots__

To prevent any further attribute to be added to an object of a class, it carries a variable named as __**slots**__. This variable is defined before __**init**__ () method. It is a list of allowed attributes to be initialized by the constructor. The **setattr()** function will first check if the second argument is in the __**slots**__ list and assign it a new value only if it exists.

Example 4.15

```
#myclass.py
class MyClass:
        __slots__=['myname', 'myage']
        def __init__(self, name=None, age=None):
                self.myname=name
                self.myage=age
        def about(self):
                print ('My name is {} and I am {}
years old'.format(self.myname,self.myage))
```

Import the modified class and check the effect of __**slots**__ variable.

Example 4.16

```
>>> from myclass import MyClass
>>> obj1=MyClass('Ashok', 21)
>>> obj1.about()
My name is Ashok and I am 21 years old
>>> setattr(obj1, 'marks', 50) #new attribute not
allowed
Traceback (most recent call last):
  File "<stdin>", line 1, in <module>
AttributeError: 'MyClass' object has no attribute
'marks'
>>> setattr(obj1, 'myage', 25) #value of existing
module can be modified
>>> obj1.about()
My name is Ashok and I am 25 years old
```

4.4 Getters/setters

Java class employs getter and setter methods to regulate access to private data members in it. Let us see if it works for a Python class. Following code modifies **myclass.py** and provides getter and setter methods for myname and myage instance attributes.

Example 4.17

```
#myclass.py
class MyClass:
        __slots__=['myname', 'myage']
        def __init__(self, name=None, age=None):
                self.myname=name
                self.myage=age
        def getname(self):
                return self.myname
        def set name(self, name):
                self.myname=name
        def getage(self):
                return self.myage
        def setage(self, age):
                self.myage=age
        def about(self):
                print ('My name is {} and I am {}
years old'.format(self.myname,self.myage))
```

The getters and setters allow instance attributes to be retrieved / modified.

Example 4.18

```
>>> from myclass import MyClass
>>> obj1=MyClass('Ashok',21)
>>> obj1.getage()
21
>>> obj1.setname('Amar')
>>> obj1.about()
My name is Amar and I am 21 years old
```

Good enough. However, this still doesn't prevent direct access to instance attributes. Why?

Example 4.19

```
>>> obj1.myname
'Amar'
>>> getattr(obj1,'myage')
21
>>> obj1.myage=25
>>> setattr(obj1,'myname', 'Ashok')
>>> obj1.about()
My name is Ashok and I am 25 years old
```

Python doesn't believe in restricting member access hence it doesn't have access controlling keywords such as public, private, or protected. In fact, as you can see, class members (attributes as well as methods) are public, being freely accessible from outside the class. **Guido Van Rossum** – who developed Python in early 1990s – once said, *"We're all consenting adults here"* justifying absence of such access restrictions. Then what is a 'Pythonic' way to use getters and setters? The built-in **property()** function holds the answer.

4.5 `property()` Function

Well, let me now make a volte-face here. It's not that Python doesn't have private/protected access restrictions. It does have. If an instance variable is prefixed with double underscore character '__', it behaves as a private variable. Let us see how:

Example 4.20

```
>>> #private variable in class
...
>>> class tester:
...       def __init__(self):
...               self.__var=10
...
>>>
```

Try declaring an object of above class and access its __var attribute.
(figure 4.5)

```
>>> t=tester()
>>> t.__var
Traceback (most recent call last):
  File "<stdin>", line 1, in <module>
AttributeError: 'tester' object has no attribute '__
var'
```

Figure 4.5 Declaring object

The **AttributeError** indicates that variable prefixed with __ is inaccessible. However, it can still be accessed from outside the class. A double underscore prefixed attribute is internally renamed as **obj._class__var**. This is called **name mangling mechanism**.

```
>>> t._tester__var
10
```

Hence, the so called private variable in Python is not really private. However, a property object acts as an interface to the getter and setter methods of a private attribute of Python class.

Python's built-in **property()** function uses getter, setter, and delete function as arguments and returns a property object. You can retrieve as well as assign to the property as if you do with any variable. When some value is assigned to a property object, its setter method is called. Similarly when a property object is accessed, its getter method is called.

```
propobj=property(fget, fset, fdel, doc)
```

In above function signature, **fget** is getter method in the class, **fset** is setter method and, **fdel** is delete method. The **doc** parameter sets the docstring of the property object.

In our ongoing **myclass.py** script, let us now define age and name properties to interface with **__myage** and **__myname** private instance attributes.

Example 4.21

```
#myclass.py
class MyClass:
        __slots__=['__myname', '__myage']
        def __init__(self, name=None, age=None):
                self.__myname=name
                self.__myage=age
        def getname(self):
                print ('name getter method')
                return self.__myname
        def setname(self, name):
                print ('name setter method')
                self.__myname=name
        def getage(self):
                print ('age getter method')
                return self.__myage
        def setage(self, age):
                print ('age setter method')
                self.__myage=age
        name=property(getname, setname, "Name")
        age=property(getage, setage, "Age")
        def about(self):
                print ('My name is {} and I am {}
years old'.format(self.__myname,self.__myage))
```

We'll now import this class and use the properties. Any attempt to retrieve or change value of property calls its corresponding getter or setter and change internal private variable. Note that the getter and setter methods have a **print()** message inserted to confirm this behaviour. The **about()** method will also show changes in private variables due to manipulations of property objects.

Example 4.22

```
>>> from myclass import MyClass
>>> obj1=MyClass('Ashok', 21)
>>> obj1.about() #initial values of object's
attributes
My name is Ashok and I am 21 years old
>>> #change age property
>>> obj1.age=30
age setter method
>>> #access name property
>>> obj1.name
name getter method
'Ashok'
>>> obj1.about() #object's attributes after property
changes
My name is Ashok and I am 30 years old
```

So, finally we get Python class to work almost similar to how OOP methodology defines. There is a more elegant way to define property objects – by using **@property** decorator.

4.6 @property Decorator

Although a detailed discussion on decorators is beyond the scope of this book, a brief introduction is necessary before we proceed to use **@ property decorator**.

Function is often termed as a **callable object**. Function is also a passable object. Just as we pass a built-in object viz. number, string, list, and so on. as argument to a function, we can define a function that receives another function as argument. Moreover, you can have function defined in another function (nested function), and a function whose return value is a function itself. Because of all these features, function is called as a first order object.

Decorator function receives a function argument. Behaviour of argument function is then extended by wrapping it in a nested function. Definition of function subjected to decoration is preceded by name of decorator prefixed with @ symbol.

Example 4.23

```
def adecorator(function):
        def wrapper():
                function()
        return wrapper
@adecorator
def decorate():
    pass
```

We shall now use **property()** function as a decorator and define a **name()** method acting as getter method for myname attribute in myclass. py code above.

Example 4.24

```
@property
def name(self):
        return self.__myname
@property
def age(self):
        return self.__myage
```

A property object's getter, setter, and deleter methods are also decorators. Overloaded **name()** and **age()** methods are decorated with **name. setter** and **age.setter** decorators respectively.

Example 4.25

```
@name.setter
def name(self,name):
        self.__myname=name
@age.setter
def age(self, age):
        self.__myage=age
```

When **@property decorator** is used, separate getter, and setter methods defined previously are no longer needed. Complete code of **myclass.py** is as below:

Example 4.26

```
#myclass.py
class MyClass:
        __slots__=['__myname', '__myage']
        def __init__(self, name=None, age=None):
                self.__myname=name
                self.__myage=age

        @property
        def name(self):
                print ('name getter method')
                return self.__myname
        @property
        def age(self):
                print ('age getter method')
                return self.__myage
        @name.setter
        def name(self,name):
                print ('name setter method')
                self.__myname=name
        @age.setter
        def age(self, age):
                print ('age setter method')
                self.__myage=age

        def about(self):
                print ('My name is {} and I am {}
years old'.format(self.__myname,self.__myage))
```

Just import above class and test the functionality of property objects using decorators.

Example 4.27

```
>>> from myclass import MyClass
>>> obj1=MyClass('Ashok', 21)
>>> obj1.about() #initial values of object's
attributes
My name is Ashok and I am 21 years old
>>> #change age property
>>> obj1.age=30
age setter method
>>> #access name property
>>> obj1.name
name getter method
'Ashok'
>>> obj1.about()
My name is Ashok and I am 30 years old
```

4.7 Class Level Attributes and Methods

In above example, MyClass defines two data variables **__myname** and **__ myage** that are instance attributes. They are invariably initialized through **__init__()** constructor. Their values are different for each object. A class however may have an attribute such that its value is same for all existing objects. In other words, such attribute is a shared or common resource and defined outside the **__init__()** method, for that matter outside any instance method.

In following script, total is a class variable of player class. It is defined with a purpose of maintaining a running sum of runs scored by each player. The player class defines name and runs as instance attributes initialized through **__init__()** method as usual which also keeps on adding runs of each object.

Example 4.28

```
#classattr.py
class player:
        __total=0
        def __init__(self, name, runs):
                self.__name=name
                self.__runs=runs
                player.__total+=self.__runs
                print ('Total runs so
far:',player.__total)
```

Let us import player class and set up a few objects. Following interpreter activity shows that the **__total** variable is being cumulatively updated by **__runs** of each object.

Example 4.29

```
>>> from classattr import player
>>> p1=player('Virat', 60)
Total runs so far: 60
>>> p2=player('Rahul', 45)
Total runs so far: 105
```

Two things are to be noted here. First, the use of += operator. It is an in-place addition operator effectively assigning addition of two operands back to the left operand. Hence **player.__total==+=self.__runs** actually becomes **player.__total=player.__total+self.__ runs**. In-place variations of other operators defined in Python are +=, -=, *=, /=, and so on.

Secondly, value of __**total** is retrieved with the help of name of class (**player.__total**) rather than **self**. This is obvious because __**total** is a class variable and not an instance variable specific to any particular object.

In view of this feature, Python has provision to define methods that can access such class attributes. A class method needs name of class to be passed to it as argument (conventionally using '**cls**' identifier). Class can also have a static method that doesn't need explicit reference to either class or object which means there's no argument to it in the form of self or cls.

Class method and static method is decorated by built-in **@classmethod** and **@staticmethod** directives.

Example 4.30

```
#classattr.py
class player:
        __total=0
        def __init__(self, name, runs):
                self.__name=name
                self.__runs=runs
                player.__total+=self.__runs
                print ('Total runs so
far:',player.__total)
        @classmethod
        def printtotal(cls):
                print ('Total runs so far:',cls.__total)
        @staticmethod
        def displaytotal():
                print ('Total runs so
far:',player.__total)
```

Output *(figure 4.6)*:

```
>>> from classattr import player
>>> p1=player('Virat',60)
Total runs so far: 60
>>> p2=player('Rahul',45)
Total runs so far: 105
>>> player.printtotal()
Total runs so far: 105
>>> player.displaytotal()
Total runs so far: 105
```

Figure 4.6 class and static methods

4.8 Inheritance

Of all features of object oriented programming methodology, inheritance is arguably the most important, and hence the most used feature in software development. Leaving aside its literary meaning, inheritance in the context of programming refers to the mechanism by which features of one class (attributes and methods) are made available to another class which has option to define additional resources or modify the functionality of inherited methods.

Python makes extensive use of inheritance. As we have seen, each class is inherited from built-in object class. Inheritance enables a template definition of properties in a parent class to be implemented by its subclass for a more specific purpose.

One such case in point is the relationship between built-in classes '**int**' and '**bool**'. Inheritance comes into picture whenever there is '**IS A**' kind of relationship between classes. Here a '**bool**' object IS A(n) '**int**' right? Hence '**int**' class is a super class of '**bool**' class. As you know a bool object has only two possible values True and False. They are equivalent to 1 and 0 respectively which are integers by the way.

Let us establish inheritance of two customized classes with following example. Ellipse an elongated circle with two radii and one radius is larger than the other. Circle can be seen as a more specific case of ellipse where two radii are equal. So circle IS A(n) ellipse! We are going to define ellipse class with two instance attributes and two methods **area()** and **perimeter()**.

Example 4.31

```
#inheritEllipse.py
import math
class ellipse:
        def __init__(self, r1, r2):
                self.radius1=r1
                self.radius2=r2
        def area(self):
                area=math.pi*self.radius1*self.radius2
                return area
        def perimeter(self):
                perimeter=2*math.pi*math.
sqrt((pow(self.radius1,2)+pow(self.radius2,2))/2)
                return perimeter
```

Note that formula for area of ellipse = π*r1*r2 and perimeter of ellipse = 2π

Let us import this class in the interpreter and declare objects as follows:

Example 4.32

```
>>> from inheritEllipse import ellipse
>>> e1=ellipse(20,30)
>>> e1.area()
1884.9555921538758
>>> e1.perimeter()
160.19042244414092
>>> e1=ellipse(20,20)
>>> e1.area()
1256.6370614359173
>>> e1.perimeter()
125.66370614359172
```

Note that in second case both radii are equal, hence ellipse happens to be a circle. We now design circle class using ellipse class as its parent. Add following lines in **inheritEllipse.py** code.

Example 4.33

```
class circle(ellipse):
        def __init__(self, r1, r2=None):
                super().__init__(r1,r2)
                self.radius2=self.radius1
```

Just import this inherited circle class, declare an object with radius as 20. Result shows that perimeter and area matches with that of ellipse object with identical radii.

Example 4.34

```
>>> from inheritEllipse import ellipse, circle
>>> c1=circle(20)
>>> c1.area()
1256.6370614359173
>>> c1.perimeter()
125.66370614359172
>>>
```

4.9 Overriding

With two similar radii for circle, equation of area of ellipse (π*r1*r2) turns out to be πr^2 and equation of perimeter of ellipse (2π effectively becomes 2πr. However, we would like to redefine **area()** and **perimeter()** methods, which are inherited by circle class, to implement these specific formulae. Such redefinition of inherited methods is called **method overriding**.

Modify circle class as per following code:

Example 4.35

```
class circle(ellipse):
        def __init__(self, r1, r2=None):
                super().__init__(r1,r2)
                self.radius2=self.radius1
        def area(self):
                area=math.pi*pow(self.radius1,2)
                return area
        def perimeter(self):
                perimeter=2*math.pi*self.radius1
                return perimeter
```

Result will be unaffected though. Python class can be inherited from multiple classes by putting names of more than one class in parentheses of class definition.

Protected?

As mentioned earlier, Python doesn't believe in restricting access of attributes. To emulate the behaviour of Java like protected access specifier, single underscore character is prefixed to the instance attribute. However, for all practical purposes, it behaves as a public attribute, not even requiring name mangling syntax as in the case of '**private**' attribute (prefixed by double underscores). The _ character serves merely as a deterrent expecting responsible programmer to refrain from using it outside inherited class.

4.10 Magic Methods

Each Python class inherits methods from its ultimate parent class – **object** class. Methods in objects are peculiarly named – having double underscores on either side. One such method is well known to you by now. The **__init__()** method. To display list of methods, we have to use built-in **dir()** function.

Example 4.36

```
>>> dir(object)
['__class__', '__delattr__', '__dir__', '__
doc__', '__eq__', '__format__', '__ge__', '__
getattribute__', '__gt__', '__hash__', '__init__',
'__init_subclass__', '__le__', '__lt__', '__ne__',
'__new__', '__reduce__', '__reduce_ex__', '__
repr__', '__setattr__', '__sizeof__', '__str__', '__
subclasshook__']
```

These double underscored methods are known as '**magic**' methods. They have very important role in Pythonic brand of object oriented programming. What is so 'magical' about them? You'll soon come to know.

These methods (sometimes referred as '**special**' or '**dunder**' – short for double underscore) in object class are really abstract methods in the sense they don't have any particular implementation. Its subclasses override them as per necessity. Take int class for example. It overrides **__str__()** method to return a printable string version of integer object.

Example 4.37

```
>>> a=123
>>> a.__str__()
```

Incidentally many of these '**dunder**' methods are rarely called **directly**. A corresponding built-in function internally calls them. The **str()** function implements the **__str__()** method.

Example 4.38

```
>>> a=123
>>> str(a)
'123'
```

Another example is **setattr()** function we used earlier in this chapter. It dynamically adds attribute to an object. It in fact performs operation of **__setattr__()** method. Have a look at following code:

Example 4.39

```
>>> class MyClass:
       pass
>>> obj1=MyClass()
>>> setattr(obj1,'myname','Madhav')
>>> #using __setattr__() method
>>> obj1.__setattr__('myage',21)
```

Even the **dir()** method used in the beginning of this section actually calls **__dir__()** magic method.

Example 4.40

```
>>> a.__dir__()
['__repr__', '__hash__', '__str__', '__
getattribute__', '__lt__', '__le__', '__eq__', '__
ne__', '__gt__', '__ge__', '__add__', '__radd__',
'__sub__', '__rsub__', '__mul__', '__rmul__', '__
mod__', '__rmod__', '__divmod__', '__rdivmod__',
'__pow__', '__rpow__', '__neg__', '__pos__', '__
abs__', '__bool__', '__invert__', '__lshift__',
'__rlshift__', '__rshift__', '__rrshift__',
'__and__', '__rand__', '__xor__', '__rxor__',
'__or__', '__ror__', '__int__', '__float__', '__
floordiv__', '__rfloordiv__', '__truediv__', '__
rtruediv__', '__index__', '__new__', 'conjugate',
'bit_length', 'to_bytes', 'from_bytes', '__
trunc__', '__floor__', '__ceil__', '__round__', '__
getnewargs__', '__format__', '__sizeof__', 'real',
'imag', 'numerator', 'denominator', '__doc__', '__
setattr__', '__delattr__', '__init__', '__reduce_
ex__', '__reduce__', '__subclasshook__', '__init_
subclass__', '__dir__', '__class__']
>>> #is equivalent to
>>> dir(int)
```

It may be noted that **dir(int)** shows lot more attributes than that of object class. These are actually inherited from abstract Number class and overridden in int class. Of particular interest are methods with names indicating arithmetic operations (such as **__add__**, **__sub__**, **__mul__**, and so on.) and logical operations (like **__ge__**, **__gt__**, **__eq__**, and so on.) They are mapped to respective operators so that a conventional arithmetic/logical operator invokes respective method. In other words, **a+b** actually performs **a.__add__(b)** call.

Example 4.41

```
>>> a=20
>>> b=10
>>> a+b
30
>>> a.__add__(b)
30
>>> a.__mul__(b)
200
>>> a*b
200
>>> a>b
True
>>> a.__le__(b)
False
```

The real magic lies ahead. You can override these methods to customize behaviour of operators to achieve operator overloading.

Example 4.42

```
#timerclass.py
class timer:
        def __init__(self, hr=None, min=None):
                self.hrs=hr
                self.mins=min
        def __add__(self, arg):
                temp=timer()
                temp.hrs=self.hrs+arg.hrs
                temp.mins=self.mins+arg.mins
                if temp.mins>=60:
                        temp.mins=temp.mins-60
                        temp.hrs=temp.hrs+1
                return temp
        def __str__(self):
                timestring='{} Hrs. {}
mins.'.format(self.hrs,self.mins)
                return timestring
```

In above script, timer class has two instance attributes hrs and mins. The **__add__**() method performs addition of two timer objects. This method is invoked in response to use of '+' operator along with two timer object operands. By the way timer class also has overridden implementation of **__str__** () method to produce string representation of its object.

Example 4.43

```
>>> from timerclass import timer
>>> t1=timer(2,45)
>>> t2=timer(3,30)
>>> t3=t1+t2
>>> print (t3)
6 Hrs. 15 mins.
>>> t3=t1.__add__(t2)
>>> print (t3)
6 Hrs. 15 mins.
```

Go ahead and overload any operator to suit needs of your application. List of all magic methods is provided in the Appendix E.

This chapter is a very brief discussion on object oriented programming as implemented in Python. Only those facets that are required in subsequent chapters of this book have been explained here.

CHAPTER 5
File IO

'**File**' is an indispensible word in the vocabulary of even an ordinary computer (even mobile) user. Every day, he is required to deal with files which may be documents, spreadsheets, presentations, images, and so on. Slightly advanced user, to whom we may call developer, prepares scripts, builds executables which are also files.

When user starts any application, he enters certain data, either through keyboard or any other device such as mouse, camera, scanner, and so on. The data goes in computer's main memory and is further processed as per the process as defined in the application. If this data - input or resulting from process - is needed for subsequent use, it is saved in computer file, because if left in the computer memory, it will be erased when computer is turned off. In this chapter, we shall discuss how data from Python program is stored in persistent disk files.

A Python console application interacts with peripheral devices through its built-in **input()** and **print()** functions. Channels of interaction between processor and peripheral devices are called **streams**. A stream is any object that sends/receives a continuous flow of data. Python's **input()** function reads data from standard input streaming device i.e. keyboard that is recognized as **sys.stdin** object defined in sys built-in module. Similarly **print()** function sends data to standard output device which is a computer display screen (monitor), defined as **sys.stdout** object.

The stdin object has **read()** and **readline()** methods to accept user input through keyboard. The **read()** method accepts data till stream is terminated by **Ctrl+D** character. On the other hand **readline()** method accepts all keystrokes till '**Enter**' key is pressed. Both methods leave '\n' at the end of input.

Example 5.1

```
>>> data=sys.stdin.read()
Hello
How are you?
>>> data
'Hello\nHow are you?\n'
>>> data=sys.stdin.readline()
Hello How are you?
>>> data
'Hello How are you?\n'
>>>
```

In fact, the **input()** function performs **stdin.readline()** and returns by stripping the trailing '**\n**' character.

The **write()** method available to stdout object does exactly what **print()** function does. It sends the argument data to default output device – the computer monitor. However, when use in interactive mode, it also displays size of object in bytes.

Example 5.2

```
>>> sys.stdout.write(data)
Hello How are you?
19
>>>
```

Any object that can send/receive stream of bytes is called *'File like object'* in Python. A file (like) object can invoke **read()** or **write()** methods depending upon the stream to which it is connected. Hence, stdin and stdout object are file like objects too. Python can perform IO operations with objects representing disk file, network sockets, memory arrays, and so on. In this chapter we shall deal with computer disk files. These files store data in a persistent manner, which is often the need as same collection of data may be needed repeatedly. Instead of laboriously keying in same data again and again from keyboard, reading it from a file becomes more efficient and less error-prone. Similarly, screen output being temporary and limited, can instead be stored in files. *(figure 5.1)*

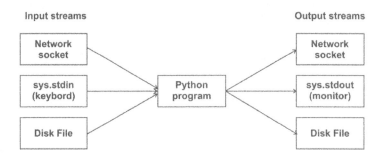

Figure 5.1: Input stream and Output stream

Standard IO streams communicating with **stdin** and **stdout** objects are always available. To use a disk file for reading/writing purpose file object needs to be declared first, by using built-in **open()** function.

5.1 Opening File

The **open()** function takes a string corresponding to disk file's name along with its path as an argument. Second argument indicates to the mode in which file is intended to be opened. Default file opening is '**r**' which stands for '**read**' mode which means data in the file is read into program variables. In order to use file as output destination, use '**w**' as value of mode parameter. The function returns a file object.

Example 5.3

```
>>> obj=open('test.txt','r')
Traceback (most recent call last):
  File "<pyshell#16>", line 1, in <module>
    obj=open('test.txt','r')
FileNotFoundError: [Errno 2] No such file or
directory: 'test.txt'
>>> obj=open('test.txt','w')
>>> obj.close()
>>>
```

Note that when in '**r**' mode **open()** function can open existing file otherwise raises **FileNotFoundError**. Always ensure that the opened file object is closed to flush data if any in the buffer.

5.2 Writing to File

The file object needs write permission to be able to save data to a file – which is done by setting mode parameter to '**w**'. Let us store a famous quote by top computer scientist Alan kay in *'top-quotes.txt'* file.

To begin with declare a file object referring to desired file with '**w**' mode enabled.

```
>>> file=open('top-quotes.txt','w')
```

The **write()** method sends a string to the file object and stores it in the underlying disk file.

Example 5.4

```
>>> quote="'The best way to predict the future is to
invent it.' - Alan Kay"
>>> file.write(quote)
64
>>> file.close()
```

Note that the interactive mode shows number of bytes written. Be sure to close the file and go ahead and view the created file using your favourite text editor software (like Notpad) to confirm that above quote is stored in it.

So, now that we have successfully created a file, let us try add a few more quotes in it as follows:

Example 5.5

```
>>> file=open('top-quotes.txt','w')
>>> quote=''''There are only two kinds of
programming languages: those people always bitch
about and those nobody uses.' - Bjarne Stroustrup
'The only way to learn a new programming language is
by writing programs in it.' -Dennis Ritchie
'A computer would deserve to be called intelligent
if it could deceive a human into believing that it
was human.' - Alan Turing'''
>>> file.write(quote)
352
>>> file.close()
```

Note the use of triple quotes to form a multi-line string. Open the file again using editor. To your surprise, the earlier string is not visible now. Why?

The reason is behaviour of '**w**' mode. It opens a file for writing purpose, erasing its earlier contents if it already exists. Here we want to add few more lines to existing file. For that we need to use '**a**' as mode parameter to let new data added to existing file. Following **table 5.1** lists other valid mode parameters and their purpose:

Table 5.1: Valid mode parameters

mode parameter	purpose
r	allows the file to be **read**. (default)
w	Opens a file for **writing** only, erases contents if existing
a	**appends** new data to existing file.
t	stores data in **text** format (default)
b	stores data in **binary** format.
+	allows **simultaneous** reading and writing in file.
x	opens file for **exclusive** creation.

Going back to our attempt to add new quotes in top-quotes.txt, change the mode parameter to '**a**'.

Example 5.6

```
>>> file=open('top-quotes.txt','a')
>>> quote=''''There are only two kinds of
programming languages: those people always bitch
about and those nobody uses.' - Bjarne Stroustrup
'The only way to learn a new programming language is
by writing programs in it.' -Dennis Ritchie
'A computer would deserve to be called intelligent
if it could deceive a human into believing that it
was human.' - Alan Turing'''
>>> file.write(quote)
352
>>> file.close()
```

The file should have earlier text intact and new quotes added after it. File object also possesses **writelines()** method to write strings in a list object. Each item in the list is treated as one line. Note that the method doesn't insert '**\n**' by itself, hence it must be explicitly provided as a part of each string.

Example 5.7

```
>>> file=open('top-quotes.txt','a')
>>> quotes=[
        'programming languages have a devious
influence. They shape our thinking habits - Edsger W.
Dijkstra\n',
'programmers do programming not because they expect
to get paid or get adulation by the public, but
because it is fun to program - Linus Torvalds\n',
'A computer would deserve to be called intelligent
if it could deceive a human into believing that it
was human - Alan Turing\n']
>>> file.writelines(quotes)
>>> file.close()
```

5.3 Reading a File

Let us now read '*top-quotes.txt*' programmatically by opening it with 'r'
mode. When in 'r' mode, the file object can call **read()**, **readline()**,
and **readlines()** methods.

Out of these, **read()** method can read specified number of bytes from
file, the size defaults to file size. However, if file is very big, the available
memory restrictions may not allow entire file to be read, so you may have
to provide size parameter to read bytes at once.

Example 5.8

```
>>> file=open('top-quotes.txt','r')
>>> text=file.read()
>>> text
"'The best way to predict the future is to invent
it.' - Alan Kay'\nThere are only two kinds of
programming languages: those people always bitch
about and those nobody uses.' - Bjarne Stroustrup\
n'The only way to learn a new programming language
is by writing programs in it.' -Dennis Ritchie\n'A
computer would deserve to be called intelligent if
it could deceive a human into believing that it was
human.' - Alan Turing\nprogramming languages have a
devious influence. They shape our thinking habits -
Edsger W. Dijkstra\nprogrammers do programming not
```

```
because they expect to get paid or get adulation
by the public, but because it is fun to program
- Linus Torvalds\nA computer would deserve to be
called intelligent if it could deceive a human into
believing that it was human - Alan Turing"
>>>file.close()
```

To read specified number of bytes from the beginning of file

Example 5.9

```
>>> file=open('top-quotes.txt','r')
>>> text=file.read(65)
>>> text
"'The best way to predict the future is to invent
it.' - Alan Kay\n"
>>> file.close()
```

Reading a File Line-by-Line

The **readline()** method reads all bytes till a newline character '**\n**' is encountered. It returns an empty string when no more lines are left to be read. Hence, we can call **readline()** method in a loop till empty string is returned. *(figure 5.2)*

```
>>> file=open('top-quotes.txt','r')
>>> while True:
        line=file.readline()
        if line=='':break
        print (line, end='')

'The best way to predict the future is to invent it.' - Alan Kay
'There are only two kinds of programming languages: those people
always bitch about and those nobody uses.' - Bjarne Stroustrup
'The only way to learn a new programming language is by writing
programs in it.' -Dennis Ritchie
'A computer would deserve to be called intelligent if it could
deceive a human into believing that it was human.' - Alan Turing
programming languages have a devious influence. They shape our
thinking habits - Edsger W. Dijkstra
programmers do programming not because they expect to get paid or
get adulation by the public, but because it is fun to program -
Linus Torvalds
A computer would deserve to be called intelligent if it could
deceive a human into believing that it was human - Alan Turing
```

Figure 5.2 Reading data from file

The file object is a data stream that acts as an iterator. An iterator serves subsequent object every time **next()** function is called till stream is exhausted and **StopIteration** exception is encountered. We can use **next()** method on file object to read a file line by line.

Example 5.10

```
f=open("top-quotes.txt","r")
while True:
        try:
                line=next(f)
                print (line, end="")
        except StopIteration:
                break
f.close()
```

Or simply use a **for** loop over each line in the file iterator:

Example 5.11

```
file=open("top-quotes.txt","r")
for line in file:
    print (line, end="")
file.close()
```

The **readlines()** method returns list of lines in the file.

```
>>> file=open('top-quotes.txt','r')
>>> lines=file.readlines()
```

5.4 Write/Read Binary File

When the mode parameter to **open()** function is set to 'w' (or 'a') value, the file is prepared for writing data in text format. Hence **write()** and **writelines()** methods send string data to the output file stream. The file is easily readable using any text editor. However, other computer files that represent pictures (.jpg), multimedia (.mp3, .mp4), executables (.exe, .com), databases (.db, .sqlite) will not be readable if opened using notepad like text editor because they contain data in binary format.

Python's **open()** function lets you to write binary data to a file. You need to add 'b' to the mode parameter. Set mode to 'wb' to open a file for writing binary data. Naturally, such file needs to be read by specifying 'rb' as file opening mode.

In case of '**wb**' mode parameter, the **write()** method doesn't accept a string as argument. Instead, it requires a bytes object. So, even if you are writing a string to a binary file, it needs to be converted to bytes first. The **encode()** method of string class converts string to bytes using one of the defined encoding schemes, such as '**utf-8**' or '**utf-16**'.

Example 5.12

```
>>> f=open('binary.dat','wb')
>>> data='Hello Python'
>>> encoded=data.encode(encoding='utf-16')
>>> encoded
b'\xff\xfeH\x00e\x001\x001\x00o\x00 \x00P\x00y\x00t\x00h\x00o\x00n\x00'
>>> f.write(encoded)
26
>>> f.close()
```

To read back data from binary file, encoded string will have to be decoded for it to be used normally, like printing it.

Example 5.13

```
>>> f=open('binary.dat','rb')
>>> encoded=f.read()
>>> data=encoded.decode(encoding='utf-16')
>>> print (data)
Hello Python
>>> f.close()
```

If you have to write numeric data to a binary file, number object is first converted to bytes and then provided as argument to **write()** method

Example 5.14

```
>>> f=open('binary.dat','wb')
>>> num=1234
>>> bin1=num.to_bytes(16, 'big')
>>> f.write(bin1)
>>> f.close()
```

To read integer data from binary file, it has to be extracted from bytes in the file.

Example 5.15

```
>>> f=open('binary.dat','rb')
>>> data=f.read()
>>> num=int.from_bytes(data,'big')
>>> num
1234
>>> f.close()
```

In **to_bytes()** and **from_bytes()** function, '**big**' is the value of byteorder parameter.

Writing float data to binary file is a little complicated. You'll need to use built-in struct module and **pack()** function from it to convert float to binary. Explanation of struct module is beyond the scope of this book.

Example 5.16

```
>>> import struct
>>> num1=1234.56
>>> f=open('binary.dat','wb')
>>> binfloat=struct.pack('f',num1)
>>> f.write(binfloat)
4
>>> f.close()
```

To read back binary float data from file, use **unpack()** function.

Example 5.17

```
>>> f=open('binary.dat','rb')
>>> data=f.read()
>>> num1=struct.unpack('f', data)
>>> print (num1)
(1234.56005859375,)
>>> f.close()
```

5.5 Simultaneous Read/Write

Modes '**w**' or '**a**' allow a file to be written to, but not to be read from. Similarly '**r**' mode facilitates reading a file but prohibits writing data to it. To be able to perform both read/write operations on a file without closing it, add '+' sign to these mode characters. As a result '**w+**', '**r+**' or '**a+**' mode will open file for simultaneous read/write. Similarly, binary read/

write simultaneous operations are enabled on file if opened with '**wb+**', '**rb+**' or '**ab+**' modes.

It is also possible to perform read or write operation at any byte position of file. As you go on writing data in a file, the **end of file (EOF)** position keeps on moving away from its beginning. By default, new data is written at current EOF position. When opened in '**r**' mode, reading starts from **0**ᵗʰ byte i.e. from beginning of file.

The **seek ()** method of file object lets you set current reading or writing position to a desired byte position in the file. It locates the desired position by counting the offset distance from beginning (0), current position (1), or EOF (2). Following example illustrates this point:

Example 5.18

```
>>> file=open("testfile.txt","w+")
>>> file.write("This is a rat race")
>>> file.seek(10,0) #seek 10th byte from beginning
>>> txt=file.read(3) #read next 3 bytes
>>> txt
'rat'
>>> file.seek(10,0) #seek 10th byte position
>>> file.write('cat') #overwrite next 3 bytes
>>> file.seek(0)
>>> text=file.read() #read entire file
>>> text
'This is a cat race'
>>> file.close()
```

Of course this may not work correctly if you try to insert new data as it may overwrite part of existing data. One solution could be to read entire content in a memory variable, modify it, and rewrite it after truncating existing file. Other built-in modules like fileinput and mmap allow modifying file in-place. However, later in this book, we are going to discuss a more sophisticated tool for manipulating databases and update data on a random basis.

5.6 File Handling using os Module

Python's built-in library has **os** module that provides useful operating system dependent functions. It also provides functions for performing low level read/write operations on file. Let us briefly get acquainted with them.

The **open()** function from **os** module (obviously it needs to be referred to as **os.open()**) is similar to the built-in **open()** function in the sense it also opens a file for read/write operations. However, it doesn't return a file or file like object but a file descriptor, an integer corresponding to file opened. File descriptor's values 0, 1 and 2 are reserved for **stdin, stdout, and stderr** streams. Other files will be given incremental file descriptor. Also, the **write()** and **read()** functions of os module needs bytes object as argument. The **os.open()** function needs to be provided one or combinations of following constants: (Table 5.2)

Table 5.2 *File handling constants*

os.O_WRONLY	open for writing only
os.O_RDWR	open for reading and writing
os.O_APPEND	append on each write
os.O_CREAT	create file if it does not exist
os.O_TRUNC	truncate size to 0
os.O_EXCL	error if create and file exists

As in case of file object, the os module defines **lseek()** function to set file r/w position at desired place from beginning, current position or end indicated by integers 0,1, and 2 respectively.

Example 5.19

```
>>> fd=os.open("testfile.txt",os.O_RDWR|os.O_CREAT)
>>> text="Hello Python"
>>> encoded=text.encode(encoding='utf-16')
>>> os.write(fd, encoded)
>>> os.lseek(fd,0,0)
>>> encoded=os.read(fd)
>>> os.path.getsize("testfile.txt") #calculate file size
>>> encoded=os.read(fd,26)
>>> text=encoded.decode('utf-16')
>>> text
'Hello Python'
```

5.7 File/Directory Management Functions

We normally use operating system's GUI utilities or DOS commands to manage directories, copy, and move files etc. The **os** module provides useful functions to perform these tasks programmatically.

os.mkdir() function creates a new directory at given path. The path argument may be absolute or relative to current directory. Use **chdir()** function to set current working directory at desired path. The **getcwd()** function returns current working directory path.

Example 5.20

```
>>> os.mkdir('mydir')
>>> os.path.abspath('mydir')
'E:\\python37\\mydir'
>>> os.chdir('mydir')
>>> os.getcwd()
'E:\\python37\\mydir'
```

You can remove a directory only if the given path to **rmdir()** function is not the current working directory path, and it is empty.

Example 5.21

```
>>> os.chdir('..') #parent directory becomes current
working directory
>>> os.getcwd()
'E:\\python37'
>>> os.rmdir('mydir')
```

The **rename()** and **remove()** functions respectively change name of a file and delete a file. Another utility function is **listdir()** which returns a list object comprising of file and subdirectory names in given path.

5.8 Exceptions

Even an experienced programmer's code does contain errors. If errors pertain to violation of language syntax, more often than not, they are detected by interpreter (compiler in case of C++/Java) and code doesn't execute till they are corrected.

There are times though, when the code doesn't show syntax related errors but errors creep up after running it. What is more, sometimes code might execute without errors and some other times, its execution abruptly terminates. Clearly some situation that arises in a running code is not tolerable to the interpreter. Such a runtime situation causing error is called exception.

Take a simple example of displaying result of two numbers input by user. Following snippet appears error free as far as syntax error is concerned.

Example 5.22

```
num1=int(input('enter a number..'))
num2=int(input('enter another number..'))
result=num1/num2
print ('result: ', result)
```

When executed, above code gives satisfactory output on most occasions, but when num2 happens to be 0, it breaks. *(figure 5.3)*

```
enter a number..12
enter another number..3
result:  4.0
enter a number..12
enter another number..0
Traceback (most recent call last):
  File "E:\python37\tmp.py", line 3, in <module>
    result=num1/num2
ZeroDivisionError: division by zero
```

Figure 5.3 ZeroDivisionError

You can see that program terminates as soon as it encounters the error without completing rest of the statements. Such abnormal termination may prove to be harmful in some cases.

Imagine a situation involving a file object. If such runtime error occurs after file is opened, abrupt end of program will not give a chance for file object to close properly and it may result in corruption of data in file. Hence exceptions need to be properly handled so that program ends safely.

If we look at the class structure of builtins in Python, there is an **Exception** class from which a number of built-in exceptions are defined. Depending upon the cause of exception in running program, object representing corresponding exception class is created. In this section, we restrict ourselves to consider file operations related exceptions.

Python's exception handling mechanism is implemented by use of two keywords – **try** and **except**. Both keywords are followed by block of statements. The **try:** block contains a piece of code that is likely to encounter an exception. The **except:** block follows the **try:** block containing statements meant to handle the exception. Above code snippet of division of two numbers is rewritten to use try – catch mechanism.

Example 5.23

```
try:
    num1=int(input('enter a number..'))
    num2=int(input('enter another number..'))
    result=num1/num2
    print ('result: ', result)
except:
    print ("error in division")
print ("end of program")
```

Now there are two possibilities. As said earlier, exception is a runtime situation largely depending upon reasons outside the program. In the code involving division of two numbers there is no exception if denominator is non-zero. In such case, **try:** block is executed completely, **except:** block is bypassed and program proceeds to subsequent statements.

If however, denominator happens to be zero, statement involving division produces exception. Python interpreter abandons rest of statements in **try:** block and sends the program flow to **except:** block where exception handling statements are given. After **except:** block rest of unconditional statements keep on executing. *(figure 5.4)*

```
enter a number..15
enter another number..5
result:  3.0
end of program
enter a number..15
enter another number..0
error in division
end of program
```

Figure 5.4 Exception Handling

Here, except block without any expression acts as a generic exception handler. To catch object of specific type of exception, corresponding Exception class is mentioned in front of **except** keyword. In this case **ZeroDivisionError** is raised, so it is mentioned in except statement. Also you can use 'as' keyword to receive exception object in an argument and fetch more information about exception.

Example 5.24

```
try:
    num1=int(input('enter a number..'))
    num2=int(input('enter another number..'))
    result=num1/num2
    print ('result: ', result)
except ZeroDivisionError as e:
    print ("error message",e)
print ("end of program")
```

File operations are always prone to raising exceptions. What if the file you are trying to open doesn't exist at all? What if you opened a file in 'r' mode but trying to write data to it? These situations will raise runtime errors (exceptions) which must be handled using try – except mechanism to avoid damage to data in files.

FileNotFoundError is a common exception encountered. It appears when attempt to read a non-existing file. Following code handles the error.

Example 5.25

```
fn=input('enter filename..')
try:
    f=open(fn,'r')
    data=f.read()
    print (data)
except FileNotFoundError as e:
    print ("error message",e)
print ("end of program")
```

Output *(figure 5.5)*:

```
E:\python37>python tmp.py
enter filename..testfile.txt
H e l l o    P y t h o n
end of program
E:\python37>python tmp.py
enter filename..nofile.txt
error message [Errno 2] No such file or directory:
'nofile.txt'
end of program
```

Figure 5.5 Output

Another exception occurs frequently when you try to write data in a file opened with 'r' mode. Type of exception is **UnsupportedOperation** defined in **io** module.

Example 5.26

```
import io
try:
    f=open('testfile.txt','r')
    f.write('Hello')
    print (data)
except io.UnsupportedOperation as e:
    print ("error message",e)
print ("end of program")
```

Output *(figure 5.6)*:

```
E:\python37>python tmp.py
error message not writable
end of program
```

Figure 5.6 Output

As we know, **write()** method of file object need a string argument. Hence argument of any other type will result in typeError.

Example 5.27

```
try:
    f=open('testfile.txt','w')
    f.write(1234)
except TypeError as e:
    print ("error message",e)
print ("end of program")
```

Output *(figure 5.7)*:

```
E:\python37>python tmp.py
error message write() argument must be str, not int
end of program
```

Figure 5.7 Output

Conversely, for file in binary mode, **write()** method needs bytes object as argument. If not, same TypeError is raised with different error message.

Example 5.28

```
try:
    f=open('testfile.txt','wb')
    f.write('Hello')
except TypeError as e:
    print ("error message",e)
print ("end of program")
```

Output *(figure 5.8)*:

```
E:\python37>python tmp.py
error message a bytes-like object is required, not
'str'
end of program
```

Figure 5.8 Output

All file related functions in os module raise **OSError** in the case of invalid or inaccessible file names and paths, or other arguments that have the correct type, but are not accepted by the operating system.

Example 5.29

```
import os
try:
    fd=os.open('testfile.txt',os.O_RDONLY|os.O_CREAT)
    os.write(fd,'Hello'.encode())
except OSError as e:
    print ("error message",e)
print ("end of program")
```

Output *(figure 5.9)*:

```
E:\python37>python tmp.py
error message [Errno 9] Bad file descriptor
end of program
```

Figure 5.9 Output

In this chapter we learnt the basic file handling techniques. In next chapter we deal with advanced data serialization techniques and special purpose file storage formats using Python's built-in modules.

CHAPTER 6
Object Serialization

Python's built-in File object and its methods performing read/write operations are undoubtedly invaluable, as the ability to store data in a persistent medium is as important as processing it. However, the File object returned by Python's built-in **open()** function has one important shortcoming, as you must have noted in the previous chapter.

When opened with **'w'** mode, the **write()** method accepts only the string object. That means, if you have data represented in any non-string form, the object of either in built-in classes (numbers, dictionary, lists or tuples) or other user-defined classes, it cannot be written to file directly.

Example 6.1

```
>>> numbers=[10,20,30,40]
>>> file=open('numbers.txt','w')
>>> file.write(numbers)
Traceback (most recent call last):
  File "<pyshell#10>", line 1, in <module>
    file.write(numbers)
TypeError: write() argument must be str, not list
>>> p1=person()
>>> class person:
        def __init__(self):
            self.name='Anil'
>>> p1=person()
>>> file=open('persons.txt','w')
>>> file.write(p1)
Traceback (most recent call last):
  File "<pyshell#20>", line 1, in <module>
    file.write(p1)
TypeError: write() argument must be str, not person
>>>
```

Before writing, you need to convert it in its string representation.

Example 6.2

```
>>> numbers=[10,20,30,40]
>>> file=open('numbers.txt','w')
>>> file.write(str(numbers))
>>> file.close()
```

In case of a user-defined class:

Example 6.3

```
>>> class person:
        def __init__(self):
                self.name='Anil'
>>> p1=person()
>>> file=open('persons.txt','w')
>>> file.write(p1.__str__())
>>> file.close()
```

To read back data from the file in the respective data type, reverse conversion needs to be done.

Example 6.4

```
>>> data=file.read()
>>> list(data)
[10, 20, 30, 40]
```

File object with '**wb**' mode requires bytes object to be provided, as an argument to **write()** method. In above case, the list of integers is converted to bytes by **bytearray()** function and then written to file as below:

Example 6.5

```
>>> numbers=[10,20,30,40]
>>> data=bytearray(numbers)
>>> file=open('numbers.txt','wb')
>>> file.write(data)
>>> file.close()
```

In case of user-defined class, attributes of its objects will have to be converted to byte objects before writing to a disk file:

Example 6.6

```
>>> file=open('persons.txt','wb')
>>> file.write(p1.name.encode())
```

This type of manual conversion of objects in the string or byte format (and vice versa) is very cumbersome and appears rather clunky. Python has better solutions for this requirement. Several built-in modules are there to store and retrieve a Python object directly to/from a file or byte string. A Python object is said to be **serialized** when it is translated in a format from which it can be reconstructed later when required. The serialized format can be stored in a disk file, byte string or can be transmitted via network sockets. When serialized data is brought back in a form identical to original, the mechanism is called **de-serialization**.

Serialization formats, used by some built-in modules, are Python-specific, whereas other modules use standard serialization protocols such as JSON, XML, and so on. **Pythonic** term for serialization is **pickling** while de-serialization is often referred to as **unpickling** in Python documentation. Python-specific serialization/de-serialization is achieved by the built-in **pickle** and **shelve** modules. Even though Python's **marshal** module offers similar functionality, it is primarily meant for internal use while reading and writing pseudo-compiled versions of Python modules with **.pyc** extension and is not recommended as a general persistence tool.

The serialized byte stream can optionally be written to a disk file. This is called as **object persistence**. The File API discussed in the previous chapter stores data persistently, but it is not in a serialized format. Python serialization libraries, that we are going to explore in this chapter, are useful for storing serialized object data to disk files.

6.1 pickle Module

The serialization format used by the `pickle` module, which is a part of Python's built-in module library, is very Python-specific. While this fact can work as an advantage that it doesn't face any restrictions by certain external standards such as JSON format, it's major disadvantage is that non-Python applications may not be able to reconstruct 'pickled' objects. Also, the pickle module is not considered secure when it comes to unpickling data received from an unauthenticated or untrusted source.

The pickle module defines module-level `dumps()` function to obtain a byte string 'pickled' representation of any Python object. It counterpart function loads () reconstructs ('unpickles') the byte string identical Python object.

Following code snippet demonstrates the use of dumps () and loads () functions:

Example 6.7

```
>>> import pickle
>>> numbers=[10,20,30,40]
>>> pickledata=pickle.dumps(numbers)
>>> pickledata
b'\x80\x03]q\x00(K\nK\x14K\x1eK(e.'
>>> #unpickled data
...
>>> unpickledata=pickle.loads(pickledata)
>>> unpickledata
[10, 20, 30, 40]
>>>
```

There are dump () and load () functions that respectively write pickled data persistently to a file like object (which may be a disk file, a memory buffer object, or a network socket object) having binary and write 'wb' mode enabled, and reconstruct identical object from file like object having 'rb' permission.

Example 6.8

```
>>> #pickle to file
...
>>> import pickle
>>> numbers=[10,20,30,40]
>>> file=open('numbers.dat','wb')
>>> pickle.dump(numbers, file)
>>> file.close()
>>> #unpickle from file
...
>>> file=open('numbers.dat','rb')
>>> unpickledata=pickle.load(file)
>>> unpickledata
[10, 20, 30, 40]
>>>
```

Almost any type of Python object can be pickled. This includes built-in types, built-in, and user-defined functions and objects of user-defined classes.

The pickle module also provides object-oriented API as a substitute for module-level dumps()/loads() and dump()/load() functions. The module has a pickler class whose object can invoke dump() or dumps() method to 'pickle' an object. Conversely, the unpickler class defines load() and loads() methods.

Following script has a **person** class whose objects are pickled in a file using pickler class. Original objects are obtained by load() method of unpickler class.

Example 6.9

```
from pickle import Pickler, Unpickler
class User:
        def __init__(self,name, email, pw):
                self.name=name
                self.email=email
                self.pw=pw
        def __str__(self):
return ('Name: {} email: {} password: {}'. \
                        format(self.name, self.email,
self.pw))
user1=User('Rajan', 'r123@gmail.com', 'rajan123')
user2=User('Sudheer', 's.11@gmail.com', 's_11')
print ('before pickling..')
print (user1)
print (user2)
file=open('users.dat','wb')
Pickler(file).dump(user1)
Pickler(file).dump(user2)
file.close()
file=open('users.dat','rb')
obj1=Unpickler(file).load()
print ('unpickled objects')
print (obj1)
obj2=Unpickler(file).load()
print (obj2)
```

Output:

```
E:\python37>python pickl-example.py
before pickling..
Name: Rajan email: r123@gmail.com password: rajan123
Name: Sudheer email: s.11@gmail.com password: s_11
unpickled objects
Name: Rajan email: r123@gmail.com password: rajan123
Name: Sudheer email: s.11@gmail.com password: s_11
E:\python37>
```

6.2 `shelve` Module

Serialization and persistence effected by functionality in this module depend on the pickle storage format, although it is meant to deal with a dictionary like object only and not with other Python objects. The shelve module defines all important **open()** function that returns the 'shelf' object representing the underlying disk file in which the 'pickled' dictionary object is persistently stored.

Example 6.10

```
>>> import shelve
>>> obj=shelve.open('shelvetest')
```

In addition to filename, the **open()** function has two more optional parameters. One is 'flag' which is by default set to 'c' indicating that the file has read/write access. Other accepted values for flag parameter are **'w'** (write only), **'r'** (read only) and **'n'** (new with read/write access). Second optional parameter is **'writeback'** whose default value is False. If this parameter is set to True, any modification made to the shelf object will be cached in the memory and will only be written to file on calling **sync()** or **close()** methods, which might result in the process becoming slow.

Once a shelf object is declared, you can store key-value pair data to it. However, the shelf object accepts only a string as the key. Value can be any valid Python object.

Example 6.11

```
>>> obj['name']='Virat Kohli'
>>> obj['age']=29
>>> obj['teams']=['India', 'IndiaU19', 'RCB',
'Delhi']
>>> obj.close()
```

In the current working directory, a file named 'shelvetest.dir' will store the above data. Since, the shelf is dictionary like object, it can invoke familiar methods of built-in dict class. Using **get()** method, one can fetch value associated with a certain key. Similarly, **update()** method can be used to add/modify k-v pairs in shelf object.

Example 6.12

```
>>> obj.get('name')
'Virat Kohli'
>>> dct={'100s':64, '50s':69}
>>> obj.update(dct)
>>> dict(obj)
{'name': 'Virat Kohli', 'age': 29, 'teams':
['India', 'IndiaU19', 'RCB', 'Delhi'], '100s': 64,
'50s': 69}
```

The shelf object also returns views of keys, values, and items,same as the built-in dictionary object.

Example 6.13

```
>>> keys=list(obj.keys())
>>> keys
['name', 'age', 'teams', '100s', '50s']
>>> values=list(obj.values())
>>> values
['Virat Kohli', 29, ['India', 'IndiaU19', 'RCB',
'Delhi'], 64, 69]
>>> items=list(obj.items())
>>> items
[('name', 'Virat Kohli'), ('age', 29), ('teams',
['India', 'IndiaU19', 'RCB', 'Delhi']), ('100s',
64), ('50s', 69)]
```

6.3 dbm Modules

These modules in Python's built-in library provide a generic dictionary like interface to different variants of DBM style databases. These databases use binary encoded string objects as key, as well as value. The **dbm. gnu** module is an interface to the DBM library version as implemented by the GNU project. On the other hand, **dbm.ndbm** module provides an interface to UNIX nbdm implementation. Another module, dbm.dumb is also present which is used as a fallback option in the event, other dbm implementations are not found. This requires no external dependencies but is slower than others.

Example 6.14

```
>>> import dbm
>>> db=dbm.open('mydbm.db','n')
>>> db['title']='Introduction to Python'
>>> db['publisher']='BPB'
>>> db['year']='2019'
>>> db.close()
```

As in the case of shelve database, user specified database name carries **'.dir'** postfix. The dbm object's **whichdb()** function tells which implementation of dbm is available on current Python installation.

Example 6.15

```
>>> dbm.whichdb('mydbm.db')
'dbm.dumb'
```

The open() function allows mode these flags: **'c'** to create a new database with read/write permission, **'r'** opens the database in read-only mode, **'w'** opens an existing database for writing, and **'n'** flag always create a new empty database with read/write permissions.

The dbm object is a dictionary like object, just as a shelf object. Hence, all dictionary operations can be performed. The following code opens 'mydbm.db' with 'r' flag and iterates over the collection of key-value pairs.

Example 6.16

```
>>> db=dbm.open('mydbm.db','r')
>>> for k,v in db.items():
        print (k,v)
b'title' : b'Introduction to Python'
b'publisher' : b'BPB'
b'year' : b'2019'
```

6.4 `csv` module

The **Comma Separated Values (CSV)** format is very widely used to import and export data in spreadsheets and RDBMS tables. The csv module, another built-in module in Python's standard library, presents the functionality to easily convert Python's sequence object in CSV format and write to a disk file. Conversely, data from CSV files is possible to be brought in Python namespace. The `reader` and `writer` classes are defined in this module that perform read/write operation on CSV files. In addition, this module also has `DictReader` and `DictWriter` classes to work with Python's dictionary objects.

The object of writer class is obtained by the `writer()` constructor which needs a file object having **'w'** mode enabled. An optional **'dialect'** parameter is given to specify the implementation type of CSV protocol, which is by default 'excel' – the format preferred by MS Excel spreadsheet software. We are now in a position to write one or more rows to the file represented by the writer object.

Example 6.17

```
>>> import csv
>>> data=[('TV','Samsung',25000),('Comput-
er','Dell',40000),('Mobile','Redmi',15000)]
>>> file=open('pricelist.csv','w', newline='')
>>> obj=csv.writer(file)
>>> #write single row
>>> obj.writerow(data[0])
>>> #write multiple rows
>>> obj.writerows(data[1:])
>>> file.close()
```

Note that, **open()** function needs **newline=''** parameter to correctly interpret newlines inside quoted fields. The 'pricelist.csv' should be created in the current working directory. Its contents can be verified by opening in any text editor, as peryour choice.

The reader object, on the other, hand returns an iterator object of rows in the CSV file. A simple for loop or next() function of an iterator can be used to traverse all rows.

Example 6.18

```
>>> file=open('pricelist.csv','r', newline='')
>>> obj=csv.reader(file)
>>> for row in obj:
        print (row)
['TV', 'Samsung', '25000']
['Computer', 'Dell', '40000']
['Mobile', 'Redmi', '15000']
>>>
```

The csv module offers powerful `DictWriter` and `DictReader` classes that can deal with dictionary objects. **DictWriter** maps the sequence of dictionary objects to rows in the CSV file. As always, the DictWriter constructor needs a writable file object. It also needs a fieldnames parameter whose value has to be a list of fields. These fields will be written as a first row in the resultant CSV file. Let us convert a list of tuples, in the above example, to list of dict objects and send it to csv format using `DictWriter` object.

Example 6.19

```
>>> data=[{'product':'TV','brand':'Sam-
sung','price':25000}, {'product':'Computer','br
and':'Dell','price':40000},{'product':'Mo-
bile','brand':'Redmi','price':15000}]
>>> file=open('pricelist.csv','w',newline='')
>>> fields=data[0].keys()
>>> obj=csv.DictWriter(file,fields)
```

The DictWriter's `writeheader()` method uses fieldnames parameter to write header row in CSV file. Each row following the header contains the keys of each dictionary item.

Example 6.20

```
>>> obj.writeheader()
>>> obj.writerows(data)
>>> file.close()
```

The resulting 'pricelist.csv' will show data, as follows:

Example 6.21

```
product,brand,price
TV,Samsung,25000
Computer,Dell,40000
Mobile,Redmi,15000
```

Reading rows in dictionary formation is easy as well. The **DictReader** object is obtained from the source CSV file. The object stores strings in first row in **fieldnames** attributes. A simple for loop can fetch subsequent rows. However, each row returns an `OrderedDict` object. Use `dict()` function to obtain a normal dictionary object out of each row.

Example 6.22

```
>>> file=open('pricelist.csv','r',newline='')
>>> obj=csv.DictReader(file)
>>> obj.fieldnames
['product', 'brand', 'price']
>>> for row in obj:
        print (dict(row))
{'product': 'TV', 'brand': 'Samsung', 'price':
'25000'}
{'product': 'Computer', 'brand': 'Dell', 'price':
'40000'}
{'product': 'Mobile', 'brand': 'Redmi', 'price':
'15000'}
```

6.5 `json` Module

JavaScript Object Notation (JSON) is an easy to use lightweight data-interchange format. It is a language-independent text format, supported by many programming languages. This format is used for data exchange between the web server and clients. Python's `json` module, being a part of Python's standard distribution, provides serialization functionality similar to the pickle module.

Syntactically speaking, json module offers identical functions for serialization and de-serialization of Python objects. Module-level functions `dumps()` and `loads()` convert Python data to its serialized string representation and vice versa. The `dump()` function uses a file object to persistently store serialized objects, whereas `load()` function reconstructs original data from the file.

Notably, dumps () function uses additional argument sort_keys. Its default value is False, but if set to True, JSON representation of Python's dictionary object holds keys in a sorted order.

Example 6.23

```
>>> import json
>>> data=[{'product':'TV','brand':'Sam-
sung','price':25000}, {'product':'Computer','br
and':'Dell','price':40000},{'product':'Mo-
bile','brand':'Redmi','price':15000}]
>>> JString=json.dumps(data, sort_keys=True)
>>> JString
'[{"brand": "Samsung", "price": 25000, "product":
"TV"}, {"brand": "Dell", "price": 40000, "product":
"Computer"}, {"brand": "Redmi", "price": 15000,
"product": "Mobile"}]'
```

The loads () function retrieves data in the original format.

Example 6.24

```
>>> string=json.loads(JString)
>>> string
[{'brand': 'Samsung', 'price': 25000, 'product':
'TV'}, {'brand': 'Dell', 'price': 40000, 'product':
'Computer'}, {'brand': 'Redmi', 'price': 15000,
'product': 'Mobile'}]
```

To store/retrieve JSONed data to/from a disk file, use dump ()   and load () functions respectively.

Example 6.25

```
>>> file=open('json.txt','w')
>>> json.dump(data,file)
>>> file=open('json.txt','r')
>>> data=json.load(file)
```

Python's built-in types are easily serialized in JSON format. Conversion is done, as per the corresponding table below:*(table 6.1)*

Table 6.1 *Python to JSON*

Python	JSON
Dict	Object
list, tuple	Array
Str	String
int, float, int- & float-derived Enums	Number
True	True
False	False
None	Null

However, converting object of a custom class is a little tricky. The json module defines `JSONEndoder` and `JSONDecoder` classes. We need to subclass them to perform encoding and decoding of objects of user-defined classes.

Following script defines a User class and an encoder class inherited from the JSONEncoder class. This subclass overrides the abstract `default()` method to return a serializable version of User class which can further be encoded.

Example 6.26

```python
import json
class User:
        def __init__(self,name, email, pw):
                self.name=name
                self.email=email
                self.pw=pw
        def __str__(self):
return ('Name: {} email: {} password: {}'. \
                                format(self.name, self.email,
self.pw))
class UserEncoder(json.JSONEncoder):
    def default(self, z):
        if isinstance(z, User):
            return (z.name, z.email, z.pw)
        else:
            super().default(self, z)
user1=User('Rajan','R@a.com','**')
encoder=UserEncoder()
obj=encoder.encode(user1)
file=open('jsonOO.txt','w')
json.dump(obj, file)
file.close()
```

To obtain the original object, we need to use a subclass of JSONDecoder. The subclass should have a method that is assigned a value of object_hook parameter. This method will be internally called when an object is sought to be decoded.

Example 6.27

```
import json
class UserDecoder(json.JSONDecoder):
        def __init__(self):
                json.JSONDecoder.__init__
(self,object_hook=self.hook)
        def hook(self,obj):
                return dict(obj)
decoder=UserDecoder()
file=open('jsonclass.txt','r')
retobj=json.load(file)
print (decoder.decode(retobj))
```

The json.tool module also has a command-line interface that validates data in string or file and delivers nice formatted output of JSON objects.

Assuming that the current working directory has 'file.txt' that contains text in JSON format, as below:

Example 6.28

```
{"name": "Rajan", "email": "r@a.com", "pw": "**"}
```

The following command produces pretty print output of the above string.

```
E:\python37>python -m json.tool file.txt
{
"name": "Rajan",
"email": "r@a.com",
"pw": "**"
}
```

It accepts a -sort-keys command line option to display keys in ascending order.

```
E:\python37>python -m json.tool file.txt --sort-keys
{
"email": "r@a.com",
"name": "Rajan",
"pw": "**"
}
```

6.6 xml Package

XML is another well-known data interchange format, used by a large number of applications. One of the main features of **eXtensible Markup Language (XML)** is that its format is both human readable and human readable. XML is widely used by applications of web services, office tools, and **Service Oriented Architectures (SOA).**

Standard Python library's xml package consists of modules for XML processing, as per different models. In this section, we discuss the **ElementTree** module that provides a simple and lightweight API for XML processing.

The XML document is arranged in a tree-like hierarchical format. The document tree comprises of elements. Each element is a single node in the tree and has an attribute enclosed in <> and </> tags. Each element may have one or more sub-elements following the same structure.

A typical XML document appears, as follows:

Example 6.29

```xml
<?xml version="1.0" encoding="iso-8859-1"?>
<pricelist>
    <product>
        <name>TV</name>
        <brand>Samsung</brand>
        <price>25000</price>
    </product>
    <product>
        <name>Computer</name>
        <brand>Dell</brand>
        <price>40000</price>
    </product>
    <product>
        <name>Mobile</name>
        <brand>Redmi</brand>
        <price>15000</price>
    </product>
</pricelist>
```

The elementTree module's class structure also has Element and SubElement objects. Each Element has a tag and attrib which is a dict object. For the root element, an attrib is an empty dictionary.

Example 6.30

```
>>> import xml.etree.ElementTree as xmlobj
>>> root=xmlobj.Element('PriceList')
>>> root.tag
'PriceList'
>>> root.attrib
{}
```

Now, we can add one or more nodes, i.e., elements under root. Each Element object may have SubElements, each having an attribute and text property.

Let us setup 'product' element and 'name', 'brand', and 'price' as its sub elements.

Example 6.31

```
>>> product=xmlobj.Element('Product')
>>> nm=xmlobj.SubElement(product, 'name')
>>> nm.text='name'
>>> brand=xmlobj.SubElement(product, 'brand')
>>> nm.text='TV'
>>> brand.text='Samsung'
>>> price=xmlobj.SubElement(product, 'price')
>>> price.text='25000'
```

The root node has append() method to add this node to it.

Example 6.32

```
>>> root.append(product)
```

Construct a tree from this root object and write its contents to the XML file.

Example 6.33

```
>>> tree=xmlobj.ElementTree(root)
>>> file=open('pricelist.xml','wb')
>>> tree.write(file)
>>> file.close()
```

The 'pricelist.xml' should be visible in the current working directory. The following script writes a list of dictionary objects to the XML file:

Example 6.34

```
import xml.etree.ElementTree as xmlobj
root=xmlobj.Element('PriceList')
pricelist=[{'name':'TV','brand':'Sam-
sung','price':'25000'},
          {'name':'Computer','brand':'Dell','pri
ce':'40000'},
          {'name':'Mobile','brand':'Red-
mi','price':'15000'}]
i=0
for row in pricelist:
        i=i+1
        print (i)
        element=xmlobj.Element('Product'+str(i))
        for k,v in row.items():
                sub=xmlobj.SubElement(element, k)
                sub.text=v
        root.append(element)
tree=xmlobj.ElementTree(root)
file=open('pricelist.xml','wb')
tree.write(file)
file.close()
```

To parse the XML file, construct document tree giving its name as file parameter in ElementTree constructor.

Example 6.35

```
import xml.etree.ElementTree as xmlobj
tree = xmlobj.ElementTree(file='pricelist.xml')
```

The getroot() method of tree object fetches root element and getchildren() returns a list of elements below it.

Example 6.36

```
root = tree.getroot()
children = root.getchildren()
```

We can now construct a dictionary object corresponding to each subelement by iterating over sub-element collection of each child node.

Example 6.37

```
for child in children:
        product={}
        pairs = child.getchildren()
        for pair in pairs:
            product[pair.tag]=pair.text
```

Each dictionary is then appended to a list returning original list of dictionary objects. Complete code parsing XML file into a list of dictionaries is as follows:

Example 6.38

```
import xml.etree.ElementTree as xmlobj
tree = xmlobj.ElementTree(file='pricelist.xml')
root = tree.getroot()
products=[]
children = root.getchildren()
for child in children:
        product={}
        pairs = child.getchildren()
        for pair in pairs:
            product[pair.tag]=pair.text
        products.append(product)
print (products)
```

Save above script from 'xmlreader.py' and run it from command line:

```
E:\python37>python xmlreader.py
[{'name': 'TV', 'brand': 'Samsung', 'price':
'25000'}, {'name': 'Computer', 'brand': 'Dell',
'price': '40000'}, {'name': 'Mobile', 'brand':
'Redmi', 'price': '15000'}]
```

Of other modules in xml package, `xml.dom` implements document object model of XML format and `xml.sax` defines functionality to implement SAX model.

6.7 `plistlib` Module

Lastly, we have a look at plist module that used to read and write 'property list' files (they usually have .plist' extension). This type of file is mainly used by MAC OS X. These files are essentially XML documents, typically used to store and retrieves properties of an object.

The functionality of plistlib module is more or less similar to other serialization libraries. It defines dumps () and loads () functions for string representation of Python objects. The load () and dump () functions read and write plist disk files.

The following script stores a dict object to a plist file.

Example 6.39

```
import plistlib
proplist = {
"name" : "Ramesh",
"class":"XII",
"div":"B",
"marks" : {"phy":50, "che":60, "maths":80}
}
fileName=open('marks.plist','wb')
plistlib.dump(proplist, fileName)
fileName.close()
```

The load () function retrieves an identical dictionary object from the file.

Example 6.40

```
with open('marks.plist', 'rb') as fp:
        pl = plistlib.load(fp)
        print(pl)
```

Another important data persistence library in Python is the sqlite3 module. It deals with read/write operations on the SQLite relational database. Before we explore its functionality, let us get acquainted with RDBMS concepts and basics of SQL, which is the next chapter.

CHAPTER 7

RDBMS Concepts

Previous chapter discussed various tools offered by Python for data persistence. While the built-in file object can perform basic read/write operations with a disk file, other built-in modules such as pickle and shelve enable storage and retrieval of serialized data to/from disk files. We also explored Python libraries that handle well-known data storage formats like CSV, JSON, and XML.

7.1 Drawbacks of Flat File

However, files created using the above libraries are flat. They are hardly useful when it comes to real-time, random access and in-place updates in them. Also, files are largely unstructured. Although CSV files do have a field header, the comma-delimited nature of data makes it very difficult to modify the contents of a certain field in a particular row. The only alternative remains, is to read the file in a Python object such as a dictionary, manipulate its contents and rewrite it after truncating the file. This approach is not feasible especially for large files as it may become time-consuming and cumbersome.

Even if we keep this issue of in-place modification of file aside for a while, there is another problem of providing concurrent r/w access to multiple applications. This may be required in the client-server environment. None of the persistence libraries of Python have built-in support to asynchronous handling of files. If required, we have to rely upon locking features of the operating system itself.

Another problem that may arise is that of data redundancy and inconsistency. This arises primarily out of the unstructured nature of data files. The term **'redundancy'** refers to the repetition of same data more than one times while describing the collection of records in a file. The first row of a typical CSV file defines the column headings, often called as fields and subsequent rows are records.

Following *table 7.1* shows a 'pricelist.csv' represented in the form of a table. Popular wordprocessors (MS Word, OpenOffice Writer) and spreadsheet programs (MS Excel, OpenOffice Calc) have this feature of converting text delimited by comma or any other character to a table.

Table 7.1 *Pricelist.csv*

InvNo	CustomerName	Product	Price	Quantity	total
1	Ravikumar	Laptop	25000	2	50000
2	John	TV	40000	1	40000
3	Divya	Laptop	25000	1	25000
4	Divya	Mobile	15000	3	45000
5	John	Mobile	15000	2	30000
6	Ravikumar	TV	40000	1	40000

As we can see, data items such as customer's name, product's name, and price are appearing repeatedly in the rows. This can lead to two issues: One, a manual error such as spelling or maintaining correct upper/lower case can creep up. Secondly, change in the value of a certain data item needs to reflect at its all occurrences, failing which it may lead to a discrepancy. For example, if the price of TV goes up to 45000, price and total columns in invoice numbers 2 and 6 should be updated. Otherwise, there will be inconsistency in further processing of data. These problems can be overcome by using a relational database.

7.2 Relational Database

The term '**database**' refers to an organized collection of data so as to remove redundancy and inconsistency, and to ensure data integrity. Over the years, different database models have been in use. Early days of computing observed the use of hierarchical and network database models. Soon, they were replaced by the **relational** database model, which is still used very predominantly. Last 10-15 years have seen emergence of **NOSQL** databases like MongoDB and Cassandra.

The relational database model, proposed by **Edgar Codd** in 1970, aims to arrange data according to the entities. Each **entity** is represented by a **table** (called **relation**). You can think of the entity as a class. Just as a class, an entity is characterized by attributes (also called fields, in the database terminology) that form columns of the table. Each instance of the entity is described in subsequent rows, below the heading row. The entity table structure provides one attribute whose value is unique for each row. Such an attribute is called '**primary key**'.

If we analyze the pricelist example above, it involves three entities, Customers, Products, and Invoices. We have prepared three tables representing them, as follows:*(figure7.1)*

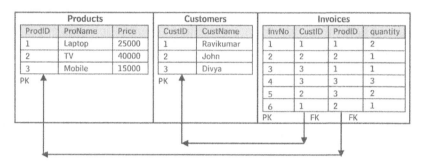

Figure 7.1 Pricelist tables

The important aspect of relational database design is to establish a relationship between tables. In the three tables above, the attributes 'prodID', 'CustID', and 'InvNo' are **primary keys** in products, customers and invoices tables respectively.

Further, structure of the 'invoices' table uses 'CustID' and 'ProductID' attributes which are the primary keys of other two tables. When primary key of one table appears in the structure of other tables, it is called '**Foreign key**' and this forms the basis of the relationship between the two.

This approach of database design has two distinct advantages. Firstly, using the relationship between primary and foreign key, details of the corresponding row can be fetched without repetition. For example, 'invoices' table has 'ProdID' foreign key which is the primary key in the 'Products' table, hence the 'name' and 'price' attributes can be fetched using this relationship. The same is true about 'CustID' which appears as the foreign key in 'invoices' and is the primary key in the 'customers' table. We can thus reconstruct the original pricelist table by using relationships.

InvNo	CustID	Customers. CustName	ProdID	Products. ProName	Products. Price	Qty	Total
1	1	Ravikumar	1	Laptop	25000	2	50000
2	2	John	2	TV	40000	1	40000

InvNo	CustID	Customers. CustName	ProdID	Products. ProName	Products. Price	Qty	Total
3	3	Divya	1	Laptop	25000	1	25000
4	3	Divya	3	Mobile	15000	3	45000
5	2	John	3	Mobile	15000	2	30000
6	1	Ravikumar	2	TV	40000	1	40000

Secondly, you need not make any changes in the 'invoices' table, if either name of product or price changes, change in 'Products' table will automatically reflect in all rows of invoices table because of the primary-foreign key relationship. Also, the database engine won't allow deleting a certain row in customers or products table, if its primary key is being used as foreign keys in the invoices table. This ensures data integrity.

Software products based on this relational model are popularly called as **Relational DataBase Systems (RDBMS)**. Some of the renowned RDBMS brands are Oracle, MySQL, MS SQL Server, Postgre SQL, DB2, SQLite, etc.

7.3 RDBMS Products

Relational Software Inc. (now Oracle Corp) developed its first SQL based RDBMS software called **Oracle V2**. IBM introduced **System-R** as its RDBMS product in 1974 and followed it by a very successful **DB2** product.

Microsoft released **SQL Server** for Windows NT in 1994. Newer versions of MS SQL server are integrated with Microsoft's .NET Framework.

SAP is an enterprise-level RDBMS product targeted towards UNIX based systems being marketed as **Enterprise Resource Planning (ERP)** product.

An open-source RDBMS product named as **MySQL**, developed by a Swedish company MySQL AB, was later acquired by Sun Microsystems, which in turn has, now, been acquired by Oracle Corporation. Being an open-source product, MySQL is a highly popular choice, after Oracle.

MS Access, shipped with Microsoft Office suite, is widely used in small-scale projects. The entire database is stored in a single file and, hence, is easily portable. It provides excellent GUI tools to design tables, queries, forms, and reports.

PostgreSQL is also an open-source object-oriented RDBMS, which has evolved from the Ingres project of the University of California, Berkley. It is available for use on diverse operating system platforms and SQL implementation is supposed to be closest to SQL standard.

SQLite is a very popular relational database used in a wide variety of applications. Unlike other databases like Oracle, MySQL, etc., SQLite is a transactional SQL database engine that is self-contained and serverless. As its official documentation describes, it is a self-contained, serverless, zero-configuration, transactional SQL database engine. The entire database is a single file that can be placed anywhere in the file system.

SQLite was developed by D. Richard Hipp in 2000. Its current version is 3.27.2. It is fully ACID compliant which ensures that transactions are atomic, consistent, isolated, and durable.

Because of its open-source nature, very small footprint, and zero configuration, SQLite databases are popularly used in embedded devices, IOT and mobile apps. Many web browsers and operating systems also use SQLite database for internal use. It is also used as a prototyping and demo of larger enterprise RDBMS.

Despite being very lightweight, it is a full-featured SQL implementation with all the advanced capabilities. SQLite database can be interfaced with most of the mainstream languages like C/C++, Java, PHP, etc. Python's standard library contains the sqlite3 module. It provides all the functionality for interfacing Python program with the SQLite database.

7.4 SQLite Installation

Installation of SQLite is simple and straightforward. It doesn't need any elaborate installation. The entire application is a self-contained executable 'sqlite3.exe'. Official website of SQLite, (https://sqlite.org/download.html) provides pre-compiled binaries for various operating system platforms containing the command line shell bundled with other utilities. All you have to do is download a zip archive of SQLite command-line tools, unzip to a suitable location and invoke **sqlite3.exe** from DOS prompt by putting name of the database you want to open.

If already existing, the SqLite3 database engine will connect to it; otherwise, a new database will be created. If the name is omitted, an in-memory transient database will open. Let us ask SQLite to open a new **mydatabase.sqlite3**.

```
E:\SQLite>sqlite3 mydatabase.sqlite3
SQLite version 3.25.1 2018-09-18 20:20:44
Enter ".help" for usage hints.
sqlite>
```

In the command window a sqlite prompt appears before which any SQL query can be executed. In addition, there "dot commands" (beginning with a dot ".") typically used to change the output format of queries, or to execute certain prepackaged query statements.

An existing database can also be opened using .open command.

```
E:\SQLite>sqlite3
SQLite version 3.25.1 2018-09-18 20:20:44
Enter ".help" for usage hints.
Connected to a transient in-memory database.
Use ".open FILENAME" to reopen on a persistent
database.
sqlite> .open test.db
```

The first step is to create a table in the database. As mentioned above, we need to define its structure specifying name of the column and its data type.

7.5 SQLite Data Types

ANSI SQL defines generic data types, which are implemented by various RDBMS products with a few variations on their own. Most of the SQL database engines (Oracle, MySQL, SQL Server, etc.) use static typing. SQLite, on the other hand, uses a more general dynamic type system. Each value stored inSQLite database (or manipulated by the database engine) has one of the following storage classes:

- NULL
- INTEGER
- REAL
- TEXT
- BLOB

A storage class is more general than a datatype. These storage classes are mapped to standard SQL data types. For example, **INTEGER** in SQLite has a type affinity with all integer types such as **int, smallint, bigint, tinyint**, etc. Similarly **REAL** in SQLite has a type affinity with float and double data type. Standard SQL data types such as **varchar, char,nchar**, etc. are equivalent to TEXT in SQLite.

SQL as a language consists of many declarative statements that perform various operations on databases and tables. These statements are popularly called queries. CREATE TABLE query defines table structure using the above data types.

7.6 CREATE TABLE

This statement is used to create a new table, specifying following details:

- Name of new table
- Names of columns (fields) in the desired table
- Type, width, and the default value of each column.
- Optional constraints on columns (PRIMARY KEY, NOT NULL, FOREIGN KEY)

Example 7.1

```
CREATE TABLE table_name (
  column1 datatype [width] [default] [constraint],
  column2 ....,
  column3 ...,
    ....
);
```

7.7 Constraints

Constraints enforce restrictions on data that a column can contain. They help in maintaining the integrity and reliability of data in the table. Following clauses are used in the definition of one or more columns of a table to enforce constraints:

PRIMARY KEY: Only one column in a table can be defined to be a primary key. The value of this table will uniquely identify each row (a record) in the table. The primary key can be set to AUTOINCREMENT if its type is INTEGER. In that case, its value need not be manually filled.

NOT NULL: By default value for any column in a row can be left as null. NOT NULL constraint ensures that while filling a new row in the table or updating an existing row, the contents of specified columns are not allowed to be null. In the above definition, to ensure that the 'name' column must have a certain value, NOT NULL constraint is applied to it.

FOREIGN KEY: This constraint is used to enforce 'exists' relationship between two tables.

Let us create a Products table in 'mydatabase' that we created above. As shown in the Figure 7.1, diagram, the 'products' table consists of ProductID, Name, and Price columns, with ProductID as its primary key.

```
sqlite> CREATE TABLE Products (
   ...>        ProductID INTEGER    PRIMARY KEY
AUTOINCREMENT,
   ...>        Name        TEXT (20),
   ...>        Price       INTEGER
   ...> );
```

(Ensure that the SQL statement ends with a semi-colon. You may span one statement over multiple lines in the console)

We also create another 'Customers' table in the same database with CustID and Name fields. CustID field should be defined as the primary key.

```
sqlite> CREATE TABLE Customers (
   ...>        CustID INTEGER    PRIMARY KEY
AUTOINCREMENT,
   ...>        Name    TEXT (20),
   ...>        GSTIN   TEXT (15)
   ...> );
```

Finally, we create another 'Invoices' table. As shown in the figure 7.1 diagram, this table has InvID as primary key and two foreign key columns referring to ProductID in 'Products' table and CustID in 'Customers' table. The 'Invoices' table also contains the 'price' column.

```
sqlite> CREATE TABLE Invoices (
   ...>        InvID       INTEGER       PRIMARY KEY
AUTOINCREMENT,
   ...>        CustID      INTEGER       REFERENCES
Customers (CustID),
   ...>        ProductID INTEGER       REFERENCES
Products (ProductID),
   ...>        Quantity INTEGER (5)
   ...> );
```

To confirm that our tables have been successfully created, use .tables command:

```
sqlite> .tables
Customers   Invoices    Products
```

SQLite stores schema of all databases in the SQLITE_MASTER table. We can fetch names of our databases and tables with following command:

```
sqlite> SELECT * FROM sqlite_master WHERE
type='table';
```

To terminate current session of SQLite3 activity use **.quit** command.

7.8 INSERT Statement

Now that we have created tables in our database, let us add few records in them. SQL provides an INSERT statement for the purpose. Itsstandard syntax is as follows:

Example 7.2

```
INSERT INTO tablename (col1, col2, …) VALUES (val1,
val2, val3, …);
```

Name of the table in which a new record (row) is to be added, follows mandatory keywords INSERT INTO. The column list is given after the name in parentheses, which is followed by the VALUES clause. The data corresponding to each column is given in another set of parentheses. Following statement adds one record in Products table:

```
sqlite> INSERT INTO Products (Name, Price) VALUES
('Laptop', 40000);
```

We insert a row in 'Customers' table by executing the following statement in SQLite console:

```
sqlite> INSERT INTO Customers (Name, GSTIN) VALUES
('Ravikumar', '27AAJPL7103N1ZF');
```

Similarly, the following statement adds a record in 'Invoices' table:

```
sqlite> INSERT INTO Invoices (CUSTID, PRODUCTID,
Quantity) VALUES (1, 1, 2);
```

Note that, in the above INSERT statements, we have not included ProductID, CustID, and InvID columns in respective column lists parentheses because they have been defined as autoincrement fields. The column list may be omitted altogether if you intend to provide values for all columns in the table (excluding autoincrement fields). They must be given in the VALUES list exactly in the same order in which their fields have been defined.

You may add a few more records in these three tables. Sample data for these tables is given below:*(table 7.3, table 7.4, and table 7.5)*

Table 7.3 *ProductsTable*

ProductID	Name	Price
1	Laptop	25000
2	TV	40000
3	Router	2000
4	Scanner	5000
5	Printer	9000
6	Mobile	15000

Table 7.4 *Customers Table:*

CustID	Name	GSTIN
1	Ravikumar	27AAJPL7103N1ZF
2	Patel	24ASDFG1234N1ZN
3	Nitin	27AABBC7895N1ZT
4	Nair	32MMAF8963N1ZK
5	Shah	24BADEF2002N1ZB
6	Khurana	07KABCS1002N1ZV
7	Irfan	05IIAAV5103N1ZA
8	Kiran	12PPSDF22431ZC
9	Divya	15ABCDE1101N1ZA
10	John	29AAEEC4258E1ZK

Table 7.5 *Invoices Table*

InvID	CustID	ProductID	Quantity
1	1	1	2
2	10	2	1
3	9	6	3
4	4	1	6
5	10	5	3

InvID	CustID	ProductID	Quantity
6	2	2	5
7	2	1	4
8	5	3	10
9	7	5	2
10	3	4	3

7.9 SELECT Statement

This is one of the most frequently used SQL statements. The purpose of SELECT statement is to fetch data from a database table and return in the form of a result set. In its simplest form SELECT statement is used as follows:

Example 7.3

```
SELECT col1, col2, .., coln FROM table_name;
```

SQLite console displays data from the named table for all rows in specified columns. SQLite console offers two useful 'dot' commands for a neat and formatted output of the SELECT statement. The **'.header on'** command will display the column names as the header of output. The **'.mode column'** command will force left alignment of data in columns.

```
sqlite> .header on
sqlite> .mode column
sqlite> select name as name, price from products;
name        Price
----------  ----------
Laptop      25000
TV          40000
Router      2000
Scanner     5000
Printer     9000
Mobile      15000
```

You can use '*' wild card character to indicate all columns in the table.

```
sqlite> .header on
sqlite> .mode column
sqlite> select * from products;
ProductID    Name          Price
----------   ----------    ----------
1            Laptop        25000
2            TV            40000
3            Router        2000
4            Scanner       5000
5            Printer       9000
6            Mobile        15000
```

The **ORDER BY** clause lists selected rows according to ascending order of data in specified column. Following statement displays records in the Products table in ascending order of price.

```
sqlite> select * from products order by price;
ProductID    Name          Price
----------   ----------    ----------
3            Router        2000
4            Scanner       5000
5            Printer       9000
6            Mobile        15000
1            Laptop        25000
2            TV            40000
```

To enforce descending order, attach 'DESC' to the ORDER BY clause.

```
sqlite> select * from products order by name desc;
ProductID    Name          Price
----------   ----------    ----------
2            TV            40000
4            Scanner       5000
3            Router        2000
5            Printer       9000
6            Mobile        15000
1            Laptop        25000
```

You can apply filter on selection of rows by using the **WHERE** clause. The WHERE keyword is followed by a logical condition having logical operators (<, >, <=, >=, =, IN, LIKE, etc.). In the following example, only those rows will be selected for which value of the 'price' column is less than 10000.

```
sqlite> select * from products where price<10000;
ProductID    Name         Price
----------   ----------   ----------
3            Router       2000
4            Scanner      5000
5            Printer      9000
```

A big advantage of the relational model comes through when data from two related tables can be fetched. In our 'Invoices' table, we have ProductID as one of the columns that is a primary key of the 'Products' table. The following example uses **WHERE** clause to join two tables - Invoices and Products - and fetch data from them in a single SELECT statement.

```
sqlite> select InvID, Products.name, Products.Price,
Quantity
    ...> from invoices, Products where invoices.
productID=Products.ProductID;
InvID        Name         Price        Quantity
----------   ----------   ----------   ----------
1            Laptop       25000        2
2            TV           40000        1
3            Mobile       15000        3
4            Mobile       15000        1
5            Printer      9000         3
6            TV           40000        5
7            Laptop       25000        4
8            Router       2000         10
9            Printer      9000         2
10           Scanner      5000         3
```

It is also possible to generate a calculated column depending on some operation on other columns. Any column heading can also be given an alias name using AS keyword.

Following SELECT statement displays **Total** column which is Products. Price*Quantity. The column shows values of this expression is named **AS** Total.

```
sqlite> select InvID, Products.name, Products.
Price, Quantity, Products.Price*Quantity as
Total
   ...> from invoices, Products where
invoices.productID=Products.ProductID;
InvID        Name         Price        Quantity
Total
----------  ----------   ----------   ----------
-  ----------
1            Laptop       25000        2            50000
2            TV           40000        1            40000
3            Mobile       15000        3            45000
4            Mobile       15000        1            15000
5            Printer      9000         3            27000
6            TV           40000        5            200000
7            Laptop       25000        4            100000
8            Router       2000         10           20000
9            Printer      9000         2            18000
10           Scanner      5000         3            15000
```

7.10 UPDATE Statement

It is possible to modify data of a certain field in given table using the UPDATE statement. The usage syntax of the UPDATE query is as follows:

Example 7.4

```
UPDATE table_name SET col1=val1, col2=val2,..,
colN=valN WHERE [expression];
```

Note that,the WHERE clause is not mandatory when executing the UPDATE statement. However, you would normally want to modify only those records satisfying a certain condition. If the WHERE clause is not specified, all records will be modified.

For example, the following statement changes the price of 'Printer' to 10000.

```
sqlite> update products set price=10000 where
name='Printer';
sqlite> select * from products;
ProductID    Name        Price
----------   ----------  ----------
1            Laptop      25000
2            TV          40000
3            Router      2000
4            Scanner     5000
5            Printer     10000
6            Mobile      15000
```

However, if you want to increase the price of each product by 10 percent, you don't have to specify the WHERE clause.

```
sqlite> update products set
price=price+price*10/100;
sqlite> select * from products;
ProductID    Name        Price
----------   ----------  ----------
1            Laptop      27500
2            TV          44000
3            Router      2200
4            Scanner     5500
5            Printer     11000
6            Mobile      16500
```

7.11 DELETE Statement

If you need to remove one or more records from a certain table, use the DELETE statement. General syntax of DELETE query is as under:

Example 7.5

```
DELETE FROM table_name WHERE [condition];
```

In most circumstances, the WHERE clause should be specified unless you intend to remove all records from the table. The following statement will remove those records from the Invoices table having Quantity>5.

```
sqlite> select customers.name, products.name,
quantity from invoices, customers, products
   ...> where invoices.productID=Products.ProductID
   ...> and invoices.CustID=Customers.CustID;
Name           Name           Quantity
----------     ----------     ----------
Ravikumar      Laptop         2
Divya          Mobile         3
Ravikumar      Mobile         1
John           Printer        3
Patel          Laptop         4
Irfan          Printer        2
Nitin          Scanner        3
```

7.12. ALTER TABLE statement

On many occasions, you may want to make changes in a table's structure. This can be done by the ALTER TABLE statement. It is possible to change the name of a table or a column, or add a new column in the table.

Following statement adds a new column in 'Customers' table:

```
sqlite> alter table customers add column address
text (20);
sqlite> .schema customers
CREATE TABLE Customers (
    CustID INTEGER    PRIMARY KEY AUTOINCREMENT,
    Name   TEXT (20),
    GSTIN  TEXT (15),
    address text (20));
```

7.13 DROP TABLE Statement

This statement will remove the specified table from the database. If you try to drop a non-existing table, the SQLite engine shows an error.

```
sqlite> drop table invoices;
sqlite> drop table employees;
Error: no such table: employees
```

When 'IF EXISTS' option is used, the named table will be deleted only if exists and the statement will be ignored if it doesn't exist.

```
sqlite> drop table if exists employees;
```

7.14 Transaction Control

As mentioned above, SQLite is a transactional database and all transactions are **ACID** compliant. ACID stands for **Atomic, Consistent, Isolated** and **Durable**. As a result, it ensures that the SQLite database doesn't lose integrity, even if transaction such as INSERT, DELETE, or UPDATE, is interrupted because of any reason whatsoever.

A transaction is the propagation of changes to the database. The operation performed by INSERT, UPDATE or DELETE statement results in a transaction.

Atomicity: When we say that a transaction should be atomic, it means that a change cannot be effected in parts. Either the entire transaction is applied or not applied.

Consistency: After any transaction is completed, the database should hold on to the changes in its state.

Isolation: It must be ensured that the transaction such as INSERT, UPDATE, or DELETE, performed by a client should only be visible to other clients after successful completion.

Durability: Result of successfully committed transactions must be permanent in the database regardless of the condition such as power failure or program crash.

SQLite provides two statements for transaction control. They are **COMMIT** and **ROLLBACK**. All CRUD (CREATE, RETRIEVE, UPDATE and DELETE) operations first take effect in memory and then they are permanently saved (committed) to the disk file. SQLite transactions are automatically committed without giving any chance to undo (rollback) the changes.

To control the commitment and rolling back manually, start transactions after issuing the directive **BEGIN TRANSACTION**. Whatever operations done thereafter will not be confirmed,until COMMIT is issued and will be annulled if ROLLBACK is issued.

```
sqlite> select * from products;
ProductID    Name         Price
---------    ---------    ---------
1            Laptop       27500
3            Router       2200
4            Scanner      5500
5            Printer      11000
6            Mobile       16500
sqlite> begin transaction;
sqlite> update products set price=2000 where
name='Router';
sqlite> select * from products;
ProductID    Name         Price
---------    ---------    ---------
1            Laptop       27500
3            Router       2000
4            Scanner      5500
5            Printer      11000
6            Mobile       16500
sqlite> rollback;
sqlite> select * from products;
ProductID    Name         Price
---------    ---------    ---------
1            Laptop       27500
3            Router       2200
4            Scanner      5500
5            Printer      11000
6            Mobile       16500
```

In the above example, the price of 'Router' is initially 2200. It was changed to 2000 but rolled back. Hence its earlier value is restored. Following example shows effect of commit statement where the effect of UPDATE statement is confirmed.

```
sqlite> begin transaction;
sqlite> update products set price=3000 where
name='Router';
sqlite> commit;
sqlite> select * from products;
ProductID    Name         Price
---------    ---------    ---------
1            Laptop       27500
3            Router       3000
4            Scanner      5500
5            Printer      11000
6            Mobile       16500
```

7.15 MySQL

So far we have learned how some basic SQL operations are performed over a relational database using SQLite console. Similar console driven interaction is possible with other RDBMS products. MySQL console works more or less similar (barring certain syntactical differences) to the SQLite console we've used in this chapter. Following piece of code shows a sample MySQL console session:

```
Welcome to the MySQL monitor. Commands end with ; or \g.
Your MySQL connection id is 17
Server version: 5.7.23 MySQL Community Server (GPL)
Copyright (c) 2000, 2018, Oracle and/or its
affiliates. All rights reserved.
Oracle is a registered trademark of Oracle
Corporation and/or its
affiliates. Other names may be trademarks of their respective
owners.
Type 'help;' or '\h' for help. Type '\c' to clear
the current input statement.
mysql> show databases;
+--------------------+
| Database           |
+--------------------+
| information_schema |
| mydb               |
| mysql              |
| performance_schema |
| sys                |
+--------------------+
5 rows in set (0.03 sec)
mysql> use mydb;
Database changed
mysql> CREATE TABLE products
    -> ( productID varchar(5),
    -> productName varchar(20),
    -> price Numeric(7,2));
Query OK, 0 rows affected (0.17 sec)
mysql> insert into products values (1, 'TV', 40000);
Query OK, 1 row affected (0.06 sec)
mysql> select * from products;
+-----------+-------------+----------+
| productID | productName | price    |
+-----------+-------------+----------+
| 1         | TV          | 40000.00 |
+-----------+-------------+----------+
1 row in set (0.05 sec)
```

MS SQL Server also has a console based frontend called **SQLCMD** which also works similarly. Command-line interface of Oracle is called **SQL*Plus**. As far as PostgreSQL is concerned, its primary command-line interface is **psql** program.

All the RDBMS products also provide GUI based environments to perform various SQL related operations instead of command-line actions. Oracle's **SQL Developer**, Microsoft's **SQL Server management studio**, **pgAdmin** for PostgreSQL, and **Workbench** for MySQL are respective examples. SQL server client is integrated with Visual Studio which helps the user to perform database operations graphically. MySQL module is shipped with various web server software bundles (for example, LAMP, XAMPP, etc.), providing a web-based interface called **PhpMyAdmin**. *(figure 7.2)*

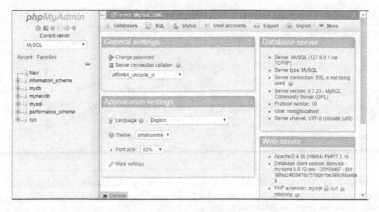

Figure 7.2 PhpMyAdmin

Although SQLite doesn't provide its own GUI tool for database management, many third-party tools are available. One such utility is **SQLiteStudio** that is very popularly used.

7.16 SQLiteStudio

SQLiteStudio is an open-source software from https://sqlitestudio.pl. It is portable, which means it can be directly run without having to install. It is powerful, fast and yet very light. You can perform CRUD operations on a database using GUI as well as by writing SQL queries.

Download and unpack zip archive of the latest version for Windows from the downloads page. Run **SQLiteStudio.exe** to launch the SqliteStudio. It's opening GUI appears as follows:*(figure 7.3)*

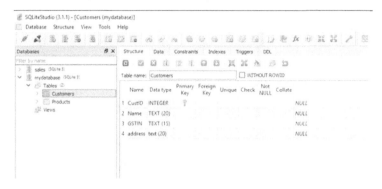

Figure 7.3 SQLiteStudio GUI

Currently attached databases appear as expandable nodes in the left column. Click any one to select and the 'Tables' sub-node shows tables in the selected database. On the right, there is a tabbed pane. The first active tab shows structure of the selected table and the second tab shows its data. The structure, as well as data, can be modified. Right-click on the Tables sub node on the left or use the Structure menu to add a new table. User-friendly buttons are provided in the Structure tab and data tab to insert/ modify column/row, commit or rollback transactions.

This concludes the current chapter on RDBMS concepts with a focus on the SQLite database. As mentioned in the beginning, this is not a complete tutorial on SQLite but a quick hands-on experience of interacting with SQLite database to understand Python's interaction with databases with DB-API that is the subject of next chapter.

CHAPTER 8
Python DB-API

The previous chapter was an overview of SQL fundamentals with the help of SQLite database. However, as mentioned there in short, there are several equally popular RDBMS in use worldwide. Some of them are open-source and others for enterprise use. Although all of them use SQL underneath them, there are lot of differences in the implementation of SQL standard by each of them. This also reflected in Python's interface modules written by individuals for interaction with databases. Since each module defined its own functionality for interaction with respective database product, its major fallout is lack of compatibility. If for some reason, a user is required to switch to different database product, almost the entire code that handles the back-end processing had to be rewritten.

To find a solution for this incompatibility issue, a 'Special Interest Group' was formed in 1996. This group (**db-sig**) recommended a set of specifications by raising 'Python Enhancement Proposal (PEP 248)' for a consistent interface to relational databases known as **DB-API**. The specifications have since been modified by subsequent enhancement proposal (PEP 249). Its recommendations are called DB-API Version 2.0.

As various Python database modules have been made DB-API compliant, most of the functionality required to interact with any database is uniform. Hence, even if the database itself is switched, only a couple of changes in the code should be sufficient.

Oracle, the world's most popular relational database can be interface with Python with more than one modules. **cx_Oracle** is a Python extension module that enables access to Oracle Database with some features of its own in addition to DB-API. It can be used with Oracle 11.2, 12.1, and 12.2 and 18.3 client libraries. There is **pyodbc** module that acts as a Python-ODBC bridge driver, can be used for Python-Oracle interaction as well.

To use Microsoft's SQL Server database with Python also, there are a couple of alternatives. The **pymysql** module is there in addition to pyodbc module.

As far as PostgreSQL is concerned, **psycopg2** module is the most popular PostgreSQL adapter for the Python programming language.

MySQL is also a very popular relational database, especially in the open-source domain. MySQL Connector/Python is a standardized database driver provided by MySQL itself. There is a **mysqldb** module for Python interface but is not still compatible with Python 3.x. You can use **pymysql** module as a drop-in replacement for mysqldb module while using Python 3.x version.

As mentioned in the previous chapter, Python's standard library consists of the **sqlite3** module which is a DB-API compliant module for handling the SQLite database through Python program. While other modules mentioned above should be installed in the current Python installation - either by **pip** utility or by using a customized installer (as in case of **MySQL Connector/ Python**), the sqlite3 module needs no such installation.

8.1 sqlite3 Module

SQLite is often used as a prototyping tool for larger databases. The fact that SQLite is extremely lightweight and doesn't require any server but still is a fully featured implementation of SQL, it is a common choice in the developmental stage of an application and is eventually replaced by enterprise RDBMS products such as Oracle. Likewise, you can think of the sqlite3 module as a prototype DB-API module. We shall explore the DB-API specifications with the help of sqlite3 module. We will soon discover how easy it is to switch to other databases just by modifying a couple of statements.

Let us start by importing the `sqlite3` module. Note that, its target SQLite library version may be different from SQLite binary downloaded by you as shown in the previous chapter.

Example 8.1:

```
>>> import sqlite3
>>> sqlite3.sqlite_version
'3.21.0'
```

8.2 Connection Object

The all important connection object is set up by module level `connect()` function. First positional argument to this function is a string representing path (relative or absolute) to a SQLite database file. The function returns a connection object referring to the database file – either existing or new. Assuming that, **'newdb.sqlite'** doesn't already exist, following statement opens it:

```
>>> conn=sqlite3.connect('newdb.sqlite')
>>> type(conn)
<class 'sqlite3.Connection'>
```

As we've seen in the previous chapter, SQLite supports in-memory database. To open the same programmatically use *":memory:"* as its path.

```
>>> conn=sqlite3.connect(":memory:")
```

The connection object has access to various methods in connection class. One of them is a cursor() method that returns a cursor object, about which we shall know in the next section. Transaction control is achieved by commit() and rollback() methods of the connection object. Connection class has important methods to define custom functions and aggregates to be used in SQL queries. Later in this chapter create_function() and create_aggregate() methods are explained.

8.3 cursor Object

After opening the database, the next step is to get a cursor object from it which is essential to perform any operation on the database. A database cursor enables traversal over the records in a database. It facilitates CRUD operations on a table. The database cursor can be considered as similar to the concept of an iterator. The cursor() method on the connection object returns the a cursor object.

```
>>> cur=conn.cursor()
>>> type(cur)
<class 'sqlite3.Cursor'>
```

Once we get hold of the cursor object, we can perform all SQL query operations, primarily with the help of its execute() method. This method needs a string argument which must be a valid SQL statement. String argument having incorrect SQL statement raises exceptions as defined in the sqlite3 module. Hence, it is recommended that a standard exception handling mechanism is used.

8.4 Creating Table

We shall now add a table in our newly created 'mydb.sqlite' database. In the following script, first two steps are as illustrated above – setting up connection and cursor objects. Next, we call **execute()** method of cursor object, giving it a string with CREATE TABLE statement inside. We shall use the same 'Products' table that we created in the previous chapter. Save following script as 'createqry.py' and execute it.

Example 8.2

```
import sqlite3
conn=sqlite3.connect('mydb.sqlite')
cur=conn.cursor()
qry='''
CREATE TABLE Products (
ProductID INTEGER    PRIMARY KEY AUTOINCREMENT,
Name       TEXT (20),
Price      INTEGER
);
'''
try:
        cur.execute(qry)
        print ('Table created successfully')
except:
        print ('error in creating table')
conn.close()
```

Products table will be created in our database. We can verify by listing out tables in this database in SQLite console, as we did in the previous chapter.

```
sqlite> .open mydb.sqlite
sqlite> .tables
Products
```

Let us also create 'Customers' and 'Invoices' tables with the same structure as used in the previous chapter. Here, we use a convenience method executescript() that is defined in cursor class. With its help, it is possible to execute multiple execute statements at once.

Example 8.3

```
import sqlite3
conn=sqlite3.connect('mydb.sqlite')
cur=conn.cursor()
qry='''
CREATE TABLE Customers (
        CustID  INTEGER   PRIMARY KEY AUTOINCREMENT,
        Name    TEXT (20),
        GSTIN   TEXT (15)
    );
CREATE TABLE Invoices (
        InvID      INTEGER     PRIMARY KEY
AUTOINCREMENT,
        CustID     TEXT        REFERENCES Customers
(CustID),
        ProductID INTEGER      REFERENCES Products
(ProductID),
        Quantity  INTEGER (5)
    );
'''
try:
        cur.executescript(qry)
        print ('Table created successfully')
except:
        print ('error in creating table')
conn.close()
```

You can go back to the SQLite console and refresh table list to confirm that all three tables are created in mydb.sqlite database.

8.5 Inserting Rows

The next step is to insert rows in the tables we have just created. We know the syntax of the INSERT statement and we have used it in console mode of SQLite in the previous chapter. To do it programmatically, declare an INSERT query string and use it as an argument to execute() method.

As noted in the previous chapter, the SQLite database engine is in auto-commit mode by default. To have better transaction control, we should commit the query operation only if it doesn't encounter any exception.

Following code inserts a record in the Products table.

Example 8.4:

```
import sqlite3
conn=sqlite3.connect('mydb.sqlite')
cur=conn.cursor()
qry="insert into Products values (1,'Laptop', 25000);"
try:
        cur.execute(qry)
        conn.commit()
        print ('Record inserted successfully')
except:
        print ('error in insert operation')
        conn.rollback()
conn.close()
```

In many cases, you may want to accept user input for field values to be inserted. You can form a query string by substituting the user inputs in the string with the help of string formatting technique, as shown below:

Example 8.5

```
>>> id=input('enter ProductID:')
enter ProductID:2
>>> nm=input('enter product name:')
enter product name:Hard Disk
>>> p=int(input('enter price:'))
enter price:5000
>>> qry="insert into products values ({}, {}, {});".
format(id, nm, p)
>>> qry
'insert into products values (2, Hard Disk, 5000);'
```

You can very well use this query string as an argument of execute() method. However, query operations using Python's string formatting is insecure as it makes the program vulnerable to SQL injection attacks. Hence, DB-API recommends the use of parameter substitution technique.

The execute() method of sqlite3 module supports the use of question mark symbols ('?') as place holders as well as named place holders in which case dictionary object of name and value pairs is given as the second argument to execute() method.

```
>>> #using '?' place holder
>>> cur.execute("insert into products values
(?,?,?)",(id,nm,p))
>>> #using named place holder
>>> cur.execute("insert into products values
(:id,:nm,:p)",{"id":id,"nm":nm,"p":p})
```

There is another useful variant of execute() method in the sqlite3
module. The first argument to executemany() method is a query string with
place holders, and the second argument is a list of parameter sequences.
The query gets executed for each sequence (itself may be a list or tuple) in
the list. Following script (*'insertqry.py'*) uses executemany() method
to insert records in the Products table, as displayed in the previous chapter.

Example 8.6

```
import sqlite3
conn=sqlite3.connect('mydb.sqlite')
cur=conn.cursor()
qry="insert into Products values (?,?,?)"
pricelist=[(1,'Laptop',25000),(2, 'TV',40000),
          (3,'Router',2000),(4,'Scanner',5000),
          (5,'Printer',9000), (6,'Mobile',15000)]
try:
        cur.executemany(qry, pricelist)
        conn.commit()
        print ('Records inserted successfully')
except:
        print ('error in insert operation')
        conn.rollback()
conn.close()
```

You can check successful insertion on SQLite console.

```
sqlite> select * from products;
ProductID   Name        Price
---------   ---------   ---------
1           Laptop      25000
2           TV          40000
3           Router      2000
4           Scanner     5000
5           Printer     9000
6           Mobile      15000
```

8.6 Updating Data

It is fairly straightforward to programmatically perform update operation on a table in SQLite database. As pointed out in previous chapter, the update query is normally conditional operation unless you intend to update all rows of a certain table. Hence a parameterized query is ideal for the purpose.

Following script (*'updateqry.py'*) asks the user to input name of the product and new price and performs update operation accordingly.

Example 8.7

```
import sqlite3
conn=sqlite3.connect('mydb.sqlite')
nm=input('enter name of product:')
p=int(input('new price:'))
qry='update Products set price=? where name=?'
cur=conn.cursor()
try:
        cur.execute(qry, (p,nm))
        print ('record updated')
        conn.commit()
except:
        print ('error in update operation')
        conn.rollback()
conn.close()
```

Run the above script from command prompt:

```
E:\python37>python updateqry.py
enter name of product:TV
new price:32000
record updated
```

The SQLite console can confirm above action.

```
sqlite> select * from products where name='TV';
ProductID    Name          Price
----------   ----------    ----------
2            TV            32000
```

8.7 Deleting Rows

Similarly, we can programmatically delete a certain record from a table. This operation is also more often than not conditional. Hence, 'WHERE' clause appears in the parameterized DELETE query. Following script (deleteqry.py) deletes row belonging to user-specified product.

Example 8.8

```python
import sqlite3
conn=sqlite3.connect('mydb.sqlite')
nm=input('enter product to delete:')
qry='delete from Products where name=?'
cur=conn.cursor()
try:
        cur.execute(qry, (nm,))
        print ('record deleted')
        conn.commit()
except:
        print ('error in delete operation')
        conn.rollback()
conn.close()
```

To delete the user input product, run above script from command prompt.

```
E:\python37>python deleteqry.py
enter product to delete:Printer
record deleted
```

Execute select query in SQLite console to verify that deleted product doesn't appear in the list.

```
sqlite> select * from products;
ProductID    Name         Price
----------   ----------   ----------
1            Laptop       25000
2            TV           32000
3            Router       2000
4            Scanner      5000
6            Mobile       15000
```

Next section explains how to programmatically retrieve records from a table.

8.8 ResultSet Object

We need to call execute() method on cursor object with a SELECT query string as its argument and a query result set is built which is similar to an iterator of rows returned in response to the query. The module provides following methods to traverse the result set:

fetchone() : Next row in the query result set is retrieved and returned in the form of a tuple. The method returns None if there are no more rows to be fetched.

fetchall() : This method returns a list of all available rows in the result set. It contains a sequence corresponding to each row. You can employ a regular for loop to traverse the rows, as follows:

Example 8.9

```
import sqlite3
conn=sqlite3.connect('mydb.sqlite')
cur=conn.cursor()
qry="select * from Products;"
cur.execute(qry)
rows=cur.fetchall()
for row in rows:
        print (row)
conn.close()
```

Run the above code ('*selectqry.py*') from command prompt.

```
E:\python37>python selectqry.py
(1, 'Laptop', 25000)
(2, 'TV', 40000)
(3, 'Router', 2000)
(4, 'Scanner', 5000)
(5, 'Printer', 9000)
(6, 'Mobile', 15000)
```

The fact that execute() method runs a parameterized query can be used to good effect to search for a certain condition in the table. Following code snippet accepts product's name as input and displays its price.

Example 8.10

```
import sqlite3
conn=sqlite3.connect('mydb.sqlite')
nm=input ('Enter name of product:')
cur=conn.cursor()
qry="select * from Products where name=?";
cur.execute(qry, (nm,))
row=cur.fetchone()
print (row)
conn.close()
```

When the above script is run from command prompt, then it above script shows following output:

```
E:\python37>python selecttqry.py
Enter name of product:TV
(2, 'TV', 40000)
```

Individual items in the 'row' tuple can be accessed by index. The row can also be unpacked in separate variables as under:

Example 8.11

```
row=cur.fetchone()
print ('ID:', row[0], 'Name:', row[1],'price:',
row[2])
id, nm, p=row
print ('ID:', id, 'Name:', nm,'price:', p)
```

8.9 User Defined Functions

The SQLite database engine by itself is equipped with several built-in functions for finding string length, changing case to upper/lower case, rounding a number, etc. However, it doesn't have the provision to define a new function with customized functionality. The sqlite3 module, however, has the provision to do so with the help of **create_function()** method available to the connection object.

In the following example, we try to represent the price of the product rounded to thousands and attach a 'k' alphabet to it. In other words, 40000 is represented by 40k. First, we define a regular Python function (myfunction) that accepts a number, divides it by 1000 and appends 'k' to its string conversion. The create_function () method has following prototype:

Example 8.12

```
create_function(SQLFunction, parameters,
PythonFunction)
```

In other words, it assigns a name to the Python function(afunction in our case) that can be used as a function in the SQL query.

Example 8.13

```
import sqlite3
conn=sqlite3.connect('mydb.sqlite')
def myfunction(num):
        return str(round(num/1000))+"k"
conn.create_function('priceinK',1,myfunction)
cur=conn.cursor()
qry="select name, priceinK(price) from products;"
cur.execute(qry)
rows=cur.fetchall()
print (rows)
conn.close()
```

Output of above code snippet is:

Example 8.14

```
[('Laptop', '25k'), ('TV', '40k'), ('Router', '2k'),
('Scanner', '5k'), ('Printer', '9k'), ('Mobile',
'15k')]
```

SQLite also has several built-in aggregate functions such as SUM, AVG, COUNT, etc. to be applied to one or more columns in a table. For example, the query 'select SUM(price) from Products' returns sum of values in the price column of all rows. Using create_aggregate() method defined to be used with the cursor object, it is possible to define customized aggregate function.

In the following script, a regular Python class named myclass is defined and it contains a **step()** method which is mandatory for user-defined aggregate function. The step() method increments count for each product name ending with 'r'. The **create_aggregate()** method attaches a name that can be used in the SQL query. When this aggregate function is called, the value returned by finalize() method of the class is in fact the result of the SELECT statement.

Example 8.15:

```
import sqlite3
conn=sqlite3.connect('mydb.sqlite')
class myclass:
        def __init__(self):
                self.count=0
        def step(self, string):
                if string.endswith('r'):
                        self.count=self.count+1
        def finalize(self):
                return self.count
conn.create_aggregate('MyF',1,myclass)
cur=conn.cursor()
qry="select MyF(name) from products;"
cur.execute(qry)
row=cur.fetchone()
print ('number of products with name ending with
'r':',(row)[0])
conn.close()
```

The output of above script is:

Example 8.16

```
number of products with name ending with : 3
```

8.10   Row Object

By default, each row in the query result set is a tuple of values belonging to the column list in SELECT statement. In the above example, the row object returns a tuple.

Example 8.17

```
>>> row=cur.fetchone()
>>> row
(2, 'TV', 40000)
>>> type(row)
<class 'tuple'>
```

The order of columns in the tuple cannot be ascertained from the object itself. The connection object has a useful '**row_factory**' property with which row in the result set can be converted into some meaningful representation. This can be done either by assigning row_factory to a user-defined function that will return a custom object, or by setting it to the constructor of Row class.

Row class has been defined in the sqlite3 module, whose primary purpose is to be used as row_factory. As a result, the row of result set is returned as a Row object. Row class defines a keys () method that returns column names used in the SELECT statement. Values are accessible using the index as well as by name.

Example 8.18

```
>>> r=cur.fetchone()
>>> type(r)
<class 'sqlite3.Row'>
>>> r.keys()
['ProductID', 'Name', 'Price']
>>> fields=r.keys()
>>> r[1]
'TV'
>>> r['name']
'TV'
>>> for nm in fields:
        print (nm, r[nm])

ProductID 2
Name TV
Price 40000
```

8.11 Backup and Restore Database

It is extremely important to secure an organization's data with periodic backup so that the same can be used to fall back in case of any damage. The sqlite3 module provides **iterdump()** function that returns an iterator of entire data of a database in the form of SQL statements. This includes CREATE TABLE statements corresponding to each table in the database and INSERT statements corresponding to rows in each table.

Let us demonstrate the effect of iterdump() with following example. First, we create a database with one table and insert a record in it. After that, we create a dump of the database. Run the following script and open the resultant backup.sql file with an editor.

Example 8.19

```
import sqlite3
conn=sqlite3.connect('sample.db')
qry='create table names (name text (20), address
text(20));'
conn.execute(qry)
qry="insert into names values('Anurag', 'Mumbai');"
cur=conn.cursor()
try:
        cur.execute(qry)
        print ('record added')
        conn.commit()
except:
        print ('error in insert operation')
        conn.rollback()
conn.close()
#creating dump
conn=sqlite3.connect('sample.db')
f=open('dump.sql','w')
for line in conn.iterdump():
        f.write('{}\n'.format(line))
f.close()
conn.close()
```

The dump file, created, will look like the following:

Example 8.20

```
BEGIN TRANSACTION;
CREATE TABLE names (name text (20), address
text(20));
INSERT INTO "names" VALUES('Anurag','Mumbai');
COMMIT;
```

To restore the database from the dumped version in 'newsample.db', we have to read its contents and execute SQL statements in it with the help of executescript() method of the cursor object.

```
>>> conn=sqlite3.connect('newsample.db')
>>> f=open('dump.sql','r')
>>> qry=f.read()
>>> f.close()
>>> cur=conn.cursor()
>>> cur.executescript(qry)
>>> conn.close()
```

New database gets constructed from the backup. To verify, run a select query on its names table and display the result.

```
>>> conn=sqlite3.connect('newsample.db')
>>> cur=conn.cursor()
>>> cur.execute('select * from names;')
>>> row=cur.fetchone()
>>> row
('Anurag', 'Mumbai')
```

As you can see the result is the same data inserted in the original database.

As mentioned earlier, SQLite recognizes NULL, INTEGER, REAL, TEXT, BLOB as native data types. They are mapped to respective Python data types as per the following table:*(table 8.1)*

Table 8.1 *Data types*

Python type	SQLite type
None	NULL
Int	INTEGER
Float	REAL
str	TEXT
bytes	BLOB

The type system of the sqlite3 module can be extended to store additional Python types in the SQLite database via object adaptation. You can let the sqlite3 module convert SQLite types to different Python types via converters. Discussion on adapters and converters is kept outside the scope of this book.

Before we discuss other DB-API compatible modules, one more thing is worth mentioning here. We have used The execute() method - and its other variants executemany() and executescript() – as defined in the cursor class of sqlite3 module. These methods are also available for use with the connection object. However, as mentioned in official documentation of the sqlite3 module, they are non-standard methods. It simply means that DB_API recommends these methods be defined in cursor class and the connection object as defined in other modules (`pymysql` or `pyodbc` module for example) may not be able to call these execute() methods.

8.12. Using `pymysql` Module

To make a Python program interact with a MySQL database, we need to install a DB-API compliant module. As mentioned earlier in this chapter, there are many alternatives available for this purpose. In this section, we shall discuss the use of **pymysql** module. In any case, the functionality of any DB-API compatible module is more or less similar, with a few differences.

The pymysql module is not a part of Python's standard library. Hence, we have to install it using pip utility.

```
E:\python37>pip3 install pymysql
```

As per the DB-API standards, the first step is to establish a connection with the database to be used. Usage of `connect()` function in pymysql module is a little different. Remember that MySQL databases are hosted on a server. Hence, the server's URL and login credentials (user ID and password) must be passed to `connect()` function. Additionally, if you are trying to connect to an existing database, its name should also be provided. If you are going to create a new database (or use existing database later), you needn't provide its name in the `connect()` function's parameter list and just connect to the server.

Example 8.21

```
>>> import pymysql
>>> con=pymysql.connect('localhost', 'root', '***')
```

MySQL provides the 'CREATE DATABASE' statement to start a new database. Execute this statement through the cursor object obtained from the connection object.

Example 8.22

```
>>> cur=con.cursor()
>>> cur.execute('create database mynewdb')
```

You can now start using this (or any other existing database) either by **select_db()** method or executing the '**USE DATABASE**' statement.

Example 8.23

```
>>> con.select_db('mynewdb')
>>> #or
>>> cur.execute('use mynewdb')
```

Now that the new database has been created and it is in use, you are now in a position to create a table and perform insert, update, delete and select operations on it exactly as we did on a SQLite database. The only thing you need to take into account is MySQL data types which are different from SQLite data types.*(Table 8.2)*

Table 8.2 *MySQL Datatypes*

Integer types	TINYINT, SMALLINT, MEDIUMINT, INTEGER, BIGINT
Float types	FLOAT, DOUBLE, DECIMAL, NUMERIC
string types	VARCHAR, TEXT, BLOB, CHAR, NCHAR
Date/time types	DATE, TIME, DATETIME
binary types	BLOB, LONGBLOB

Accordingly, CREATE TABLE query string for MySQL will be as follows:

Example 8.24

```
>>> qry='''
CREATE TABLE Products (
ProductID INTEGER   PRIMARY KEY AUTO_INCREMENT,
Name       VARCHAR (20),
Price      INTEGER
)
'''
>>> cur.execute(qry)
```

You can follow the process, as detailed in previous sections of this chapter, for insert, delete, and select operations.

8.13 pyodbc **Module**

ODBC is a language and operating system independent API for accessing relational databases. The pyodbc module enables access to any RDBMS for which the respective ODBC driver is available on the operating system. Most of the established relational database products (Oracle, MySQL, PostgreSQL, SQL Server, etc.) have ODBC drivers developed by the vendors themselves or third-party developers.

In this section, we access 'mydb' database deployed on MySQL server. First of all, verify if your OS has a corresponding ODBC driver installed. If not, download **MYSQL/ODBC** connector compatible with your OS, MySQL version and hardware architecture from MySQL's official download page: https://dev.mysql.com/downloads/connector/odbc/ and perform installation as per instructions.

Following discussion pertains to MySQL ODBC on Windows OS. You need to open **ODBC Data Sources** app in Administrative Tools section of control panel, add newly installed MySQL driver, if it doesn't have the same already and configure it to identify by a **DSN** (Data Source Name) with the help of MySQL sever's user ID and password, pointing towards 'mydb' database.*(figure 8.1)*

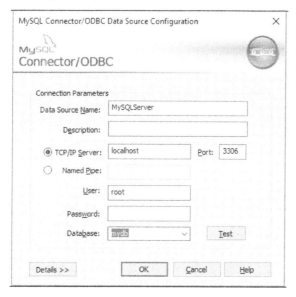

Figure 8.1 ODBC Data Source

This 'MySQLDSN' is now available for use to any application including our Python interpreter. You need to install pyodbc module for that purpose.

Start the Python interpreter and import this module. Its `connect()` function takes the DSN and other login credentials as arguments.

Example 8.25

```
>>> con=pyodbc.connect("DSN=MYSQLDSN;UID=root")
```

Once we obtain the connection object, the rest of the operations are exactly similar to that described with reference to sqlite3 module. You can try creating Customers and Invoices tables in mydb database using their earlier structure and sample data.

In conclusion, we can say that the DB-API specification has made database handling very easy and more importantly uniform. However, data in SQL tables is stored basically in primary data types only which are mapped to corresponding built-in data types of Python. Python's user-defined objects can't be persistently stored and retrieved to/from SQL tables. The next chapter deals with the mapping of Python classes to SQL tables.

CHAPTER 9
Python - SQLAlchemy

The concluding paragraph of previous chapter briefly talked about disparity between type systems of SQL and object oriented programming languages such as Python. Apart from Python's Number (that too int and float only, not complex) and string types (which are generally called scalar types), SQL doesn't have equivalent data type for others such as dict, tuple, list, or any user defined class.

If you have to store such object in a relational database, it must be deconstructed into SQL data types first, before performing INSERT operation. On the other hand, a Python object of desired type will have to be constructed by using data retrieved from a SQL table, before a Python script is able to process it.

Let's take a case of 'Products' table in **SQLite** database used in previous chapter. Its structure is as follows:

Example 9.1

```
CREATE TABLE Products (
ProductID INTEGER   PRIMARY KEY AUTOINCREMENT,
Name        TEXT (20),
Price       INTEGER
);
```

On the other side, Python script has a Products class and its object is populated with data as below:

Example 9.2

```
class Product:
        def __init__(self, id, name, price):
                self.id=id
                self.name=name
                self.price=price
p1=Product(1,'Laptop',25000)
```

Following **sqlite3** module syntax, following statement will insert p1 object in the Products table:

Example 9.3

```
cur.execute("insert into products values
(?,?,?);",(self.id, self.name, self.price))
```

Similarly, following statements will store retrieved data in an object of Products class.

Example 9.4

```
cur.execute('select * from products where name=?',
('Laptop',))
row=cur.fetchone()
p1=Products(row[0], row[1],row[2])
```

As you can see, this involves a tedious and explicit packing and unpacking of Python object in order to be compatible with SQL data types.

This is where **Object Relational Mappers** are useful.

9.1 What is ORM?

An **Object Relation Mapper (ORM)** library provides a seamless interface between a class and a SQL table. A class is mapped to a certain table in database, so that cumbersome to and fro conversion between object and SQL types is automated. The products class in Python code can be mapped to Products table in the database. As a result, all **CRUD** operations are done with the help of object only, not requiring hard coded SQL queries to be used in Python script.

ORMs thus provide an abstraction layer over the raw SQL queries, thus enabling rapid application development. Such ORM libraries are available for most programming languages including Python. **SQLAlchemy** is a popular database toolkit widely used by Python developers. SQLALchemy's ORM system transparently synchronizes all changes in state of an object of user defined class with its related row in the database table.

SQLAlchemy interacts with certain type of database in association with respective DB-API compliant module. Its dialect system is able to establish interaction with a database through latter's DB-API driver. That means, you should have corresponding DB-API module also installed along with SQLAlchemy to be able to use particular type of RDBMS.

As a matter of fact, SQLALchemy library also contains, in addition to ORM API, the SQL **Expression Language (SQLAlchemy Core)** that executes primitive constructs of the relational database directly. While our focus in this chapter is on **SQLALChemy ORM**, we shall also briefly SQL Expression language in the end. *(figure 9.1)*

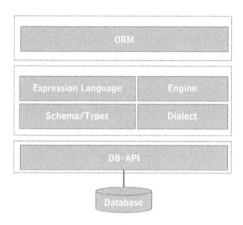

Figure 9.1 SQLAlchemy

In most cases, SQLAlchemy is installed with the help of pip utility. As explained in --, a virtual environment with SQLAlchemy installed will be used for this chapter. We need to activate it and start Python interpreter.

Example 9.5

```
E:\SQLAlchemyEnv>scripts\activate
(SQLAlchemyEnv) E:\SQLAlchemyEnv>python
Python 3.7.2 (tags/v3.7.2:9a3ffc0492, Dec 23 2018,
23:09:28) [MSC v.1916 64 bit (AMD64)] on win32
Type "help", "copyright", "credits" or "license" for
more information.
>>>
```

9.2 SQLAlchemy ORM

First step is to connect to a database by using **create_engine()** function in sqlalchemy module. This function should be provided with URL of the database. Easiest way is to connect to an in-memory SQLite database.

Example 9.6

```
>>> from sqlalchemy import create_engine
>>> engine=create_engine('sqlite:///:memory:')
```

To connect to a SQLite database file use URL similar to following:

```
engine =create_engine('sqlite:///mydb.sqlite')
```

As you know, Python library has in-built support for SQLite in the form of DB-API compatible **sqlite3** module. However, for other databases its respective module needs to be installed. In order to connect to a different database (other than SQLite), its corresponding connection string includes the dialect and module. The general format of use of **create_engine()** function is as follows:

```
dialect+driver://username:password@host:port/
database
```

Hence, to connect to a MySQL database using **pymysql** module, we need to use following statement:

```
engine = create_engine('mysql+pymydsql://root@
localhost/mydb')
```

This assumes that MySQL server's username is '*root*' with no password set. The **create_engine()** function returns Engine object. It represents the interface to the database. The ORM doesn't use the Engine directly once created but is used behind the scenes. This function can accept optional 'echo' argument which is False by default. If set to True, it causes the generated SQL to be displayed by Python interpreter.

```
>>> engine=create_
engine('sqlite:///:memory:',echo=True)
```

9.3 ORM - Table Object and Mapped Class

Next step is to describe the database tables and define the mapping classes. An object of a metaclass, called **Declarative Base class** that stores a catalog of user defined classes and mapped tables is first obtained. This Declarative Base class is defined in sqlalchemy.ext.declarative sub-module.

```
>>> from sqlalchemy.ext.declarative import
declarative_base
>>> base=declarative_base()
```

Use this 'base' class to define mapped classes in terms of it. We define Products class and map it to Products table in the database. Its **__tablename__** property defines this mapping. Other attributes are column names in the table.

Example 9.7

```
#myclasses.py
from sqlalchemy.ext.declarative import declarative_
base
from sqlalchemy import Column, Integer, String
base=declarative_base()
class Product(Base):
    __tablename__ = 'Products'

    ProductID = Column(Integer, primary_key=True)
    name = Column(String)
    price = Column(Integer)
```

Column is a SQLAlchemy schema object that represents column in the database table. Its constructor defines name, data type, and constraint parameters. The Column data type can be any of the following generic data types that specify the type in which Python data can be read, written, and stored. SQLAlchemy will choose the best database column type available on the target database when issuing a CREATE TABLE statement.

- BigInteger
- Boolean
- Date
- DateTime
- Float
- Integer
- Numeric
- SmallInteger
- String

- Text
- Time

Even though this class defines mapping, it's a normal Python class, in which there may be other ordinary attributes and methods as may be required by application.

The `Table` object is created as per the specifications in the class, and is associated with the class by constructing a Mapper object which remains behind-the-scene and we normally don't need to deal with directly.

The **Table** object created in Declaraive system is a member of MetaData attribute of declarative base class. The **create_all()** method is called on **metadata**, passing in our Engine as a source of database connectivity. It will emit **CREATE TABLE** statements to the database for all tables that don't yet exist.

```
base.metadata.create_all(engine)
```

Complete process explained above is stored as a script (*addproducts.py*) in the root folder of our virtual environment.

Example 9.8

```
from sqlalchemy import Column, Integer, String
from sqlalchemy.ext.declarative import declarative_
base
from sqlalchemy import create_engine
from myclasses import Product, base
engine = create_engine('sqlite:///mydb.sqlite',
echo=True)
base.metadata.create_all(engine)
```

We run this script from command prompt (from within our virtual environment of course). The command window will show, apart from other logging information, the equivalent CREATE TABLE statement emitted by SQLALchemy. *(figure 9.1)*

```
(SQLAlchemyEnv) E:\SQLAlchemyEnv>python class-table-
mapping.py
PRAGMA table_info("Products")
()
CREATE TABLE "Products" (
        "ProductID" INTEGER NOT NULL,
        name VARCHAR,
        price INTEGER,
        PRIMARY KEY ("ProductID")
)

()
COMMIT
```

Figure 9.1 CREATE TABLE statement emitted by SQLALchemy

(Some logging data not displayed)

9.4 ORM - Session object

Now that we have created Products table in the database, next step is to start transaction session. Session object is a handle used to interact with the database. We define a Session class which will serve as a factory for new Session objects with the help of **sessionmaker()** function.

```
from sqlalchemy.orm import sessionmaker
Session = sessionmaker(bind=engine)
```

Here engine is the Engine object that represents connection with our database. Whenever you need to have a conversation with the database, you instantiate a Session:

```
sessionobj = Session()
```

The session remains in force till changes to the database are committed and/or the **close()** method is called on session object.

9.5 ORM - Add Data

To add data in 'Products' table, first initialize an object of its mapped Products class, add it to the session and commit the changes.

Example 9.9

```
p1 = Products(name='Laptop', price=25000)
sessionobj.add(p1)
sessionobj.commit()
```

Add above code snippets to **addproducts.py**. It now looks like this:

```
from sqlalchemy import Column, Integer, String
from sqlalchemy import create_engine
from myclasses import Products,base
engine = create_engine('sqlite:///mydb.sqlite',
echo=True)
base.metadata.create_all(engine)
from sqlalchemy.orm import sessionmaker
Session = sessionmaker(bind=engine)
sessionobj = Session()
p1 = Product(name='Laptop', price=25000)
sessionobj.add(p1)
sessionobj.commit()
```

Run above script from command prompt. SQLAlchemy will emit equivalent parameterized INSERT query that will be echoed on the terminal as shown below in figure 9.2:

```
(SQLAlchemyEnv) E:\SQLAlchemyEnv>addproducts.py
PRAGMA table_info("Products")
()
BEGIN (implicit)
INSERT INTO "Products" (name, price) VALUES (?, ?)
('Laptop', 25000)
COMMIT
```

Figure 9.2 addproducts.py

If you want to confirm, open the database in SQLite console and view rows in Products table. *(figure 9.3)*

```
sqlite> .head on
sqlite> .mode column
sqlite> .open mydb.sqlite
sqlite> select * from products;
ProductID    name         price
---------    ---------    ---------
1            Laptop       25000
```

Figure 9.3: SQLite console

To add multiple records at once, call **add_all()** method on session object. It requires list of objects to be added.

Example 9.10

```
p2=Products(name='TV',price=40000)
p3=Products(name='Router',price=2000)
p4=Products(name='Scanner',price=5000)
p5=Products(name='Printer',price=9000)
p6=Products(name='Mobile',price=15000)
sessionobj.add_all([p2,p3,p4,p5,p6])
sessionobj.commit()
```

Go ahead and add 'Customers' class mapped to 'Customers' table. Add data as per sample data given. (We shall add 'Invoices' class and 'Invoices' table a little later)

Example 9.11

```
class Customer(base):
    __tablename__='Customers'
    CustID=Column(Integer, primary_key=True)
    name=Column(String)
    GSTIN=Column(String)
```

We have to add this table in the database schema by executing following statement again:

```
base.metadata.create_all(engine)
```

9.6 ORM - Querying

In order to fetch data from a database table, we need to obtain query object. The **query()** method is defined in the Session class. It needs the mapped class as argument.

```
q=sessionobj.query(Product)
```

The query object itself has access to various methods to fetch rows from the underlying table and return objects of mapped class.

The **query.get()** method accepts the primary key as argument and returns the corresponding object. For example, following statement returns object with ProductID=2 (ProductID being primary key of Products table)

```
p=q.get(2)
```

Because 'echo' parameter is set to True in Engine constructor, the console shows corresponding SQL statement generated by SQLAlchemy as below:

Example 9.12

```
BEGIN (implicit)
SELECT "Products"."ProductID" AS "Products_
ProductID", "Products".name AS "Products_name",
"Products".price AS "Products_price"
FROM "Products"
WHERE "Products"."ProductID" = ?
sqlalchemy.engine.base.Engine (2,)
```

Attributes of the object (p.name and p.price) can now be displayed. Still better, provide a **__str__()** method in Products class. Modify it in myclasses.py script as under:

Example 9.13

```
class Product(base):
    __tablename__ = 'Products'

    ProductID = Column(Integer, primary_key=True)
    name = Column(String)
    price = Column(Integer)
    def __str__(self):
        return 'name:{} price: {}'.format(self.name,
self.price)
```

The **query.all()** method returns a list of all objects which can be traversed using a loop. Here is a fetchllrecs.py script:

Example 9.14

```
#fetchallrecs.py
from sqlalchemy import Column, Integer, String
from sqlalchemy import create_engine
from myclasses import Product,base, Customers
engine = create_engine('sqlite:///mydb.sqlite',
echo=True)
base.metadata.create_all(engine)
from sqlalchemy.orm import sessionmaker
Session = sessionmaker(bind=engine)
sessionobj = Session()
q=sessionobj.query(Products)
rows=q.all()
for row in rows:
        print (row)
```

Shown below is the output of this script along with shortened log in the console window *(figure 9.4)*:

```
(SQLAlchemyEnv) E:\SQLAlchemyEnv>python
fetchallrecs.py
PRAGMA table_info("Products")
()
BEGIN (implicit)
SELECT "Products"."ProductID" AS "Products_
ProductID", "Products".name AS "Products_name",
"Products".price AS "Products_price"
FROM "Products"
()
name:Laptop price: 25000
name:TV price: 40000
name:Router price: 2000
name:Scanner price: 5000
name:Printer price: 9000
name:Mobile price: 15000
```

Figure 9.4 Output of script of example 9.14

9.7 ORM - Filter Criteria

The query object has **filter ()** method that implements **WHERE** clause as used in raw SQL SELECT statement. Argument to filter can be any Boolean expression. In following snippet, filter is 'price>20000'.

```
rows=q.filter(Product.price>20000)
```

This will translate into corresponding SQL statements as under:

Example 9.15

```
SELECT "Products"."ProductID" AS "Products_
ProductID", "Products".name AS "Products_name",
"Products".price AS "Products_price"
FROM "Products"
WHERE "Products".price > ?
(20000,)
```

SQLAlchemy supports the use of wild cards for filter operations on string columns. The LIKE keyword in SQL is implemented by applying **like ()** filter. **Products.name.like('%er')** filters rows with product name ending with '*er*'

```
rows=q.filter(Product.name.like('%er'))
```

In effect above statement is equivalent to following SQL query:

Example 9.16

```
SELECT "Products"."ProductID" AS "Products_
ProductID", "Products".name AS "Products_name",
"Products".price AS "Products_price"
FROM "Products"
WHERE "Products".name LIKE ?
('%er',)
```

As you will expect, following output will be displayed:

```
name:Router price: 2000
name:Scanner price: 5000
name:Printer price: 9000
```

The **fileter ()** can have AND/OR conjunctions implemented by **and_ ()** and or_ () .

Following filter returns products with price between 10000 and 30000

```
from sqlalchemy import and_
rows=q.filter(and_(Product.price>10000, Product.
price<30000))
```

Here is the generated SQL:

Example 9.17

```
SELECT "Products"."ProductID" AS "Products_
ProductID", "Products".name AS "Products_name",
"Products".price AS "Products_price"
FROM "Products"
WHERE "Products".price > ? AND "Products".price < ?
(10000, 30000)
```

The OR operation is performed by following statement

Example 9.18

```
from sqlalchemy import or_
rows=q.filter(or_(Product.price>20000, Product.name.
like('%er')))
```

which is equivalent to following SQL statement:

Example 9.19

```
SELECT "Products"."ProductID" AS "Products_
ProductID", "Products".name AS "Products_name",
"Products".price AS "Products_price"
FROM "Products", "Customers"
WHERE "Products".price <= ? OR "Customers".name LIKE
?
(5000, '%er')
```

9.8 ORM - Update Data

Modifying attributes of an object is very easy in SQLAlchemy. First, you have to fetch a desired object, either by the primary key (using **get()** method) or by applying proper filter. All you have to do is assign new value to its attribute and **commit** the change.

Following code will fetch an object from 'Products' table whose ProductID=2 (Product name is TV and price is 40000 as per sample data)

Example 9.20

```
p=q.get(2)
SELECT "Products"."ProductID" AS "Products_
ProductID", "Products".name AS "Products_name",
"Products".price AS "Products_price"
FROM "Products"
WHERE "Products"."ProductID" = ?
2,)
```

Change the price to 45000 and commit the session.

```
p.price=45000
sessionobj.commit()
```

SQLAlchemy internally executes following UPDATE statement:

```
UPDATE "Products" SET price=? WHERE
"Products"."ProductID" = ?
(45000, 2)
COMMIT
```

9.9 ORM - Relationships

In case of raw SQL, we establish relationship among tables using the **FOREIGN KEY** constraint. This section describes how relationships are built between tables and mapped classes.

In previous chapter, our **mydb.sqlite** database contained Invoices table that had relationship with 'Products' and 'Customers' table. These relationships were established with foreign keys. We shall now declare Invoice class (that maps Invoices table) and relate it to Product class and Customer class with the help of **ForeignKey()** function imposed on **ProductID** and **CustID** columns in it. This is very similar to definition of table in raw SQL.

Example 9.21

```
from sqlalchemy import ForeignKey
class Invoice(base):
    __tablename__='Invoices'
    InvID=Column(Integer, primary_key=True)
    CustID=Column(Integer, ForeignKey('Customers.
CustID'))
    ProductID=Column(Integer, ForeignKey('Products.
ProductID'))
    quantity=Column(Integer)
```

However, this will not establish relationship amongst classes. SQLAlchemy's ORM provides **relationship()** function for this purpose. In the Invoice class, 'prod' is a **relationship** property that sets up link with the Product class, and 'cst' attribute is a relationship that establishes relation between Invoice and Customer class.

```
    prod=relationship("Customer", back_
populates="Invoices")
    cst=relationship("Product", back_
populates="Invoices")
```

The 'back_populates' parameter indicates that *'prod'* and *'cst'* properties have to be placed on the related mapped classes (Product and Customer respectively) that will handle this relationship in the other direction. The backward relationship is established by following directives:

Example 9.22

```
Product.Invoices=relationship('Invoice', order_
by=Invoice.InvID, back_populates='cst')
Customer.Invoices=relationship('Invoice', order_
by=Invoice.InvID, back_populates='prod')
```

Complete code of Invoice class is given below. Add it to myclasses. py script and recreate the metadata schema by executing **create_ all(engine)** function.

Example 9.23

```
from sqlalchemy import ForeignKey
from sqlalchemy.orm import relationship
class Invoice(base):
    __tablename__='Invoices'
    InvID=Column(Integer, primary_key=True)
    CustID=Column(Integer, ForeignKey('Customers.
CustID'))
    ProductID=Column(Integer, ForeignKey('Products.
ProductID'))
    prod=relationship("Customer", back_
populates="Invoices")
    cst=relationship("Product", back_
populates="Invoices")
    quantity=Column(Integer)
Product.Invoices=relationship('Invoice', order_
by=Invoice.InvID, back_populates='cst')
Customer.Invoices=relationship('Invoice', order_
by=Invoice.InvID, back_populates='prod')
```

Structure of newly created Invoices table will be echoed on the command terminal:

Example 9.24

```
PRAGMA table_info("Invoices")
()
CREATE TABLE "Invoices" (
        "InvID" INTEGER NOT NULL,
        "CustID" INTEGER,
        "ProductID" INTEGER,
        quantity INTEGER,
        PRIMARY KEY ("InvID"),
        FOREIGN KEY("CustID") REFERENCES "Customers"
("CustID"),
        FOREIGN KEY("ProductID") REFERENCES
"Products" ("ProductID")
)
()
COMMIT
```

Using **Session** object, we can now add data in this table as follows:

Example 9.25

```
from sqlalchemy.orm import sessionmaker
Session = sessionmaker(bind=engine)
sessionobj = Session()
i1=Invoice(InvID=1, CustID=1, ProductID=1,
quantity=2)
sessionobj.add(i1)
sessionobj.commit()
```

Likewise, you can add rest of records as given in sample data in previous chapter.

9.10 Querying related tables (ORM)

The query object we used earlier in this chapter can act on more than one mapped classes. By equating relating columns in two tables using **filter()** function we can simulate implicit join effected by **WHERE** clause in SQL syntax.

The snippet give blow, we display name of product and its price of ProductID in Invoices table. The **filter()** establishes join on the basis of equal values of ProductID in Invoices and Products tables.

Example 9.26

```
from sqlalchemy import Column, Integer, String
from sqlalchemy import create_engine, and_, or_
from myclasses import Product,base, Customer,
Invoice
engine = create_engine('sqlite:///mydb.sqlite',
echo=True)
base.metadata.create_all(engine)
from sqlalchemy.orm import sessionmaker
Session = sessionmaker(bind=engine)
sessionobj = Session()
q=sessionobj.query(Invoice,Product)
for i,p in q.filter(Product.ProductID==Invoice.
ProductID).all():
        print (i.InvID, p.name, p.price, i.quantity)
```

The equivalent SQL expression emitted by SQLAlchemy will be echoed as follows:

Example 9.27

```
SELECT "Invoices"."InvID" AS "Invoices_InvID",
"Invoices"."CustID" AS "Invoices_CustID",
"Invoices"."ProductID" AS "Invoices_ProductID",
"Invoices".quantity AS "Invoices_quantity",
"Products"."ProductID" AS "Products_ProductID",
"Products".name AS "Products_name", "Products".price
AS "Products_price"
FROM "Invoices", "Products"
WHERE "Products"."ProductID" =
"Invoices"."ProductID"
```

Output of above script:

```
1  Laptop 25000 2
2  TV 40000 1
3  Mobile 15000 3
4  Laptop 25000 6
5  Printer 9000 3
6  TV 40000 5
7  Laptop 25000 4
8  Router 2000 10
9  Printer 9000 2
10 Scanner 5000 3
```

To join 'Invoices' table with 'Customers' table and display name of corresponding Customer as well, add another condition in filter – equating their CustID columns). Change the looping statement as follows:

Example 9.28

```
print ("InvID,Customer,Product,Price,Quantity")
for i,p,c in q.filter \
    (and_(Product.ProductID==Invoice.ProductID, \
        Customer.CustID==Invoice.CustID)).all():
    print ('{},{},{},{}'.format(i.InvID,
c.name,p.name, p.price, i.quantity))
```

Set the `echo` parameter to False and run the script to obtain following result:

```
InvID,Customer,Product,Price,Quantity
1,Ravikumar,Laptop,25000
2,John,TV,40000
3,Divya,Mobile,15000
4,Nair,Laptop,25000
5,John,Printer,9000
6,Patel,TV,40000
7,Patel,Laptop,25000
8,Shah,Router,2000
9,Irfan,Printer,9000
10,Nitin,Scanner,5000
```

As mentioned in the beginning of this chapter, SQLAlchemy defines schema specific SQL Expression Language which is at the core of domain-centric ORM model. Functionality of Expression Language is closer to raw SQL than ORM which offers a layer of abstraction over it. In following section a brief overview of SQLAlchemy's Expression Language is covered.

9.11 SQLAlchemy Core

We have to use the same process (as used in ORM) to connect to the database i.e. using **create-engine()** function that returns Engine object.

```
from sqlalchemy import create_engine
engine = create_engine('sqlite:///mydb.sqlite',
echo=True)
```

If you plan to use any other database dialect, ensure that you install its respective DB-API module.

```
engine = create_engine('mysql+pymydsql://root@
localhost/mydb')
```

In order to create tables in this database, first we have to set up a MetaData object which stores table information and other schema related information.

```
from sqlalchemy import MetaData
meta=MetaData()
```

The Table class in sqlalchemy module needs this metadata object as one of the arguments to its constructor.

```
TableName=Table("name", meta, Column1, Column2, ...)
```

As we have used before, Column object represents a column in the database table and needs its name, data type, and constraints (if any) to be specified.

Example 9.29

```
from sqlalchemy import create_engine, MetaData,
Table, Column, Integer, String
engine = create_engine('sqlite:///mydb.sqlite',
echo=True)
meta=MetaData()
Products = Table('Products', meta,
Column('ProductID', Integer, primary_key=True),
Column('name', String), Column('Price', Integer), )
meta.create_all(engine)
```

The **create_all()** function emits equivalent SQL query as follow:

Example 9.30

```
CREATE TABLE "Products" (
        "ProductID" INTEGER NOT NULL,
        name VARCHAR,
        "Price" INTEGER,
        PRIMARY KEY ("ProductID")
)
```

9.12 Core - Inserting Records

Next is how to insert a record in this table? For this purpose, use **insert()** construct on the table. It will produce a template **INSERT** query.

Example 9.31

```
>>> ins=Products.insert()
>>> str(ins)
'INSERT INTO "Products" ("ProductID", name, "Price")
VALUES (:ProductID, :name, :Price)'
```

We need to put values in the place holder parameters and submit the **ins** object to our database engine for execution.

Example 9.32

```
ins.values(name="Laptop",Price=25000)
con=engine.connect()
con.execute(ins)
```

Selecting data from table is also straightforward. There is a **select()** function that constructs a new Select object.

Example 9.33

```
>>> s=Products.select()
>>> str(s)
'SELECT "Products"."ProductID", "Products".name,
"Products"."Price" \nFROM "Products"'
```

Provide this Select object to **execute()** function. It now returns a result set from which one (**fetchone**) or all records (**fetchall**) can be fetched.

Example 9.34

```
>>> result=con.execute(s)
>>> for row in result:
... print (row)
```

9.13 Core - Updating Records

SQLalchemy's core API defines **update()** function which lets value of one or more columns in one or more rows be modified.

```
table.update().where(condition).values(Col=newval)
```

For example, to update price of TV to 45000, use

```
qry=Products.update().where(Products.c.name=="TV").
values(name=45000)
con.execute(qry)
```

Similarly, to delete a certain record from table, use the following statement:

```
qry=Products.delete().where(Products.c.name='TV')
con.execute(qry)
```

At the outset, there appears to be some overlap among the usage patterns of the **ORM** and the Expression Language. However, the similarity is rather superficial. ORM approach is from the perspective of a user-defined domain model. SQL Expression Language looks at it from perspective of literal schema and SQL expression representations.

While an application may use either approach exclusively, sometimes, in advanced scenarios, it may have to make occasional usage of the Expression Language directly in otherwise ORM oriented application where specific database interactions are required.

SQLAlchemy library is extensively used in Python based web frameworks such as **Flask** and **bottle**. There are **Flask-SQLAlchemy** and **Bottle_SQLAlchemy** extensions specifically written for them. Other popular ORM libraries are **SQLObject** and **Django ORM**.

CHAPTER 10

Python and Excel

Interactive spreadsheet applications have been in use for quite long. Over the years, Microsoft Excel has emerged as the market leader in this software category. Early versions of MS Excel used a proprietary data representation format. After 2003, Microsoft has adopted **Office Open XML (OOXML)** file format for its later versions of MS Excel.

OOXML is an **ECMA** standard file format. This has led to the development of programming interfaces for Excel in many programming environments including Python. Out of many Python packages, **openpyxl** is the most popular and can read/write Excel files with **.xlsx** extension. **Pandas** is a very popular Python library. It has various tools for performing analysis of data stored in different file formats. Data from Excel sheet, CSV file, or SQL table can be imported in Pandas dataframe object for processing.

In this chapter, first we shall learn to use **openpyxl** to programmatically perform various operations on an Excel files uch as copy a range, define, and copy formula, insert image, create chart, and so on.

In second part of this chapter, we get acquainted to **Pandas** library – specifically how to read/write data from/to an Excel worksheet.

Before proceeding further, here is a brief recap of important terms used in Excel spreadsheet. An Excel document is called as **workbook** and is saved as **.xlsx** file. A workbook may have multiple worksheets. Each worksheet is a grid of large number of cells, each of which can store one piece of data - either value or formula. Each Cell in grid is identified by its row and column number. Columns are identified by alphabets, A, B, C, ..., Z, AA, AB, and so on. Rows are numbered starting from 1. *(figure 10.1)*

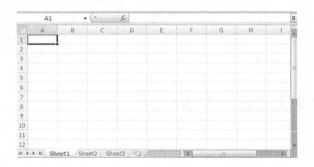

Figure 10.1 Excel sheet

10.1. Excel with `openpyxml`

The `openpyxl` is an open source package. Its installation is straightforward by using `pip` utility. It is recommended that you set a virtual environment first and then install `openpyxl` in it using following command:

Example 10.1

```
E:\>cd excelenv
E:\excelenv>scripts\activate
(excelenv) E:\excelenv>scripts\pip3 install openpyxl
Collecting openpyxl
  Using cached https://files.pythonhosted.org/packag-
es/5f/f8/a5d3a4ab669f99154f87ab531192dd84ac79aae62e-
fab662bd2d82a72194/openpyxl-2.6.1.tar.gz
Collecting jdcal (from openpyxl)
  Using cached https://files.pythonhosted.org/packag-
es/a0/38/dcf83532480f25284f3ef13f8ed63e03c58a65c9d-
3ba2a6a894ed9497207/jdcal-1.4-py2.py3-none-any.whl
Collecting et_xmlfile (from openpyxl)
  Using cached https://files.pythonhosted.org/
packages/22/28/a99c42aea746e18382ad9fb36f64c-
1c1f04216f41797f2f0fa567da11388/et_xmlfile-1.0.1.tar.
gz
Installing collected packages: jdcal, et-xmlfile,
openpyxl
  Running setup.py install for et-xmlfile ... done
  Running setup.py install for openpyxl ... done
Successfully installed et-xmlfile-1.0.1 jdcal-1.4
openpyxl-2.6.1
```

10.2 Creating a workbook

An object of Workbook class represents an empty workbook with one worksheet. Set it to be active so that data can be added to it.

Example 10.2

```
>>> from openpyxl import Workbook
>>> wb=Workbook()
>>> sheet1=wb.active
>>> sheet1.title='PriceList'
```

Each cell in the worksheet is identified by a string made of Column name and row number. Top left cell is 'A1'. Normal assignment operator is used to store data in a cell.

```
>>> sheet1['A1']='Hello World'
```

(NB: These operations as well as others that will be described in this chapter will not be immediately visualized in Python environment itself. The workbook so created needs to be saved and then opened using Excel application to see the effect)

There is another way to assign value to a cell. The **cell()** method accepts row and column parameters with integer values. Column names A, B, C, and so on; will be denoted by 1,2,3, and so on. Rows are also numbered from 1.

```
>>> sheet1.cell(row=1, column=1).value='Hello World'
```

Contents of cell are retrieved from its **value** attribute.

```
>>> sheet1['a1'].value
'Hello World'
```

Use **save()** method to store the workbook object as Excel document. Later, open it to verify above process. *(figure 10.2)*

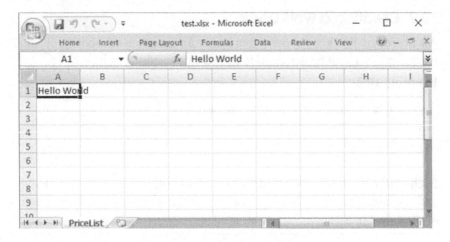

Figure 10.2 test.xlsx

10.3 Read Data from Worksheet

To read data from an existing Excel document, we need to load it with **load_workbook()** function.

```
>>> from openpyxl import load_workbook
>>> wb=load_workbook(filename='test.xlsx')
```

Set the desired worksheet as active and retrieve value of any cell.

Example 10.3

```
>>> sheet1.cell(row=1, column=1).value
'Hello World'
>>> #or
>>> sheet1['A1'].value
'Hello World'
```

Following script writes data in a list object, each item being a tuple comprising of ProductID, name, and price.

Example 10.4

```
#saveworkbook.py
from openpyxl import Workbook
wb = Workbook()
sheet1 = wb.active
sheet1.title='PriceList'
sheet1.cell(column=1, row=1, value='Pricelist')
pricelist=[('ProductID', 'Name', 'Price'),
          (1,'Laptop',25000),(2, 'TV',40000),
          (3,'Router',2000),(4,'Scanner',5000),
          (5,'Printer',9000), (6,'Mobile',15000)]
for col in range(1,4):
        for row in range(1,7):
                sheet1.cell(column=col, row=1+row,
value=pricelist[row-1][col-1])
wb.save(filename = "test.xlsx")
```

The Excel document in the current directory looks like: *(figure 10.3)*

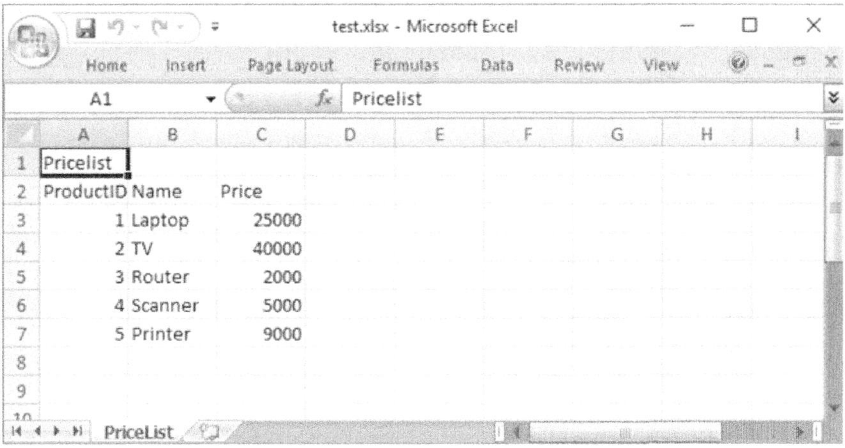

Figure 10.3 Excel document in the current directory

Let us find out how to perform certain formatting actions on worksheet data.

10.4. Read Cell Range to List

First of all let us read back the data from **A2:C7** in a Python list object by traversing the range with two nested loops. Each row is collected in a tuple and appended to a list.

Example 10.5

```
sheet1 = wb['PriceList']
pricelist=[]
for row in range(1,7):
        prod=[]
        for col in range(1,4):
                val=sheet1.cell(column=col,
row=2+row).value
                prod.append(val)
        pricelist.append(tuple(prod))
print (pricelist)
```

The result will be as shown below:

```
[(1, 'Laptop', 25000), (2, 'TV', 40000), (3,
'Router', 2000), (4, 'Scanner', 5000), (5,
'Printer', 9000)]
```

10.5 Merge and Center

To merge A1-C1 cells use **merge_cells()** method.

```
sheet1.merge_cells('A1:C1')
```

The **openpyxl.styles** module defines Alignment and Font classes. Apply '*Center*' alignment to text in '*A1*'

```
cell=sheet1['A1']
cell.alignment=Alignment(horizontal='center')
```

The Font object can be configured by defining attributes like name, size, color, and so on. Font constructor also accepts bold, italic, underline, and strike as Boolean attributes (True/False).

```
cell.font=Font(name='Calibri',size=20,bold=True)
```

10.6 Define Formula

It is very easy to define a formula in a cell. Just assign string representation of cell formula as would appear in the formula bar of Excel. For example, if you want to set cell 8 to sum of cells between C3 to 7, assign it to '=SUM(C3:C7)'

Example 10.6

```
sheet1['B8']='SUM'
sheet1['C8']='=SUM(C3:C7)'
sheet1['C9']='=AVERAGE(C3:C7)'
```

All above actions are collected in following script. Run it from command prompt and then open the workbook. *(figure 10.4)*

Example 10.7

```
#readworkbook.py
from openpyxl import load_workbook
wb = load_workbook('test.xlsx')
sheet1 = wb['PriceList']
#copy range to list
pricelist=[]
for row in range(1,7):
        prod=[]
        for col in range(1,4):
                val=sheet1.cell(column=col,
row=2+row).value
                prod.append(val)
        pricelist.append(tuple(prod))
print (pricelist)
#merge and center
sheet1.merge_cells('A1:C1')#merge
cell=sheet1['A1']
cell.alignment=Alignment(horizontal='center')
#apply font
cell.font=Font(name='Calibri',size=20,bold=True)
#define formula
sheet1['b8']='SUM'
sheet1['C8']='=SUM(C3:C7)'
sheet1['C9']='=AVERAGE(C3:C7)'
```

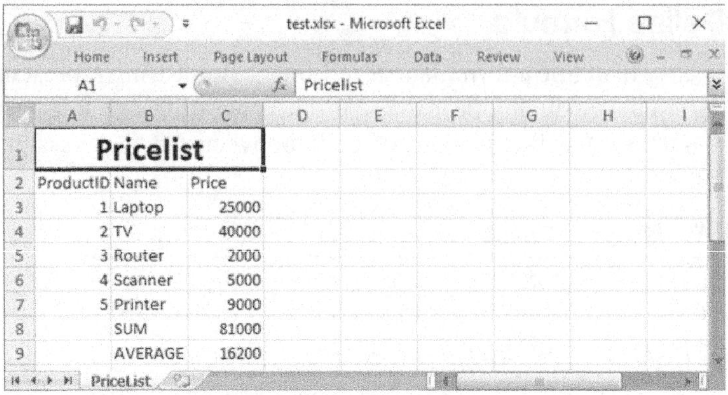

Figure 10.4 Output of Example 10.7

10.7. Copy Formula

One of the important features of Excel software is ability of copying a cell formula either with relative or absolute address to other cell or range. In the above worksheet, we calculate difference of each price and average and store it in Column D. Accordingly formula for D4 should be C4-C9. It is to be copied for range D5:D9

The **openpyxml.formula** module defines Translator class having **translate_formula()** function that copies formula at original cell (D4) to the required range.

Example 10.8

```
from openpyxl.formula.translate import
Translator#copy formula
sheet1['D2']='DIFF'
sheet1['D3']='=C$9-C3'
sheet1['D4'] = Translator("=C$9-C3", origin="D3").
translate_formula("D4")
for row in range(4,8):
        coor=sheet1.cell(column=4, row=row).
coordinate#copy formula to range
        sheet1.cell(column=4, row=row).
value=Translator("=C$9-C3", origin="D3"). \

translate_formula(coor)
```

Using the **translate_formula**, we can also copy a range of cells to other location. Following snippet copies range **A2:D2** which is the table's heading row to **A10:D10** cell range.

Example 10.9

```
sheet1['A10'] = '=A2'
for col in range(1,4):
        coor=sheet1.cell(column=col,row=3).coordinate
      coor1=sheet1.cell(column=col, row=10).coordinate
        print (coor,coor1)
        sheet1.cell(column=col, row=10).
value=Translator("=A2", origin="A10"). \

translate_formula(coor1)
```

After copying the formula and range, the worksheet appears as follows: (*figure 10.5*)

	A	B	C	D	E	F	G	H	I
1	**Pricelist**								
2	ProductID	Name	Price	DIFF					
3	1	Laptop	25000	-8800					
4	2	TV	40000	-23800					
5	3	Router	2000	14200					
6	4	Scanner	5000	11200					
7	5	Printer	9000	7200					
8		SUM	81000						
9		AVERAGE	16200						
10	ProductID	Name	Price						
11									

A10   *fx* =A2

Figure 10.5 Worksheet of example 10.9

10.8 Charts

One of the most attractive features of MS Excel application is to dynamically generate various types of charts based upon data in worksheet. The **openpyxl** package has a chart module that offers the required functionality. In this section we shall see how we can render charts programmatically.

Sample data for this demonstration is stored in *'example.xlsx'* as below: *(figure 10.6)*

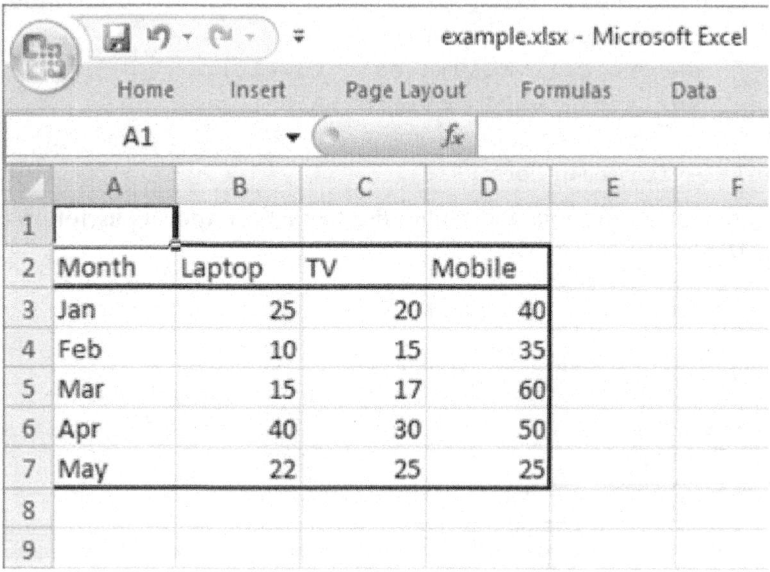

Figure 10.6 Sample data for demonstration

The chart module defines classes for all types of charts such as **BarChart** and **LineChart**. Chart requires data range and category range to be defined. These ranges are defines with **Reference()** function. It stipulates row and column numbers of top-left and bottom-right cells of desired range.

In above worksheet, B2:D7 is the data range including the column labels and A1:A7 range is the categories range.

Example 10.10

```
from openpyxl import load_workbook
wb = load_workbook('example.xlsx')
ws = wb.active
from openpyxl.chart import BarChart, Reference
values = Reference(ws, min_col=2, min_row=2, max_
col=4, max_row=7)
ctg=Reference(ws, min_col=1,min_row=3, max_col=1,
max_row=7)
```

The chart object is configured by **add_data()** and **set_ categories()** methods. The **add_data()** method takes the data range as first parameter. If **titles_from_data** parameter is set to True, first row in the data range is used for series legend title. The title of chart, X axis and Y axis is also set by respective properties.

Example 10.11

```
c1 = BarChart()
c1.add_data(values, titles_from_data=True
c1.title = "Bar Chart"
c1.x_axis.title = 'Months'
c1.y_axis.title = 'Sales'
ws.add_chart(c1, "A10")
c1.set_categories(ctg)
wb.save(filename='example.xlsx')
```

Run above script and then open the workbook document. It will now have the bar chart stored in it. *(figure 10.7)*

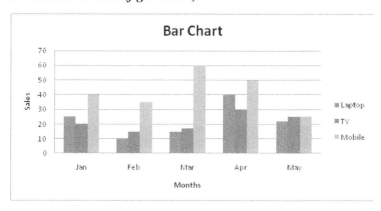

Figure 10.7 Bar chart

Another example of Line chart is explained below. The chart configuration has only one change. The chart object itself is of **LineChart()** type.

Example 10.12

```
from openpyxl.chart import LineChart
c2 = LineChart()
c2.add_data(values, titles_from_data=True)#legends
c2.title = "Line Chart"
c2.x_axis.title = 'Months'
c2.y_axis.title = 'Sales'
ws.add_chart(c2, "F2")
c2.set_categories(ctg)
```

Line chart is stored in the **'example.xlsx'**. Open it to view. *(figure 10.8)*

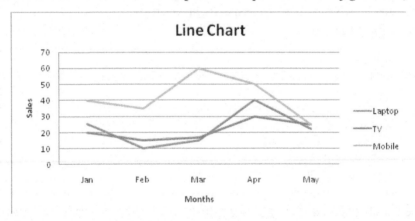

Figure 10.8 Line chart

10.9 Insert Image

First, install **pillow** library in your current Python environment. It is an open source Python image library that provides support for opening, saving and manipulating image files.

```
pip3 install pillow
```

Let us create a new worksheet in *'example.xlsx'* in which we shall insert an image.

```
wb = load_workbook('example.xlsx')
sheet2=wb.create_sheet(title="image")
```

Now import Image class from **openpyxl.drawing.image** module. Obtain the Image object from the image file to be inserted. Finally call **add_image()** method of the worksheet. This method needs image object and location. *(figure 10.9)*

Example 10.13

```
from openpyxl.drawing.image import Image
img = Image('openpyxl.jpg')
sheet2.add_image(img, 'A1')
wb.save(filename='example.xlsx')
```

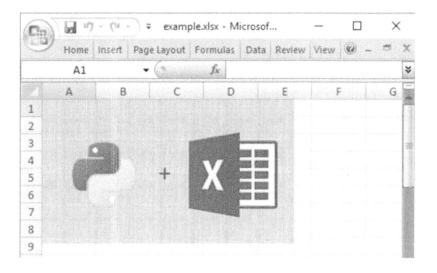

Figure 10.9 example.xlsx

10.10 Excel with Pandas

Pandas library is extremely popular with data scientists as it provides easy-to-use tools for data manipulation and analysis. Different types of data structures are available in Pandas. Of which, dataframe is most commonly used. **Dataframe** in **Pandas** represents a two dimensional tabular data structure with labelled columns which may be of different data types.

Before we explore **DataFrame** object and its relationship with Excel, we have to ensure that Pandas package is installed in current Python environment. If you are using Anaconda distribution, **Pandas** is already installed in it. Otherwise you may have to get it using pip utility in the virtual environment we have created for this chapter.

```
E:\excelenv>scripts\activate
(excelenv) E:\excelenv>scripts\pip3 install pandas
```

During installation, few more libraries like **NumPy** and others are also installed as they are internally used by **Pandas**.

As mentioned earlier, DataFrame object of Pandas is a two-dimensional table-like structure, with labelled columns which may be of different data types (This is similar to **SQL** table isn't it?). It can be constructed using various data objects as inputs such as Python list or dictionary. Of particular relevance to us in this chapter is creating a **DataFrame** object using a list of **dictionary** items.

Let us first define a list, each item in which is a dictionary object. It has three k-v pairs as shown below:

Example 10.14:

```
>>> pricelist=[{'ProductID':1, 'Name':'Laptop',
'price':25000},
          {'ProductID':2, 'Name':'TV',
'price':40000},
          {'ProductID':3, 'Name':'Router',
'price':2000},
          {'ProductID':4, 'Name':'Scanner',
'price':5000},
          {'ProductID':5, 'Name':'Printer',
'price':9000}]
```

Use this list object as argument to constructor of **DataFrame** object.

Example 10.15

```
>>> import pandas as pd
>>> df=pd.DataFrame(pricelist)
>>> df
        Name  ProductID  price
0    Laptop          1  25000
1        TV          2  40000
2    Router          3   2000
3   Scanner          4   5000
4   Printer          5   9000
```

Note the left-most column of index of each row. The index numbers by default start with 0. The Pandas library presents number of functions for manipulation of dataframe (such as indexing, slicing, grouping, iteration, statistical functions – sum, average, and so on.)

10.11 Pandas DataFrame to Excel

What we are interested in is to save this dataframe as an Excel worksheet. The DataFrame object itself has **to_excel()** method needing name of Excel document to be created and worksheet title.

```
>>> df.to_excel("dataframe.xlsx", sheet_
name='sheet1')
```

An Excel document of given name will be readily created in current working directory for you to verify. *(figure 10.10)*

Figure 10.10 dataframe.xlsx

10.12 Read worksheet to Pandas DataFrame

On the other hand, a worksheet in Excel document can be loaded in a DataFrame object with the use of **read_excel()** method.

Example 10.16

```
>>> df=pd.read_excel('dataframe.xlsx', sheet_
name='sheet1')
>>> df
       Name  ProductID  price
0   Laptop          1  25000
1       TV          2  40000
2   Router          3   2000
3  Scanner          4   5000
4  Printer          5   9000
```

Incidentally, conversion to/from DataFrame and many other data formats is possible. This includes JSON, CSV, pickle, SQL, and so on. As a quick example, we shall try to read a SQLite table data, using **read_sql_query()** function.

Example 10.17

```
>>> import pandas as pd
>>> import sqlite3
>>> con=sqlite3.connect('mydb.sqlite')
>>> df = pd.read_sql_query("SELECT * FROM
Products;", con)
>>> df
   ProductID     Name  Price
0          1   Laptop  27500
1          3   Router   3000
2          4  Scanner   5500
3          5  Printer  11000
4          6   Mobile  16500
```

At the conclusion of this chapter, you must have got a fair idea of how you can use Python to manipulate Excel workbook document. While **openpyxl** package is all about automating functionality of Excel software, data in Excel sheets can be brought in Pandas dataframes for high-level manipulations and analysis and exported back.

Next two chapters of this book deal with the exciting world of **NOSQL** databases and the way Python can interact with two of very popular **NOSQL** databases – **MongoDB,** and **Cassandra.**

CHAPTER 11

Python – PyMongo

11.1 What is NOSQL?

In today's era of real-time web applications, NoSQL databases are becoming increasingly popular. The term NoSQL originally referred to "non SQL" or "non-relational", but its supporters prefer to call "Not only SQL" to indicate that SQL-like query language may be supported alongside.

NoSQL is touted as open-source, distributed and horizontally scalable schema-free database architecture. NoSQL databases are more scalable and provide superior performance as compared to RDBMS. This primarily because it requires that schemas (table structure, relationships, etc.) be defined before you can add data. Some of the popular NoSQL databases extensively in use today include **MongoDB, CouchDB, Cassendra, HBase**, etc.

Several NoSQL products are available in the market. They are classified into four categories based on the data model used by them.

Key-Value store: Uses a hash table (also called a dictionary). Each item in the database is stored as a unique attribute name (or 'key'), associated with its value. The key-value model is the simplest type of NoSQL database. Examples of key-value databases are **Amazon simpleDB, Oracle BDB, Riak**, and **Berkeley DB**.

Column Oriented: This type of databases store and process very large amount of data distributed over multiple machines. Keys point to multiple columns. The columns are arranged by column family. Examples of column-oriented databases are **Cassandra** and **HBase**.

Document oriented: Database of this category is an advanced key-value store database. The semi-structured documents are stored in formats like JSON. Documents can contain many different key-value pairs, or key-array pairs, or even nested documents.

Graph Based: Databases of this type are used to store information about networks of data, such as social connections. A flexible graph model can scale across multiple machines. Graph stores include Neo4J and Giraph.

In this chapter, we shall get acquainted with a hugely popular document-oriented database, **MongoDB** and how it can be interfaced with Python through **PyMongo** module.

11.2 MongoDB

NoSQL databases typically have huge amount of data. Hence, more often than not, power of a single CPU is not enough when it comes to fetching data corresponding to a query. MongoDB uses a **sharding** technique which splits data sets across multiple instances. A large collection of data is split across multiple physical servers called **'shards'**, even though they behave as one collection. Query request from the application is routed to appropriate shard and the result is served. Thus, MongoDB achieves horizontal scalability. *(figure 11.1)*

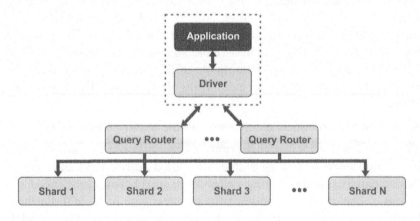

Figure 11.1 MongoDB

The **Document** is the heart of a MongoDB database. It is a collection of key-value pairs – similar to Python's dictionary object. We can also think of it being similar to single row in a table of SQL based relational database.

Collection in MongoDB is analogous to a table in the relational database. However, it doesn't have a predefined schema. The Collection has a dynamic schema in the sense each document may of a variable number of k-v pairs not necessarily with the same keys in each document.

Each document is characterized by a special key called "_**id**" having a unique value, again similar to a primary key in the entity table of a relational database.

MongoDB server has a command-line interface from inside which different database operations can be performed.

11.3 Installation of MongoDB

MongoDB server software is available in two forms: Community edition (open source release) and Enterprise edition (having additional features such as administration, and monitoring).

The MongoDB community edition is available for Windows, Linux as well as MacOS operating systems at https://www.mongodb.com/download-center/community. Choose appropriate version as per the OS and architecture of your machine and install it as per the instructions on the official website. Examples in this chapter assume that MongoDB is installed on Windows in e:\mongodb folder.

Start MongoDB server from command terminal using the following command:

```
E:\mongodb\bin>mongod
..
waiting for connections on port 27017
```

The server is now listening to connection request from client at port number 22017 of the localhost. (Server's startup logs are omitted in the above display). To stop it, press ctrl-C. MongoDB databases are stored in the bin\data directory. You can specify alternative location though by specifying --dbpath option as follows:

Example 11.1

```
E:\mongodb\bin>mongod --dbpath e:\test
```

Now, start **Mongo** shell in another terminal.

```
E:\mongodb\bin>mongo
MongoDB shell version v4.0.6
connecting to:
mongodb://127.0.0.1:27017/?gssapiServiceName=mongodb
Implicit session: session { "id" : UUID("0d848b11-
acf7-4d30-83df-242d1d7fa693") }
MongoDB server version: 4.0.6
---
>
```

Mongo shell is a Javascript interface to MongoDB server. It is similar to the SQLite shell or MsSQL console, as we have seen earlier chapter. The **CRUD** operations on MongoDB database can be performed from here.

11.4 MongoDB - Create Database

To display the current database in use, there's **db** command. Default database in use is **test**.

```
> db
Test
```

With **'use'** command any other database is set as current. If the named database doesn't exist, a new one is created.

```
> use mydb
switched to db mydb
```

However, until you store data (such as collection or document) in it, is the database is not created. The following command inserts a document in 'products' collection under the current database.

11.5 MongoDB - Insert Document

Appropriately, insertone() method is available to a collection object in a database. A document is provided to it as a parameter.

```
> db.products.insertone({"ProductID":1,
"Name":"Laptop", "Price":25000})
WriteResult({ "nInserted" : 1 })
```

Result of above (for that matter any insert/update/delete operation) command returns **WriteResult** object. The insert() method inserts multiple documents if the argument is an array of documents. In that case, the result is **BulkWriteResult** object.

```
> var pricelist=[{'ProductID':1, 'Name':'Laptop',
'price':25000},
... {'ProductID':2, 'Name':'TV', 'price':40000},
... {'ProductID':3, 'Name':'Router', 'price':2000},
... {'ProductID':4, 'Name':'Scanner', 'price':5000},
... {'ProductID':5, 'Name':'Printer', 'price':9000}]
> db.products.insert(pricelist);
BulkWriteResult({
"writeErrors" : [ ],
"writeConcernErrors" : [ ],
"nInserted" : 5,
"nUpserted" : 0,
"nMatched" : 0,
"nModified" : 0,
"nRemoved" : 0,
"upserted" : [ ]
})
```

The `insert()` function inserts single document or array whereas a single document is inserted with `inserOne()` method and array whereas `insert_many()` method is used with an array.

11.6 MongoDB - Querying Collection

Retrieving data from the database is always an important operation. MongoDB's collection has `find()` method with which documents are fetched. Without any argument, `find()` method returns a result set of all documents in a collection. In effect, it is equivalent to **'SELECT * FROM \<table>'** in SQL.

```
> db.products.find()
{ "_id" : ObjectId("5c8d420c7bebaca49b767db3"),
"ProductID" : 1, "Name" : "Laptop", "price" : 25000
}
{ "_id" : ObjectId("5c8d420c7bebaca49b767db4"),
"ProductID" : 2, "Name" : "TV", "price" : 40000 }
{ "_id" : ObjectId("5c8d420c7bebaca49b767db5"),
"ProductID" : 3, "Name" : "Router", "price" : 2000 }
{ "_id" : ObjectId("5c8d420c7bebaca49b767db6"),
"ProductID" : 4, "Name" : "Scanner", "price" : 5000
}
{ "_id" : ObjectId("5c8d420c7bebaca49b767db7"),
"ProductID" : 5, "Name" : "Printer", "price" : 9000
}
```

Note that, '**_id**' key is automatically added to each document. The value of each _id is of **ObjectId** type and is unique for each document.

Invariably, you would want to apply to the result set returned by find(). It is done by putting the key-value pair in its parenthesis. In its generalized form, the conditional query is written as follows:

Example 11.2

```
db.collection.find({"key":"value"})
```

The following statement retrieves a document whose 'Name' key has 'TV' value.

Example 11.3

```
> db.products.find({"Name":"TV"})
{ "_id" : ObjectId("5c8d420c7bebaca49b767db4"),
"ProductID" : 2, "Name" : "TV", "price" : 40000 }
```

MongoDB doesn't use traditional logical operator symbols. Instead, it has its own operators, as listed below: *(table 11.1)*

Table 11.1 *Logical operators*

MongoDB operator	Description
$eq	equal to (==)
$gt	greater than (>)
$gte	greater than or equal to (>=)
$in	if equal to any value in array
$lt	less than (<)
$lte	less than or equal to (<=)
$ne	not equal to (!=)
$nin	if not equal to any value in array

The operators are used in find() method to apply filter. The following statement returns products with price>10000.

```
> db.products.find({"price":{$gt:10000}})
{ "_id" : ObjectId("5c8d420c7bebaca49b767db3"),
"ProductID" : 1, "Name" : "Laptop", "price" : 25000
}
{ "_id" : ObjectId("5c8d420c7bebaca49b767db4"),
"ProductID" : 2, "Name" : "TV", "price" : 40000 }
```

The **$and** as well as **$or** operators are available for compound logical expressions. Their usage is, as follows:

Example 11.4

```
db.collection.find($and:[{"key1":"value1"},
{"key2":"value2"}])
```

Use the following command to fetch products with price between 1000 and 10000.

```
> db.products.find({$and:[{"price":{$gt:1000}},
{"price":{$lt:10000}}]})
{ "_id" : ObjectId("5c8d420c7bebaca49b767db5"),
"ProductID" : 3, "Name" : "Router", "price" : 2000 }
{ "_id" : ObjectId("5c8d420c7bebaca49b767db6"),
"ProductID" : 4, "Name" : "Scanner", "price" : 5000
}
{ "_id" : ObjectId("5c8d420c7bebaca49b767db7"),
"ProductID" : 5, "Name" : "Printer", "price" : 9000
}
```

11.7 MongoDB - Update Document

Predictably, there is an update() method available to collection object. Just as in SQL UPDATE, the **$set** operator assigns updated value to a specified key. Its primary usage is, as below:

Example 11.5

```
db.collection.update({"key":"value"},
{$set:{"key":"newvalue"}})
```

For example, the following statement changes the price of 'TV' to 50000.

```
> db.products.update({"Name":"TV"},
{$set:{"price":50000}})
WriteResult({ "nMatched" : 1, "nUpserted" : 0,
"nModified" : 1 })
```

The WriteResult() confirms the modification. You can also use Boolean operators in the update criteria. To perform update on multiple documents, use updateMany() method. The following command use **$inc** operator to increment the price by 500 for all products with ProductID greater than 3.

```
> db.products.updateMany({"ProductID":{$gt:3}},
{$inc:{"price":500}})
{ "acknowledged" : true, "matchedCount" : 2,
"modifiedCount" : 2 }
```

11.8 MongoDB - Delete Document

The `remove()` method deletes one or more documents from the collection based on the provided criteria. The following statement will result in removal of a document pertaining to price>40000 (in our data it happens to be with name='TV').

```
> db.products.remove({"price":{$gt:40000}})
WriteResult({ "nRemoved" : 1 })
```

Run the `find()` method in the shell to verify the removal.

Now that, we have attained some level of familiarity with MongoDB with the help of shell commands.,let us concentrate on our main objective – use MongoDB in Python.

11.9 PyMongo Module

`PyMongo` module is an official Python driver for MongoDB database developed by Mongo Inc. It can be used on Windows, Linux, as well as MacOS. As always, you need to install this module using pip3 utility.

```
pip3 install pymongo
```

Before attempting to perform any operation on a database, ensure that you have started the server using 'mongod' command and the server is listening at port number 22017.

To let your Python interpreter interact with the server, establish a connection with the object of **MongoClient** class.

Example 11.6

```
>>> from pymongo import MongoClient
>>> client=MongoClient()
```

The following syntax is also valid for setting up connection with server.

Example 11.7

```
>>> client = MongoClient('localhost', 27017)
#or
client = MongoClient('mongodb://localhost:27017')
```

In order to display currently available databases use **list_database_
names()** method of `MongoClient` class.

Example 11.8

```
>>> client.list_database_names()
['admin', 'config', 'local', 'mydb']
```

11.10 PyMongo – Add Collection

Create a new database object by using any name currently not in the list.

Example 11.9

```
>>> db=client.newdb
```

The Database is actually created when first document is inserted. The
following statement will implicitly create a 'products' collection and
multiple documents from the given list of dictionary objects.

Example 11.10

```
>>> pricelist=[{'ProductID':1, 'Name':'Laptop',
'price':25000},{'ProductID':2, 'Name':'TV',
'price':40000},{'ProductID':3, 'Name':'Router',
'price':2000},{'ProductID':4, 'Name':'Scanner',
'price':5000},{'ProductID':5, 'Name':'Printer',
'price':9000}]
>>> db.products.insert_many(pricelist)
```

You can confirm the insertion operation by `find()` method in the Mongo
shell, as we have done earlier.

We create a collection object explicitly by using **create_collection()**
method of the database object.

Example 11.11

```
>>> db.create_collection('customers')
```

Now, we can add one or more documents in it. The following script adds
documents in 'customers' collection.

Example 11.12

```
from pymongo import MongoClient
client=MongoClient()
db=client.newdb
db.create_collection("customers")
cust=db['customers']
custlist=[{'CustID':1,'Name':'Ravikumar','GS-
TIN':'27AAJPL7103N1ZF'},
{'CustID':2,'Name':'Patel','GSTIN':'24ASDFG1234N-
1ZN'},
{'CustID':3,'Name':'Nitin','GSTIN':'27AABBC7895N-
1ZT'},
{'CustID':4,'Name':'Nair','GSTIN':'32MMAF8963N1ZK'},
{'CustID':5,'Name':'Shah','GSTIN':'24BADEF2002N-
1ZB'},
{'CustID':6,'Name':'Khurana','GSTIN':'07KABCS1002N-
1ZV'},
{'CustID':7,'Name':'Irfan','GSTIN':'05IIAAV5103N-
1ZA'},
{'CustID':8,'Name':'Kiran','GSTIN':'12PPSD-
F22431ZC'},
{'CustID':9,'Name':'Divya','GSTIN':'15ABCDE1101N-
1ZA'},
{'CustID':10,'Name':'John','GS-
TIN':'29AAEEC4258E1ZK'}]
cust.insert_many(custlist)
client.close()
```

11.11 PyMongo - Querying Collection

PyMongo module defines find() method to be used with a collection object. It returns a `cursor` object which provides a list of all documents in the collection.

Example 11.13

```
>>> products=db['products']
>>> docs=products.find()
>>> list(docs)
[{'_id': ObjectId('5c8dec275405c12e3402423c'),
'ProductID': 1, 'Name': 'Laptop', 'price': 25000},
{'_id': ObjectId('5c8dec275405c12e3402423d'),
'ProductID': 2, 'Name': 'TV', 'price': 50000},
{'_id': ObjectId('5c8dec275405c12e3402423e'),
'ProductID': 3, 'Name': 'Router', 'price': 2000},
{'_id': ObjectId('5c8dec275405c12e3402423f'),
'ProductID': 4, 'Name': 'Scanner', 'price': 5000},
{'_id': ObjectId('5c8dec275405c12e34024240'),
'ProductID': 5, 'Name': 'Printer', 'price': 9000}]
```

This `cursor` object is an iterator that serves one document for every call of the `next()` method. Each document is a dictionary object of k-v pairs. The following code displays the name and GSTIN of all customers.

Example 11.14

```
#mongofind.py
from pymongo import MongoClient
client=MongoClient()
db=client.newdb
cust=db['customers']
docs=cust.find()
while True:
        try:
                doc=docs.next()
                print (doc['Name'], doc['GSTIN'])
        except StopIteration:
                break
client.close()
```

Run above script from command prompt.

```
E:\python37>python mongofind.py
Ravikumar 27AAJPL7103N1ZF
Patel 24ASDFG1234N1ZN
Nitin 27AABBC7895N1ZT
Nair 32MMAF8963N1ZK
Shah 24BADEF2002N1ZB
Khurana 07KABCS1002N1ZV
Irfan 05IIAAV5103N1ZA
Kiran 12PPSDF22431ZC
Divya 15ABCDE1101N1ZA
John 29AAEEC4258E1ZK
```

You can, ofcourse, employ a regular 'for' loop to traverse the cursor object to obtain one document at a time.

Example 11.15

```
for doc in docs:
        print (doc['Name'], doc['GSTIN'])
```

The logical operators of MongoDB (described earlier in this chapter) are used to apply filter criteria for find() method. As an example, products with price>10000 are fetched with the following statement:

Example 11.16

```
>>> products=db['products']
>>> docs=products.find({'price':{'$gt':10000}})
>>> for doc in docs:
        print (doc.get('Name'), doc.get('price'))
Laptop 25000
TV 50000
```

11.12 PyMongo – Update Document

PyMongo offers two collection methods for modification of data in one or more documents. They are update_one() and update_many(). Both require a filter criteria and a new value of one or more keys. The update_one() updates only the first document that satisfies filter criteria. On the other hand, update_many() performs update on all documents that satisfy the filter criteria.

Example 11.17

```
collection.update_one(filter, newval)
```

Following Python script accepts name of the product from user and displays the current price. It is updated to the new price input by the user.

Example 11.18

```
#mongoupdate.py
from pymongo import MongoClient
client=MongoClient()
db=client.newdb
prod=input('enter name:')
doc=db.products.find_one({'Name':prod})
print (doc['Name'], doc['price'])
price=int(input('enter price:'))
db['products'].update_
one({'Name':prod},{"$set":{'price':price}})
client.close()
```

Execute above script from the command prompt:

```
E:\python37>python mongoupdate.py
enter name:Printer
Printer 9000
enter price:12500
```

11.13 PyMongo - Relationships

MongoDB is a non-relational database. However, you can still establish relationships between documents in a database. MongoDB uses two different approaches for this purpose. One is an embedded approach and the other is a referencing approach.

Embedded Relationship

In this case, the documents appear in a nested manner where another document is used as the value of a certain key. The following code represents a 'customer' document showing a customer (with '_id'=1) buys two products. A list of two product documents is the value of 'prods' key.

Example 11.19

```
>>> cust.insert_one({'_id':1,'name':'Ravi',
                 'prods':[
                         { 'Name':'TV',
'price':40000},

{'Name':'Scanner','price':5000}
                         ]
                 })
```

Querying such an embedded document is straightforward as all data is available in the parent document itself.

Example 11.20

```
>>> doc=cust.find_one({'_id':1},{'prods':1})

>>> doc
{'_id': 1, 'prods': [{'Name': 'TV', 'price': 40000},
{'Name': 'Scanner', 'price': 5000}]}
```

The embedded approach has a major drawback. The database is not normalized and, hence, data redundancy arises. As size grows, it may affect the performance of read/write operations.

Reference Relationship

This approach is somewhat similar to the relations in a SQL based database. The collections (equivalent to RDBMS table) are normalized for optimum performance. One document refers to other with its '_id' key.

Recollecting that instead of automatically generated random values for '_id', they can be explicitly specified while inserting document in a collection, following is the constitution of 'products' collection.

Example 11.21

```
>>> list(prod.find())

[{'_id': 1, 'Name': 'Laptop', 'price': 25000}, {'_
id': 2, 'Name': 'TV', 'price': 40000}, {'_id': 3,
'Name': 'Router', 'price': 2000}, {'_id': 4, 'Name':
'Scanner', 'price': 5000}, {'_id': 5, 'Name':
'Printer', 'price': 9000}]
```

We now create 'customers' collection.

Example 11.22

```
>>> db.create_collection('customers')
>>> cust=db['customers']
```

The following document is inserted with one key 'prods' being a list of
'_id's from products collection.

Example 11.23

```
>>> cust.insert_one({'_id':1, 'Name':'Ravi',
'prods':[2,4]})
```

However, in such a case, you may have to run two queries: one on the
parent collection, and another on related collection. First, fetch the _ids
of related table.

Example 11.24

```
>>> doc=cust.find_one({'_id':1},{'prods':1})
>>> prods
[2, 4]
```

Then, iterate over the list and access required field from the related
document.

Example 11.25

```
>>> for each in prods:
        doc=prod.find_one({'_id':each})
        print (doc['Name'])

TV
Scanner
```

Reference approach can be used to build one-to-one or one-to-many type
of relationships. The choice of approach (embedded or reference) largely
depends on data usage, projected growth of size of the document and the
atomicity of the transaction.

In this chapter, we had an overview of MongoDB database and its Python
interface in the form of PyMongo module. In the next chapter, another
NoSQL database – **Cassandra** – is going to be explained along with its
association with Python.

Python - Cassandra

In this last chapter, we are going to deal with another important NOSQL database – Cassandra. Today some of the biggest IT giants (including FaceBook, Twitter, Cisco, and so on) use Cassandra because of its high scalability, consistency, and fault-tolerance. **Cassandra** is a distributed database from Apache Software Foundation. It is a **wide column** store database. Large amount of data is stored across many commodity servers which makes data highly available.

12.1 Cassandra Architecture

The fundamental unit of data storage is a node. A **node** is a single server in which data is stored in the form of keyspace. For understanding, you can think of **keyspace** as a single database. Just as any server running a SQL engine can host multiple databases, a node can have many keyspaces. Again, like in a SQL database, keyspace may have multiple column families which are similar to tables.

However, the architecture of Cassandra is logically as well as physically different from any SQL oriented server (Oracle, MySQL, PostgreSQL, and so on). Cassandra is designed to be a foolproof database without a single point of failure. Hence, data in one node is replicated across a peer-to-peer network of nodes. The networks is called a **data center**, and if required, multiple data centers are interconnected to form a **cluster**. Replication strategy and replication factor can be defined at the time of creation of a keyspace. *(figure 12.1)*

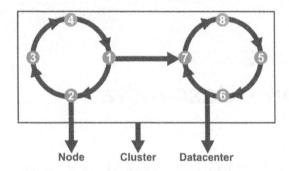

Node   Cluster   Datacenter

Figure 12.1 Cassandra architecture

Each 'write' operation over a keyspace is stored in Commit Log, which acts as a crash-recovery system. After recording here, data is stored in a **Mem-table**. Mem-table is just a cache or buffer in the memory. Data from the mem-table is periodically flushed in SSTables, which are physical disk files on the node.

Cassandra's data model too, is entirely different from a typical relational database. It is often, described as a **column store** or column-oriented NOSQL database. A keyspace holds one or more column families, similar to the table in RDBMS. Each **table** (column family) is a collection of rows, each of which stores columns in an ordered manner. **Column**, therefore, is the basic unit of data in Cassandra. Each column is characterized by its name, value, and timestamp.

The difference between a SQL table and Cassandra's table is that the latter is schema-free. You don't need to define your column structure ahead of time. As a result, each row in a Cassandra table may have columns with different names and variable numbers.*(figure 12.2)*

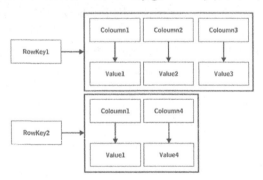

Figure 12.2 Cassandra table

12.2 Installation

The latest version of Cassandra is available for download at http://cassandra. apache.org/download/. Community distributions of Cassandra (DDC) can be found at https://academy.datastax.com/planet-cassandra/cassandra. Code examples in this chapter are tested on DataStax distribution installed on Windows OS.

Just as any relational database uses SQL for performing operations on data in tables, Cassandra has its own query language **CQL** which stands for **Cassandra Query Language**. The DataStax distribution comes with a useful front-end IDE for CQL. All operations such as creating keyspace and table, running different queries, and so on can be done both visually as well as using text queries. The following diagram shows a view of DataStax DevCenter IDE.*(figure 12.3)*

Figure 12.3 DataStax DevCenter IDE

12.3 CQL Shell

Cassandra installation also provides a shell inside which you can execute **CQL** queries. It is similar to MySQL console, SQLite console, or Oracle's SQL Plus terminal.*(figure 12.4)*

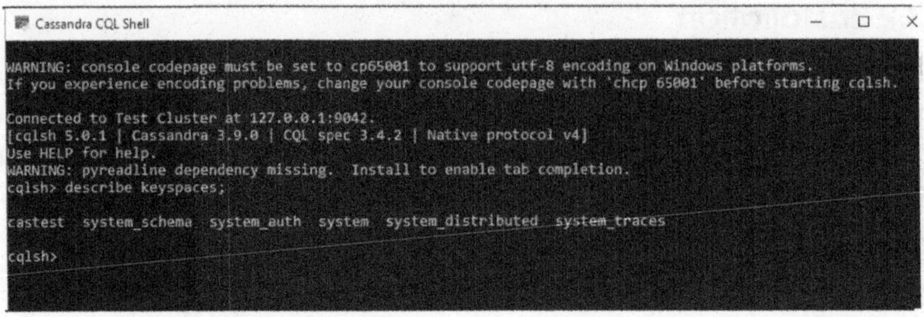

Figure 12.4 CQL Shell

We shall first learn to perform basic CRUD operations with Cassandra from inside **CQLSH** and then use Python API for the purpose.

12.4 Create Keyspace

As mentioned above, Cassandra Query Language (CQL) is the primary tool for communication with Cassandra database. Its syntax is strikingly similar to SQL. The first step is to create a **keyspace**.

A keyspace is a container of column families or tables. CQL provides CREATE KEYSPACE statement to do exactly the same – create a new keyspace. The statement defines its name and replication strategy.

Example 12.1

```
CREATE KEYSPACE name with replication {options}
```

The **replication** clause is mandatory and is characterized by **class** and **replication_factor** attributes. The 'class' decides the replication strategy to be used for the keyspace. Its value is, by default, **SimpleStrategy** indicating that data will be spread across the entire cluster. Another value of `class` is **NetworkTopologyStrategy**. It is a production-ready strategy with the help of which replication factor can be set independently on each data center.

The **replication_factor** attribute defines number of replicas per data center. Set its value to 3, which is considered optimum, so that the data availability is reasonably high.

The following statement creates 'MyKeySpace' with 'SimpleStrategy' and replication_factor of 3.

```
cqlsh> create keyspace mykeyspace with
    ... replication={'class': 'SimpleStrategy',
'replication_factor' : 3};
```

Note that, the name of keyspace is case-insensitive unless given in double-quotes. CQL provides the **use** keyword to set a certain keyspace as current. (Similar to MySQL 'use' statement isn't it?). To display list of keyspaces in the current cluster, there is **DESCRIBE** keyword.

```
cqlsh> describe keyspaces;
castest          system_auth   mykeyspace
system_traces
system_schema   system        system_distributed
cqlsh> use mykeyspace;
cqlsh:mykeyspace>
```

Create New Table

As mentioned earlier, one or more column families or tables may be present in a keyspace. The CREATE TABLE command in CQL creates a new table in the current keyspace. Remember the same command was used in SQL?

The general syntax is, as follows:

Example 12.2

```
create table if not exists table_name
(
col1_definition,
col2_definition,
..
..
)
```

Column definition contains its name and data type, optionally setting it as the **primary key**. The primary key can also be set after the list of columns have been defined. The 'if not exists' clause is not mandatory but is recommended to avoid error if the table of the given name already exists.

The following statement creates the 'Products' table in mykeyspace.

```
cqlsh:mykeyspace> create table if not exists
products
            ... (
            ... productID int PRIMARY KEY,
            ... name text,
            ... price int
            ... );
```

Following definition is also identical:

```
cqlsh:mykeyspace> create table products
            ... (
            ... productID int,
            ... name text,
            ... price int,
            ... primary key (productID)
            ... );
```

Partition Key

Partition key determines on which node will a certain row will be stored. If a table has single primary key (as in above definition), it is treated as **partition key** as well. The hash value of this partition key is used to determine the node or replica on which a certain row is located. Cassandra stores rows having primary key in a certain range on one node. For example, rows with a productID value between 1 to 100 are stored on Node A, between 2 to 200 on node B, and so on.

The primary key may comprise of more than one column. In that case, the first column name acts as the partition key and subsequent columns are **cluster keys**. Let us change the definition of Products table slightly as follows:

```
cqlsh:mykeyspace> create table products
            ... (
            ... productID int,
            ... manufacturer text,
            ... name text,
            ... price int,
            ... primary key(manufacturer,
productID)
            ... );
```

In this case, the 'manufacturer' column acts as the partition key and 'productID' as a cluster key. As a result, all products from the same manufacturer will reside on the same node. Hence a query to search for products from a certain manufacturer will return results faster.

12.5 Inserting Rows

INSERT statement in CQL is exactly similar to one in SQL. However, the column list before the 'VALUES' clause is not optional as is the case in SQL. That is because, in Cassandra, the table may have variable number of columns.

```
cqlsh:mykeyspace> insert into products (productID,
name, price) values (1, 'Laptop',25000);
```

Issue INSERT statement multiple number of times to populate 'products' table with sample data given in chapter 9. You can also import data from a CSV file using copy command, as follows:

```
cqlsh:mykeyspace> copy products (productID, name,
price)
              ... from 'pricelist.csv' with
delimiter=',' and header=true;
```

12.6 Querying Cassandra Table

Predictably, CQL also has SELECT statement to fetch data from a Cassandra table. Easiest usage is employing '*' to fetch data from all columns in a table.

```
cqlsh:mykeyspace> select * from products;
 productid | name      | price
-----------+-----------+-------
        5 | 'Printer' |  9000
        1 | 'Laptop'  | 25000
        2 |      'TV' | 40000
        4 | 'Scanner' |  5000
        6 | 'Mobile'  | 15000
        3 | 'Router'  |  2000
(6 rows)
```

All conventional logical operators are allowed in the filter criteria specified with the WHERE clause. The following statement returns product names with price greater than 10000.

```
cqlsh:mykeyspace> select * from products where
price>10000 allow filtering;
 productid | name      | price
-----------+-----------+--------
         1 | 'Laptop'  | 25000
         2 |      'TV' | 40000
         6 | 'Mobile'  | 15000

(3 rows)
```

Use of **ALLOW FILTERING** is necessary here. By default, CQL only allows select queries where all records read will be returned in the result set. Such queries have predictable performance. The ALLOW FILTERING option allows to explicitly allow (some) queries that require filtering. If the filter criteria consists of partition key columns only = and IN operators are allowed.

UPDATE and **DELETE** statements of CQL are used as in SQL. However, both must have filter criteria based on the primary key. (Note the use of '--' as a commenting symbol)

```
cqlsh:mykeyspace> --update syntax
cqlsh:mykeyspace> update newproducts set price=45000
where productID=2;
cqlsh:mykeyspace> --delete syntax
cqlsh:mykeyspace> delete from newproducts where
productID=6;
```

12.7 Table with Compound Partition Key

In the above example, the products table had been defined to have a partition key with a single primary key. Rows in such a table are stored in different nodes depending upon hash value of the primary key. However, data is stored across the cluster using a slightly different method when the table has a compound primary key. The following table's primary key comprises of two columns.

```
cqlsh:mykeyspace> create table products
              ... (
              ... productID int,
              ... manufacturer text,
              ... name text,
              ... price int,
              ... primary key(manufacturer, productID)
              ... );
```

For this table, 'manufacturer' is the partition key and 'productID' behaves as a cluster key. As a result, products with similar 'manufacturer' are stored in the same node. Let us understand with the help of the following example. The table contains following data:

Example 12.3

```
cqlsh:mykeyspace> select * from products;
 productid | manufacturer | name        | price
-----------+--------------+-------------+-------
         5 |      'Epson' |   'Printer' |  9000
        10 |      'IBall' |  'Keyboard' |  1000
         1 |       'Acer' |    'Laptop' | 25000
         8 |       'Acer' |       'Tab' | 10000
         2 |    'Samsung' |        'TV' | 40000
         4 |      'Epson' |   'Scanner' |  5000
         7 |      'IBall' |     'Mouse' |   500
         6 |    'Samsung' |    'Mobile' | 15000
         9 |    'Samsung' |        'AC' | 35000
         3 |      'IBall' |    'Router' |  2000
(10 rows)
```

Rows in the above table will be stored among nodes such that products from the same manufacturer are together. *(figure 12.5)*

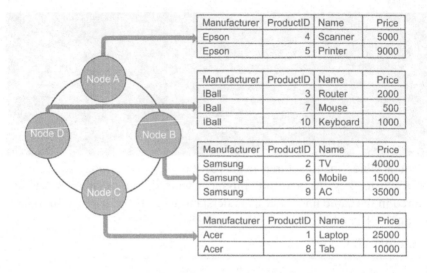

Manufacturer	ProductID	Name	Price
Epson	4	Scanner	5000
Epson	5	Printer	9000

Manufacturer	ProductID	Name	Price
IBall	3	Router	2000
IBall	7	Mouse	500
iBall	10	Keyboard	1000

Manufacturer	ProductID	Name	Price
Samsung	2	TV	40000
Samsung	6	Mobile	15000
Samsung	9	AC	35000

Manufacturer	ProductID	Name	Price
Acer	1	Laptop	25000
Acer	8	Tab	10000

Figure 12.5 Compound Partition Key

12.8 Python Cassandra Driver

Cassandra's Python module has been provided by apache itself. It works with the latest version CQL version 3 and uses Cassandra's native protocol. This Python driver also has ORM API in addition to core API which is similar in many ways to DB-API.

To install this module, use the pip installer as always.

```
E:\python37>scripts\pip3 install cassandra-driver
```

Verify successful installation by following commands:

Example 12.4

```
>>> import cassandra
>>> print (cassandra.__version__)
3.17.0
```

To execute CQL queries, we have to set up a **Cluster** object, first.

Example 12.5

```
>>> from cassandra.cluster import Cluster
>>> clstr=Cluster()
```

Next up, we need to start a session by establishing a connection with our keyspace in the cluster.

Example 12.6

```
>>> session=clstr.connect('mykeyspace')
```

The ubiquitous `execute()` method of session object is used to perform all CQL operations. For instance, the primary SELECT query over the 'products' table in 'mykeypace' returns a result set object. Using a typical for loop, all rows can be traversed.

Example 12.7

```
#cassandra-select.py
from cassandra.cluster import Cluster
clstr=Cluster()
session=clstr.connect('mykeyspace')
rows=session.execute("select * from products;")
for row in rows:
        print ('Manufacturer: {} ProductID:{}
Name:{} price:{}'.format(row[1],row[0], row[2],
row[3]))
```

Output

```
E:\python37>python cassandra-select.py
Manufacturer: 'Epson' ProductID:5 Name:'Printer'
price:9000
Manufacturer: 'IBall' ProductID:10 Name:'Keyboard'
price:1000
Manufacturer: 'Acer' ProductID:1 Name:'Laptop'
price:25000
Manufacturer: 'Acer' ProductID:8 Name:'Tab'
price:10000
Manufacturer: 'Samsung' ProductID:2 Name:'TV'
price:40000
Manufacturer: 'Epson' ProductID:4 Name:'Scanner'
price:5000
Manufacturer: 'IBall' ProductID:7 Name:'Mouse'
price:500
Manufacturer: 'Samsung' ProductID:6 Name:'Mobile'
price:15000
Manufacturer: 'Samsung' ProductID:9 Name:'AC'
price:35000
Manufacturer: 'IBall' ProductID:3 Name:'Router'
price:2000
```

12.9 Parameterized Queries

The **cassandra.query** submodule defines following **Statement** classes:

SimpleStatement: A simple, unprepared CQL query contained in a query string. For example:

Example 12.8

```
from cassandra.query import SimpleStatement
stmt=SimpleStatement("select * from products;")
rows=session.execute(stmt)
```

BatchStatement: A batch combines multiple DML operations (such as INSERT, UPDATE, and DELETE) and executes at once to achieve atomicity. For the following example, firs,t create a 'customers' table in the current keyspace.

```
create table customers
... (
... custID int primary key,
... name text,
... GSTIN text
... );
```

Customer data is provided in the form of a list of tuples. Individual INSERT query is populated with each tuple and added in a BatchStatement. Batch is then executed at once.

Example 12.9

```
#cassandra-batch.py
from cassandra.cluster import Cluster
clstr=Cluster()
session=clstr.connect('mykeyspace')
custlist=[(1,'Ravikumar','27AAJPL7103N1ZF'),
        (2,'Patel','24ASDFG1234N1ZN'),
        (3,'Nitin','27AABBC7895N1ZT'),
        (4,'Nair','32MMAF8963N1ZK'),
        (5,'Shah','24BADEF2002N1ZB'),
        (6,'Khurana','07KABCS1002N1ZV'),
```

```
        (7,'Irfan','05IIAAV5103N1ZA'),
        (8,'Kiran','12PPSDF22431ZC'),
        (9,'Divya','15ABCDE1101N1ZA'),
        (10,'John','29AAEEC4258E1ZK')]
from cassandra.query import SimpleStatement,
BatchStatement
batch=BatchStatement()
for cst in custlist:
        batch.add(SimpleStatement("INSERT INTO
customers (custID,name,GSTIN) VALUES (%s, %s, %s)"),
\
            (cst[0], cst[1],cst[2]))
session.execute(batch)
```

Run above code and then check rows in 'customers' table in CQL shell.

```
cqlsh:mykeyspace> select * from customers;
 custid | gstin              | name
--------+--------------------+----------
      5 | 24BADEF2002N1ZB    |     Shah
     10 | 29AAEEC4258E1ZK    |     John
      1 | 27AAJPL7103N1ZF    | Ravikumar
      8 | 12PPSDF22431ZC     |    Kiran
      2 | 24ASDFG1234N1ZN    |    Patel
      4 | 32MMAF8963N1ZK     |     Nair
      7 | 05IIAAV5103N1ZA    |    Irfan
      6 | 07KABCS1002N1ZV    |  Khurana
      9 | 15ABCDE1101N1ZA    |    Divya
      3 | 27AABBC7895N1ZT    |    Nitin
(10 rows)
```

PreparedStatement: Prepared statement contains a query string that is parsed by Cassandra and then saved for later use. Subsequently, it only needs to send the values of parameters to bind. This reduces network traffic and CPU utilization because Cassandra does not have to re-parse the query each time. The **Session.prepare()** method returns a **PreparedStatement** instance.

Example 12.10

```
#cassandra-prepare.py
from cassandra.cluster import Cluster
from cassandra.query import PreparedStatement
clstr=Cluster()
session=clstr.connect('mykeyspace')
stmt=session.prepare("INSERT INTO customers (custID,
name,GSTIN) VALUES (?,?,?)")
boundstmt=stmt.bind([11,'HarishKumar',
'12PQRDF22431ZN'])
session.execute(boundstmt)
```

Each time, the prepared statement can be executed by binding it with a new set of parameters. Note that, the PreparedStatement uses '?' as place holder and not '%s' as in BatchStatement.

12.10 User-defined Types

While executing the queries, Python data types are implicitly parsed to corresponding CQL types as per the following table:*(figure 12.1)*

Table 12.1 *Data types*

Python Type	CQL Type
None	NULL
bool	boolean
float	float, double
int, long	int, bigint, varint, smallint, tinyint, counter
decimal.Decimal	Decimal
str, unicode	ascii, varchar, text
buffer, bytearray	Blob
Date	Date
Datetime	Timestamp
Time	Time
list, tuple, generator	List
set, frozenset	Set
dict, OrderedDict	Map
uuid.UUID	timeuuid, uuid

In addition to the above built-in CQL data types, Cassandra table may have a column of a user-defined type to which an object of Python class can be mapped.

Cassandra provides a **CREATE TYPE** statement to define a new user-defined type which be used as a type for a column in a table defined with the CREATE TABLE statement.

In the script given below (Cassandra-udt.py), we define a Cassandra user-defined type named as 'contacts' and use it as the data type of 'contact' column in 'users' table. The **register_user_type()** method of cluster object helps us to map Python class 'ContactInfo' to the user-defined type.

Example 12.11

```
#cassandra-udt.py
from cassandra.cluster import Cluster
cluster = Cluster(protocol_version=3)
session = cluster.connect()
session.set_keyspace('mykeyspace')
session.execute("CREATE TYPE contact (email text,
phone text)")
session.execute("CREATE TABLE users (userid int
PRIMARY KEY, name text, contact frozen<contact>)")
class ContactInfo:
    def __init__(self, email, phone):
        self.email = email
        self.phone = phone
cluster.register_user_type('mykeyspace', 'contact',
ContactInfo)
# insert a row using an instance of ContctInfo
session.execute("INSERT INTO users (userid, name,
contact) VALUES (%s, %s, %s)",
                (1, 'Admin', ContactInfo("admin@
testserver.com", '9988776655')))
```

The following display of CQL shell confirms the insertion operation of the above script.

```
cqlsh:mykeyspace> select * from users;
 userid | contact
| name
--------+-----------------------------------------------------
----------+-------
      1 | {email: 'admin@testserver.com', phone:
'9988776655'} | Admin
(1 rows)
```

In this chapter, we learnt about the basic features of the Cassandra database, and importantly how to perform read/write operations on it with Python.

Final thoughts

This is also the last chapter of this book. Starting with the basics of Python, we learned how to work with different data storage formats. This work is neither a Python handbook nor a SQL/NoSQL database guide. Instead, it is intended to be a simple and practical explanation of Python interfaces with different data persistence avenues available today.

This book concentrates primarily on basic CRUD operations on SQL and NoSQL databases and other data file formats. However, these techniques are merely complementary to the real data crunching a data scientist needs to perform. The next logical thing for a curious reader would be to acquire data manipulation and visualization skills for which Python has very rich and powerful libraries.

I hope you enjoyed this book as much as I did bringing to you. Feedback, suggestions, and corrections if any are most welcome so that subsequent edition can be improved.

Thanks.

APPENDIX A
Alternate Python Implementations

The official distribution of Python hosted at https://www.python.org/ is a reference implementation. Since it is written in C, it is called CPython implementation. Several alternative implementations are available as follows:

IronPython: An implementation of Python for the .NET framework. It can use both Python and .NET framework libraries and exposes Python code to other languages in the .NET framework. Python Tools for Visual Studio integrates IronPython directly into the Visual Studio development environment.

Jython: An implementation that compiles Python code to Java bytecode and executed by the JVM (Java Virtual Machine). It can import and use any Java class like a Python module.

PyPy: A fast python implementation with a JIT compiler. The interpreter implemented is a restricted subset of the Python language called RPython.

Stackless Python: An enhanced version of the CPython. It provides the benefits of thread-based programming without compromise on performance.

MicroPython: A lean and efficient implementation of the Python 3 programming language that includes a small subset of the Python standard library and is optimized to run on microcontrollers.

Appendix B
Alternate Python Distributions

In addition to standard distribution available at https://www.python.org, many other third party organizations distribute CPython bundled with additional modules and packages specifically for certain applications such as scientific computing, machine learning, etc.

ActiveState ActivePython: Available as a commercial and community version. It includes scientific computing modules.

Pythonxy: Free distribution for scientific applications, numerical computations, data analysis, and visualization based on Qt GUI and Spyder IDE.

Winpython: A portable scientific Python distribution for Windows.

Conceptive Python SDK: Commercial distribution that targets the development of business, desktop, and database applications.

Enthought Canopy: A scientific and analytic Python package distribution having integrated tools for iterative data analysis, visualization, and application development.

Anaconda Python:A full Python package consisting a large number of data science libraries and has its own package management system called conda.

eGenix PyRun: Single file executable is a portable Python runtime, complete with stdlib, frozen into a single 3.5MB - 13MB executable file.

Appendix C
Built-in Functions

abs()	Return the absolute value of a number.
all()	Return True if all elements of the iterable are true
any()	Return True if any element of the iterable is true.
ascii()	Return a string containing a printable representation of an object.
bin()	Convert an integer to binary string prefixed with "0b".
bool()	Return a Boolean value, i.e. one of True or False.
breakpoint()	This function drops you into debugger at the call site.
bytearray()	Return a new array of bytes.
bytes()	Return a new "bytes" object.
callable()	Return True if object argument appears callable.
chr()	Return string representing a character whose Unicode code point is the integer i.
@classmethod	Transform a method into a class method.
compile()	Compile the source into a code or AST object.
complex()	Return a complex number with the value real + imag*1j
delattr()	The function deletes named attribute, provided the object allows it.
dict()	Create a new dictionary object is the dictionary class.
dir()	Without arguments, return list of names in current local scope. With an argument, attempt to return a list of valid attributes for that object.
divmod()	Take two (non complex) numbers as arguments and return a pair of numbers consisting of their quotient and remainder.
enumerate()	Return an enumerate object.
eval()	The expression argument is parsed and evaluated as a Python expression

exec()	This function supports dynamic execution of Python code.
filter()	Construct an iterator from those elements of iterable for which function returns true.
float()	Return a floating point number constructed from a number or string.
format()	Convert a value to a "formatted" representation, as controlled by format_spec.
frozenset()	Return a new frozenset object.
getattr()	Return the value of the named attribute of object.
globals()	Return a dictionary representing current global symbol table.
hasattr()	The result is True if the string is the name of one of the object's attributes, False if not.
hash()	Return the hash value of the object (if it has one).
help()	Invoke the built-in help system.
hex()	Convert integer to lowercase hexadecimal string prefixed with "0x".
id()	Return the "identity" of an object.
input()	The function reads a line from input, returns a string.
int()	Return an integer from a number or string x.
isinstance()	Return true if argument is an instance of the classinfo argument.
issubclass()	Return true if class is a subclass of classinfo.
iter()	Return an iterator object.
len()	Return the length (the number of items) of an object.
list()	Rather than being a function, list is actually a mutable sequence type.
locals()	Update and return a dictionary representing the current local symbol table.
map()	Return an iterator that applies function to every item of iterable, yielding the results.
max()	Return the largest item in an iterable or the largest of two or more arguments.
memoryview()	Return a "memory view" object from given argument.
min()	Return the smallest item in an iterable or the smallest of two or more arguments.

next()	Retrieve next item from iterator by calling its __next__() method. If iterator exhausts, StopIteration is raised.
object()	Return a new featureless object. object is a base for all classes. It has the methods that are common to all instances of Python classes.
oct()	Convert an integer number to an octal string prefixed with "0o".
open()	Open file and return a corresponding file object.
ord()	Return an integer representing the Unicode code point of that character.
pow()	Return x to the power y.
print)	Print objects to the text stream file, separated by sep and followed by end. sep, end, file and flush.
property()	Return a property attribute.
range()	Rather than being a function, range is actually an immutable sequence type.
repr()	Return a string containing a printable representation of an object.
reversed()	Return a reverse iterator.
round()	Return number rounded to ndigits precision after the decimal point.
set()	Return a new set object, with elements from iterable.
setattr()	The function assigns the value to the attribute, provided the object allows it.
slice()	Return a slice object representing the set of indices specified by range(start, stop, step).
sorted()	Return a new sorted list from the items in iterable.
@staticmethod	Transform a method into a static method.
str()	Return a str version of object.
sum()	Sums start and the items of an iterable from left to right and returns the total. start defaults to 0.
super()	Return a proxy object that delegates method calls to a parent class.
tuple()	Rather than being a function, tuple is actually an immutable sequence type.
type()	With one argument, return the type of an object. With three arguments, return a new type object.

vars()	Return the __dict__ attribute for a module, class, instance, or any other object with a __dict__ attribute.
zip()	Make an iterator that aggregates elements from each of the iterables.
__import__()	This function is invoked by the import statement.

Built-in Modules

Text Processing Services	
string	Common string operations
re	Regular expression operations
Binary Data Services	
struct	Interpret bytes as packed binary data
codecs	Codec registry and base classes
Data Types	
datetime	Basic date and time types
calendar	General calendar-related functions
collections	Container datatypes
array	Efficient arrays of numeric values
copy	Shallow and deep copy operations
pprint	Data pretty printer
enum	Support for enumerations
Numeric and Mathematical Modules	
math	Mathematical functions
cmath	Mathematical functions for complex numbers
decimal	Decimal fixed point and floating point arithmetic
fractions	Rational numbers
random	Generate pseudo-random numbers
statistics	Mathematical statistics functions
Functional Programming Modules	
itertools	Functions creating iterators for efficient looping
functools	Higher-order functions on callable objects
operator	Standard operators as functions
File and Directory Access	
pathlib	Object-oriented filesystem paths

os.path	Common pathname manipulations
filecmp	File and Directory Comparisons
linecache	Random access to text lines
shutil	High-level file operations
Data Persistence	
pickle	Python object serialization
shelve	Python object persistence
marshal	Internal Python object serialization
dbm	Interfaces to Unix "databases"
sqlite3	DB-API 2.0 interface for SQLite databases
Data Compression and Archiving	
zlib	Compression compatible with gzip
gzip	Support for gzip files
zipfile	Work with ZIP archives
File Formats	
csv	CSV File Reading and Writing
configparser	Configuration file parser
plistlib	Generate and parse Mac OS X .plist files
Cryptographic Services	
hashlib	Secure hashes and message digests
secrets	Generate secure random numbers
Generic Operating System Services	
os	Miscellaneous operating system interfaces
io	Core tools for working with streams
time	Time access and conversions
argparse	Parser for command-line options and arguments
getopt	C-style parser for command line options
getpass	Portable password input
curses	Terminal handling for character-cell displays
Concurrent Execution	
threading	Thread-based parallelism
multiprocessing	Process-based parallelism
subprocess	Subprocess management
queue	A synchronized queue class

_thread	Low-level threading API
Networking and Interprocess Communication	
asyncio	Asynchronous I/O
socket	Low-level networking interface
ssl	TLS/SSL wrapper for socket objects
signal	Set handlers for asynchronous events
mmap	Memory-mapped file support
Internet Data Handling	
email	An email and MIME handling package
json	JSON encoder and decoder
mailcap	Mailcap file handling
mailbox	Manipulate mailboxes in various formats
Structured Markup Processing Tools	
html	HyperText Markup Language support
xml.etree.ElementTree	The ElementTree XML API
xml.dom	The Document Object Model API
xml.sax	Support for SAX2 parsers
Internet Protocols and Support	
webbrowser	Convenient Web-browser controller
cgi	Common Gateway Interface support
wsgiref	WSGI Utilities and Reference Implementation
urllib	URL handling modules
http	HTTP
ftplib	FTP protocol client
poplib	POP3 protocol client
imaplib	IMAP4 protocol client
smtplib	SMTP protocol client
smtpd	SMTP Server
telnetlib	Telnet client
ipaddress	IPv4/IPv6 manipulation library
Internationalization	
gettext	Multilingual internationalization services
locale	Internationalization services

Program Frameworks	
turtle	Turtle graphics
cmd	Support for line-oriented command interpreters
shlex	Simple lexical analysis
Graphical User Interfaces with Tk	
tkinter	Python interface to Tcl/Tk
IDLE	Python IDE
Development Tools	
pydoc	Documentation generator and online help system
doctest	Test interactive Python examples
unittest	Unit testing
2to3	Automated Python 2 to 3 code translation
test	Regression tests package for Python
Debugging and Profiling	
bdb	Debugger framework
pdb	The Python Debugger
timeit	Measure execution time of small code snippets
trace	Trace or track Python statement execution
Software Packaging and Distribution	
distutils	Building and installing Python modules
ensurepip	Bootstrapping the pip installer
venv	Creation of virtual environments
zipapp	Manage executable Python zip archives
Python Runtime Services	
sys	System-specific parameters and functions
sysconfig	Access to Python's configuration information
builtins	Built-in objects
dataclasses	Data Classes
contextlib	Utilities for with-statement contexts
abc	Abstract Base Classes
gc	Garbage Collector interface
inspect	Inspect live objects

Custom Python Interpreters	
code	Interpreter base classes
codeop	Compile Python code
Importing Modules	
zipimport	Import modules from Zip archives
importlib	The implementation of import
Python Language Services	
pyclbr	Python class browser support
py_compile	Compile Python source files
compileall	Byte-compile Python libraries
dis	Disassembler for Python bytecode
MS Windows Specific Services	
msilib	Read and write Microsoft Installer files
msvcrt	Useful routines from the MS VC++ runtime
winreg	Windows registry access
Unix Specific Services	
posix	The most common POSIX system calls
pwd	The password database
syslog	Unix syslog library routines

Magic Methods

Magic Methods	equivalent operator
__add__(self, other)	addition (+) operator
__sub__(self, other)	subtraction (-) operator.
__mul__(self, other)	multiplication (*) operator.
__floordiv__(self, other)	floor division (//) operator.
__div__(self, other)	division (/) operator.
__mod__(self, other)	modulo (%) operator.
__pow__(self, other[, modulo])	exponentiation (**) operator.
__lt__(self, other)	less than (<) operator.
__le__(self, other)	less thsn or equal to (<=) operator.
__eq__(self, other)	is equal to (==) opcrator.
__ne__(self, other)	not equal to (!=) operator.
__ge__(self, other)	greater than (>=) operator.
__iadd__(self, other)	add and assign (+=) operator
__isub__(self, other)	subtract and assign (-=) operator.
__imul__(self, other)	multiply and assign (*=) operator.
__ifloordiv__(self, other)	floor division and assign (//=) operator.
__idiv__(self, other)	divide and assign (/=) operator.
__imod__(self, other)	modulo and assign (%=) operator.
__ipow__(self, other)	exponentiation and assign (**=) operator.

SQLite Dot Commands

.backup ?DB? FILE	Backup DB (default "main") to FILE
.binary on|off	Turn binary output on or off. Default OFF
.cd DIRECTORY	Change the working directory to DIRECTORY
.changes on|off	Show number of rows changed by SQL
.clone NEWDB	Clone data into NEWDB from the existing database
.databases	List names and files of attached databases
.dbinfo ?DB?	Show status information about the database
.dump ?TABLE? ...	Dump the database in an SQL text format if TABLE specified, only dump tables matching LIKE pattern TABLE.
.echo on|off	Turn command echo on or off
.headers on|off	Turn display of headers on or off
.help	Show this message
.import FILE TABLE	Import data from FILE into TABLE
.indexes ?TABLE?	Show names of all indexes
.limit ?LIMIT? ?VAL?	Display or change the value of an SQLITE_LIMIT
.load FILE ?ENTRY?	Load an extension library
.log FILE|off	Turn logging on or off. FILE can be stderr/stdout

.mode MODE ?TABLE?	Set output mode where MODE is one of
	ascii	Columns/rows delimited by 0x1F and 0x1E
	csv	Comma-separated values
	column	Left-aligned columns. (See .width)
	html	HTML <table> code
	insert	SQL insert statements for TABLE
	line	One value per line
	list	Values delimited by "|"
	quote	Escape answers as for SQL
	tabs	Tab-separated values
	tcl	TCL list elements

.once FILENAME	Output for the next SQL command only to FILENAME
.open ?OPTIONS? ?FILE?	Close existing database and reopen FILE. The --new option starts with an empty file
.output ?FILENAME?	Send output to FILENAME or stdout
.print STRING...	Print literal STRING
.prompt MAIN CONTINUE	Replace the standard prompts
.quit	Exit this program
.read FILENAME	Execute SQL in FILENAME
.restore ?DB? FILE	Restore content of DB (default "main") from FILE
.save FILE	Write in-memory database into FILE
.separator COL ?ROW?	Change the column separator and the row separator
.shell CMD ARGS...	Run CMD ARGS... in a system shell
.show	Show the current values for various settings
.stats ?on|off?	show stats or turn stats on or off
.system CMD ARGS...	Run CMD ARGS... in a system shell
.tables ?TABLE?	List names of tables
.timeout MS	Try opening locked tables for MS milliseconds
.timer on|off	Turn SQL timer on or off
.trace FILE|off	Output each SQL statement as it is run
.width NUM1 NUM2 ...	Set column widths for "column" mode

APPENDIX G
ANSI SQL Statements

AND / OR	logical operators used in WHERE clause
ALTER TABLE	add/delete/modify columns in existing table
AS	set another name for table or column
BETWEEN	in WHERE clause to check if expression is between certain range
CREATE DATABASE	create a new database
CREATE TABLE	create new table
CREATE INDEX	create new index
CREATE VIEW	create new view
DELETE	delete one or more rowssatisfying WHERE condition in a table
DROP DATABASE	drop a database
DROP INDEX	drop an index
DROP TABLE	drop a table
EXISTS	check whether a table exists or not
GROUP BY	used with aggregate functions
HAVING	used with SELECT statement
IN	specify multiple values in WHERE clause
INSERT INTO	insert a row in table
INNER JOIN	selects records with matching values in both tables
LEFT JOIN	selects all records from left and matched records in right table
RIGHT JOIN	selects all records from right and matched records from left table
FULL JOIN	selects records that match condition in either table

LIKE	used in WHERE clause to set filter criteria using wild cards
ORDER BY	return result set in ascending/descending order
SELECT	returns a result set containing listed columns from rows based on filter criteria if any.
SELECT *	used in SELECT to specify all columns in a table
SELECT DISTINCT	to force only distinct values of a certain column be selected
SELECT INTO	insert selected data from one table in another table.
SELECT TOP	returns first n number of rows from the result set
TRUNCATE TABLE	delete rows from table keeping structure intact.
UNION	Combine distinct values from result set of two SELECT statements
UNION ALL	combine all values from two SELECT statements even if repreated
UPDATE	Modify value of a certain column of existing rows in a table
WHERE	sets a filter criteria for SELECT/UPDATE/DELETE queries.

PyMongo API Methods

Database Level Operations

Database()	Get a database by client and name.
create_collection()	Create a new Collection in this database.
drop_collection()	Drop a collection.
get_collection()	Get a Collection with the given name and options
validate_collection()	Validate a collection.

MogoClient: Tools for connecting to MongoDB

MongoClient()	Client for a MongoDB instance, a replica set, or a set of mongoses.
close()	Cleanup client resources and disconnect from MongoDB.
db_name	Get the db_name Database on MongoClient c.
address	(host, port) of the current standalone, primary, or mongos,
list_databases()	Get a cursor over the databases of the connected server.
list_database_names()	Get a list of the names of all databases on the connected server.
drop_database()	Drop a database.
get_database()	Get a Database with the given name and options.
server_info()	Get information about the MongoDB server we're connected to.

Cursor: iterating over query results

Cursor()	Create a new cursor.
add_option()	Set arbitrary query flags using a bitmask.
address	The (host, port) of the server used, or None.

alive	Does this cursor have the potential to return more data?
clone()	Get a clone of this cursor.
close()	Explicitly close / kill this cursor.
collection	The Collection that this Cursor is iterating.
cursor_id	Returns the id of the cursor
distinct()	Get a list of distinct values for key among all documents in the result set of this query.
next()	Advance the cursor.
rewind()	Rewind this cursor to its unevaluated state.
session	The cursor's ClientSession
sort()	Sorts this cursor's results.
where()	Adds a $where clause to this query.

Collection level operations

Collection()	Get / create a Mongo collection.
name	The name of this Collection.
database	The Database that this Collection is a part of.
bulk_write()	Send a batch of write operations to the server.
insert_one()	Insert a single document.
insert_many()	Insert an iterable of documents.
replace_one()	Replace a single document matching the filter.
update_one()	Update a single document matching the filter.
update_many()	Update one or more documents that match the filter.
delete_one()	Delete a single document matching the filter.
delete_many()	Delete one or more documents matching the filter.
aggregate()	Perform an aggregation using the aggregation framework on this collection.
find(filter)	Query the database. The filter argument is a prototype document that all results must match.
find_one()	Get a single document from the database.
find_one_and_replace()	Finds a single document and replaces it, returning either the original or the replaced document.
find_one_and_update()	Finds a single document and updates it, returning either the original or the updated document.
create_index()	Creates an index on this collection.
drop()	Alias for drop_collection().

Cassandra CQL Shell Commands

CAPTURE	Captures output of a command and adds it to a file.
CONSISTENCY	Shows the current consistency level, or sets a new consistency level.
COPY	Copies data to and from Cassandra to a file.
CLS/CLEAR	Clears the console.
DESCRIBE KEYSPACES	Output the names of all keyspaces.
DESCRIBE KEYSPACE	Output CQL commands that could be used to recreate the given keyspace, and the objects in it (such as tables, types, functions, etc.).
DESCRIBE TABLES	Output the names of all tables in the current keyspace
DESCRIBE TABLE	Output CQL commands that could be used to recreate the given table.
DESCRIBE INDEX	Output the CQL command that could be used to recreate the given index.
DESCRIBE CLUSTER	Output information about the connected Cassandra cluster
DESCRIBE SCHEMA	Output CQL commands that could be used to recreate the entire (non-system) schema.
DESCRIBE TYPE	Output the CQL command that could be used to recreate the given user-defined-type.
DESCRIBE FUNCTION	Output the CQL command that could be used to recreate the given user-defined-function.
DESCRIBE AGGREGATE	Output the CQL command that could be used to recreate the given user-defined-aggregate.
EXPAND	Enables or disables expanded (vertical) output.
SHOW VERSION	Shows version and build of the connected Cassandra instance, CQL spec version and the Thrift protocol

EXIT/QUIT	Exits cqlsh.
HELP	Gives information about cqlsh commands.
LOGIN	Login using the specified username and password.
PAGING	Enables or disables query paging.
SHOW HOST	Shows where cqlsh is currently connected.
SHOW SESSION	Pretty-prints the requested tracing session.
SOURCE	Executes a file containing CQL statements.
TRACING	Enables or disables request tracing.